# A MENTAL
## REVOLUTION

HISTORICAL PERSPECTIVES ON BUSINESS
ENTERPRISE SERIES
Mansel G. Blackford and K. Austin Kerr, EDITORS

Henry E. Huntington and the Creation of Southern
California
WILLIAM B. FRIEDRICKS

Making Iron and Steel: Independent Mills in Pittsburgh,
1820–1920
JOHN N. INGHAM

Eagle-Picher Industries: Strategies for Survival in the
Industrial Marketplace
DOUGLAS KNERR

Rebuilding Cleveland: The Cleveland Foundation and Its
Evolving Urban Strategy
DIANA TITTLE

Daniel Willard and Progressive Management on the
Baltimore & Ohio Railroad
DAVID M. VROOMAN

# A MENTAL REVOLUTION

## Scientific Management since Taylor

EDITED BY Daniel Nelson

Ohio State University Press • COLUMBUS

Library of Congress Cataloging-in-Publication Data
A Mental revolution : scientific management since Taylor /
    edited by Daniel Nelson.
        p.        cm. — (Historical perspectives on business
    enterprise series)
    Includes bibliographical references and index.
    ISBN 0–8142–0567–4
    1. Industrial management — United States — History —
20th century. I. Nelson, Daniel, 1941–   .   II. Series.
HD70.U5M426   1992
658 — dc20                                                           91–33381
                                                                              CIP

Text and jacket design by Jim Brisson.
Type set in Bembo by Focus Graphics, St. Louis, MO.
Printed by Cushing-Malloy, Ann Arbor, MI.

9   8   7   6   5   4   3   2   1

Scientific management is not any efficiency device. . . . It is not a new system of figuring costs; it is not a new system of paying men . . . it is not holding a stop watch on a man and writing things down about him . . . it is not motion study nor an analysis of the movements of men. . . . It is not divided foremanship . . . it is not any of the devices which the average man calls to mind when scientific management is spoken of. . . . In this sense, scientific management involves a complete mental revolution.

FREDERICK W. TAYLOR, 1912

It is still necessary to go back to Taylor for definitions and fundamental principles. But scientific management is a dynamic thing; its principles are the principles of growth and change and it is for that reason that its progress since the war has been sure and swift.

EDWARD EYRE HUNT, 1924

# CONTENTS

# A MENTAL
## REVOLUTION

# INTRODUCTION

Scientific management has attracted surprisingly little attention in the United States in recent years. The handful of books and essays that have appeared since the 1950s have focused on Frederick W. Taylor (1856–1915), the engineer, inventor, and publicist who became the first American management theorist to reach a large, nontechnical audience. They assume or imply that Taylor's influence did not die with him in 1915 but provide only the most general indication of the character of that influence. As a result, Edward Eyre Hunt's *Scientific Management Since Taylor* (1924) remains the last, best word on American scientific management in the post-Taylor era. In the meantime, historians and social scientists specializing in European affairs have discovered or rediscovered indigenous scientific management movements that drew inspiration from the American pioneers but soon developed identities of their own. The results of the new scholarship are most striking in the case of France, which had the most ambitious management movement outside the United States, but impressive studies in German, British, Russian, Italian, and Japanese history have documented the spread of ideas and techniques once assumed to be peculiarly American. While it may be premature to speak of an international history of scientific management, it is clear that Taylor found enthusiastic disciples everywhere and that scientific management measurably affected the performance of institutions in many countries.

In recent years there has been a reawakening of interest in the United States as well, particularly among younger scholars. Their research promises to close the gap between European and American scholarship and to permit authoritative generalizations about the impact of scientific management on managerial theory and practice. This volume is a preliminary report of their work. It makes no pretense of covering every aspect of the post-1915 scientific management movement, of treating every subject or decade equally, or of providing an unmistakable trail for those who follow. The authors have tried, as the saying goes, to do a few things well.

Although the authors have worked as individuals, with varying perspectives and values, they share several assumptions. First, scientific management did not begin or end with Taylor. The starting point for organized, self-conscious activity was his synthesis and extension of systematic management, the late nineteenth century effort to bring order and system to manufacturing. But Taylor was one creative individual among many; he cast a long shadow because he told people what they were ready to hear. The movement associated with him and his work evolved during his lifetime and continued to evolve after his death.

Second, though it drew on a rich intellectual and administrative heritage, scientific management in practice was highly disruptive. This characteristic accounted for the controversies that often accompanied its introduction, for the popularity of short cuts designed to preserve the benefits and minimize the trauma of scientific management, and for Taylor's attempt to explain his objective in nontechnical language. The latter effort led him to identify his work with "a complete mental revolution," suggesting the transcendent possibilities of improved management on the shop floor and in society.

Third, scientific management cannot be discussed solely in terms of manufacturing operations or work or business administration. From the beginning it had wider potential applications. Taylor and his followers emphasized ideas and activities—research, planning, communications, standards, incentives, feedback—that were applicable to any institution. Their ideal factory was a metaphor for a better society. They also spoke the language of anti-establishment rebels. Their scorn for the income statement and the marketplace as yardsticks of economic success gave them a common bond with progressives, socialists, and revolutionaries on both sides of the Atlantic.

The essays in this volume are a step toward a new understanding of the role of scientific management in America, but many gaps remain. There is still little information about the operation of industrial enterprises under scientific management and even less about the service organizations, large and small, that embraced the engineers' ideas and methods. Equally notable is the comparative neglect of American mobilization in World War II, the ultimate triumph of scientific management and mass production. In the political realm, the link with Herbert Hoover and his associates is well documented, but the role of scientific management in the New Deal remains to be explored, despite the fact that most nonacademic leaders of scientific management in the 1930s had become federal government officials by the end of the decade. Nor is there any study of the intellectual impact of scientific management on government comparable to accounts of the rise of Keynesian theory. Most important, perhaps, there is little information on the apparent exhaustion of scientific management in the 1950s and after, as planning, standardization, and other fundamentals of scientific management became clichés and marketing and finance increasingly overshadowed production. The list could be extended almost indefinitely.

A final note on terminology. Before 1910, Taylor and his followers used various labels to describe their work. At the instigation of Louis Brandeis, they agreed to employ the term *scientific management*, one of the phrases they had used informally. For the next twenty years scientific management meant the ideas and techniques of Taylor, his disciples, and those who followed in their footsteps. After World War II, when American social scientists rediscovered Taylor's work, they often substituted the word *Taylorism*, which had been widely used in Europe and which enabled them to avoid disputes over what was and what was not genuinely scientific. In this volume the terms are considered synonymous.

DANIEL NELSON

I    Scientific Management in Retrospect

In January 1912, Frederick W. Taylor, the center of a highly publicized controversy over the effects of "scientific management," testified before a House of Representatives committee investigating his handiwork. His first objective, he explained, was to "sweep away a good deal of rubbish." Scientific management was "not any efficiency device. . . . It is not a new system of figuring costs; it is not a new system of paying men . . . it is not holding a stop watch on a man . . . it is not time study; it is not motion study. . . ." In fact, it was "not any of the devices which the average man calls to mind when scientific management is spoken of." On the contrary, it was "a complete mental revolution on the part of the workingman" and an "equally complete mental revolution on the part of those on management's side. . . . And without this complete mental revolution on both sides scientific management does not exist."[1]

Taylor's identification of scientific management with a "mental revolution" had several purposes. It was the culminating step in a long campaign to sell his approach to industrial management as a system rather than a series of palliatives for specific problems. It was also a defense against criticisms that had arisen from piecemeal installations and the association of scientific management with hostility to unions. Finally, it emphasized a point that Taylor

The author gratefully acknowledges the comments and suggestions of K. Austin Kerr, Patrick Fridenson, Heidrun Homburg, Barbara Clements, Eisuke Daito, and the authors of the other essays in this volume.

himself had only recently begun to articulate: that successful management depended on ideas that were applicable to many different kinds of organizations. Taylor's imagery evoked an enthusiastic response from engineers and factory managers and from a larger group whose interests extended to virtually every institution.[2] From this point scientific management was both a detailed plan for improving the operations of a plant or office and a set of prescriptions for improving any activity. Its popularity underlined the significance of Taylor's metaphor.

## Taylor and the Origins of Scientific Management

The journey that ultimately led Taylor to define his work as "a complete mental revolution" was long and arduous. It included experiences in a variety of industrial enterprises, involvement in the emerging engineering profession and in the existing management movement, and associations with a corps of associates who disseminated the Taylor system.

The events of Taylor's early years played a large and controversial part in these activities.[3] Born in 1856 into an aristocratic Philadelphia family, Taylor had the benefit of tutors and exclusive schools, extended travel, and associations with the Philadelphia elite. After attending Phillips Exeter Academy, he rejected a university education in favor of a traditional apprenticeship and an industrial career, which began in the machine shop of the Midvale Steel Company in 1878. He rose rapidly, thanks to ability and hard work and to close personal ties with the Clark family, the principal owners of Midvale. In 1885, after receiving an engineering degree via correspondence courses from the Stevens Institute of Technology, he became the company's chief engineer. His prospects of rising still further received a severe jolt the following year when the Clarks sold Midvale to a local industrialist who had a son of similar age and experience. As a result, Taylor resigned in 1889 to head a company that a group of New York financiers had organized to exploit a novel paper-making process. This experience proved to be equally frustrating. The new technology was defective, the company lost money, and Taylor and his wife were unhappy in the Maine frontier town where they had to live. With considerable bitterness, Taylor left in 1893 to become a self-employed consultant.

By that time he had taken important steps toward a new role. He had a substantial reputation as an inventor of industrial machinery and broad experience as an industrial manager. He had also undertaken several experiments that forced him to think more explicitly about organizations and people. One of these, an effort to compute operating times for machine tools with a stopwatch, would envolve into time and motion study, his signature contribution to industrial management.

Most of all, Taylor had become associated with two enterprises that were reshaping the industrial environment. The first was the rapidly maturing engineering profession, whose advocates sought an identity based on rigorous formal education, frequent contact, mutually accepted standards of behavior, and social responsibility. In factories, mines, and railroad yards, they rejected the empiricism of the practitioner for scientific experimentation and analysis. They acknowledged the primacy of the profit motive, but they insisted that reason and truth were essential to continued financial success.[4] The second, closely related development was the systematic management movement, an effort among engineers and sympathizers to substitute administrative systems for the informal methods of industrial management that had evolved with the factory system. Systematic management was a rebellion against tradition, empiricism, and the assumption that common sense, personal relationships, and craft knowledge were sufficient to run a small factory. In the large, capital intensive, technologically advanced operations of the late nineteenth century, "rule-of-thumb" methods resulted in confusion and waste. The revisionists' answer was to replace traditional managers with engineers and to substitute managerial systems for guesswork and ad hoc evaluations.[5]

By the time Taylor began his career as an engineer and manager, cost accounting systems, methods for planning and scheduling production and organizing materials, and incentive wage plans were staples of engineering publications and trade journals. Their objective was an unimpeded flow of materials and information. In human terms, proponents of systematic management sought to transfer power from the first-line supervisor to the plant manager and to force all employees to pay greater attention to the manager's goals. Most threatening, perhaps, they advocated decisions based on performance rather than on personal qualities and associations.[6]

In the 1890s, Taylor became the most ambitious and vigorous proponent of systematic management. As a consultant he introduced accounting systems that permitted managers to use operating records to guide their actions, production control systems that allowed managers to know more precisely what was happening on the shop floor, piece rate systems that encouraged workers to follow orders and instructions, and related measures. In 1895 he employed a colleague, Sanford E. Thompson, to continue his time study research with the goal of calculating standards for various occupations that would be published and sold to employers. Between 1898 and 1901, as a consultant to the Bethlehem Iron Company, Taylor introduced all of his systems and vigorously pursued his research. This experience, punctuated by controversy and escalating conflict with the company's managers, was the capstone of his creative career. Two developments were of special importance. Taylor's discovery of "high speed steel," which improved the performance of metal cutting tools, assured his fame as an inventor. In addition, his effort to introduce systematic methods in many areas of the company's operations forced him to develop an integrated view of managerial innovation and a broader conception of the manager's role. By 1901 Taylor had fashioned scientific management from systematic management.[7]

As the events of Taylor's career make clear, the two approaches were intimately related. Systematic and scientific management had common roots, attracted the same kinds of people, and had the same business objectives. Yet in retrospect the differences stand out. Systematic management was diffuse and utilitarian, a series of isolated measures that did not add up to a larger whole or have recognizable implications beyond day-to-day industrial operations. Scientific management added significant detail and a larger view. In 1901, when he left Bethlehem, Taylor resolved to devote his time and ample fortune to promoting both. His first report on his work, "Shop Management" (1903), portrayed an integrated complex of systematic management methods, supplemented by refinements and additions like time study.[8]

At first Taylor was disappointed with the response to his work. He could talk about a larger, integrated conception of management but most manufacturers wanted solutions to specific problems. Furthermore, their preoccupation with the particulars, notably time study and incentive wage plans, threatened more serious difficulties. Many machine shop owners, for example, introduced time study and an incentive wage to raise output and wean employees from the International Association of Machinists (IAM) and other trade unions. Taylor and his followers, who had little sympathy for unions, were slow to realize the dangers of this course. By 1910 the IAM and the American Federation of Labor (AFL) had become implacable enemies of scientific management and Taylor was embroiled in a public controversy that would haunt him for the rest of his life.[9]

Taylor responded to these problems with two tactical adjustments. First, he began to rely more heavily on anecdotes from his career — "object lessons" — to convey his message to audiences that had little interest in technical detail. Taylor liberally interpreted his experiences to make his point. Thus the tale of "Schmidt," the oxlike Bethlehem laborer whose stupidity Taylor had supposedly overcome with an incentive wage, was largely apocryphal.[10] Second, apart from the object lessons, Taylor spoke less about factory operations and more about the significance and general applicability of his ideas. Between 1907 and 1909, with the aid of one of his shrewdest associates, Morris L. Cooke, he wrote a sequel to "Shop Management" that ultimately became *The Principles of Scientific Management* (1911). Rather than discuss the specific methods he introduced in factories and shops, Taylor used colorful stories and language to illuminate "principles" of management. To suggest the integrated character and broad applicability of scientific management, he equated it with a "complete mental revolution."[11]

Taylor's reformulation of scientific management as a series of principles and as a mental revolution made him a celebrity. "Shop Management" had reached an audience of engineers and industrialists; the *Principles* potentially appealed to everyone. Building on the momentum of other efficiency movements devoted to natural resource conservation, improved government service, more effective education, and similar goals, Taylor invited readers to extrapolate.[12] How did scientific management apply to their circumstances? Could they duplicate Taylor's successes? What were the possibilities of rational organization, time study, and material incentives? What costs could they anticipate? Taylor's book became an inspiration to those on both sides of the Atlantic who equated industrial or social progress with increased efficiency.

As Taylor's name became a household word, his role in the management movement paradoxically declined. The popularity of the *Principles* created more demands for appearances and statements than any individual could satisfy, and Taylor had little choice but to turn to others to assist him. Initially, he had no qualms about this step. For years he had attracted devoted followers. At first they were employees like Thompson, who performed specific tasks. After Taylor's retirement in 1901 they became more independent, introducing the techniques he had developed and refined at Bethlehem. In addition, Taylor attracted other individuals who were intrigued both by his methods and by the larger implications of his activities. They soon began to play creative roles in their own right. In 1910 Louis Brandeis, the distinguished lawyer and reformer, skillfully used their testimony in the celebrated Eastern Rate Case before the Interstate Commerce Commission to publicize scientific management. By the time the *Principles* appeared and Taylor testified before the Congressional investigating committee, Taylor's followers were well prepared to apply scientific management in industry and to explain its significance to an eager public. Their competence and fidelity became a major concern of Taylor's later years; the tensions that arose from his concerns have in turn been a feature of most histories of scientific management.[13]

The most influential disciples were Henry L. Gantt and Morris L. Cooke, whom Taylor trusted and generally endorsed; Frank B. Gilbreth and Harrington Emerson, whom he grew to dislike and distrust; and Harlow S. Person, who became a major figure in the scientific management movement after his death. Gantt was Taylor's first important follower, the creator of valuable refinements such as the task and bonus wage plan and the charts that became his trademark. He was also the first of the Taylor group to recognize the common ground between scientific management and personnel work.[14] Cooke was the most political of Taylor's followers, the principal link between scientific management and progressive reform. He became known for his applications of scientific management to public administration and for his overtures to union leaders.[15] Gilbreth's colorful activities often obscured his substantive contributions to the analysis of work. Emerson was a creative publicist who grasped the potential of scientific management as a business, and Person was the foremost theorist of scientific management after Taylor's death. As head of the Taylor Society, the association of Taylor's professional and intellectual disciples, in the 1920s and 1930s, he identified scientific management with the liberal business community of that era. Among other important individuals with ties to the Taylor circle, Richard A. Feiss and Mary Van Kleeck symbolized the diverse potential of scientific management.

## Scientific Management in Industry

During Taylor's lifetime, scientific management was first and foremost a plan for enhanced business performance that Taylor's followers and other consultants installed for fees. Taylor and his allies argued that their work increased profits, enhanced productivity, and eliminated class divisions and labor unrest. Critics charged that it encouraged excessive specialization, degraded work, and encouraged personal competition, hostility, and a sense of alienation. The conflicting charges were so sweeping that it was (and is) impossible to reconcile them.[16] However, historical research has addressed several pertinent issues, including the extent to which scientific management was adopted in industry, the character of the changes that occurred in those plants, and the impact of such activities on the work and well-being of employees.

Between 1901 and 1915 Taylor's associates introduced scientific management in nearly 200 American businesses, 181 or eighty percent of which were factories.[17] Some of the plants were large and modern, like the Pullman and Remington Typewriter companies; others were small and technologically primitive. Approximately one-third of the total were large volume producers for mass markets, but scientific management initially had limited appeal among the managers of mass production plants.[18] A majority of the 181 firms fell into one of two broad categories. First were those whose activities required the movement of large quantities of materials between numerous work stations (such as textile mills, railroad repair shops, and automobile plants). Their managers sought to reduce delays and bottlenecks and increase throughput, the volume of production per unit of time. The second group consisted of innovative firms, mostly small, that were already committed to managerial reform. Their executives were attracted to Taylor's promise of social harmony and improved working conditions. A significant minority of the total fell in both categories. Many of the textile mills, for example, were leaders in welfare work.[19]

The history of scientific management in these plants provides little support for the contention, common to many later accounts, that Taylor's central concern was the work of the individual employee. Consultants devoted most of their time and energies to machine operations, tools and materials, production schedules, routing patterns, and cost and other record systems. In one-third of the factories these activities generated such controversy that time and motion studies were never undertaken. In others, such as the Franklin Automobile Co. and several textile mills, the installation consisted almost exclusively of improvements in schedules and routing. As a result at least one-half of the employees of the 181 firms were essentially onlookers. They may have experienced fewer delays, used different tools, or found that their supervisor's authority had diminished, but their own activities were unaffected.[20]

What about the other employees? Taylor promised that they would receive higher wages and have more opportunities for promotion and less reason for conflict with their supervisors. Most assessments of these claims have concluded that Taylor promised more than his associates could or would deliver. By the same token, the union leaders and other critics exaggerated the dangers of scientific management. They argued that skilled workers would forfeit their skills and creativity, that scientific management would promote speedups, fatigue, and rate cuts, and that average workers would lose their jobs.[21] Taylor's followers mocked the deskilling argument; Gilbreth compared it to the notion that surgeons or dentists were deskilled general practitioners.[22] In recent years, however, it has reappeared in social science texts and in radical critiques of the economy, notably in the influential work of Harry Braverman. The modern critics extrapolated from the *Principles* rather than from the experiences of the 181 plants or other historical data.[23] They reasoned that industrial jobs had become intellectually and psychologically unrewarding since Taylor's time; that Taylor was the architect of modern work (or so the text writers insisted); and therefore, that Taylor had tipped his hand when he referred, in the *Principles* to "gathering together all of the traditional knowledge which in the past has been possessed by the workmen."

The most important effect of the deskilling argument may have been to obscure the more serious charges that scientific management led to speedups, rate cuts, and the discharge of employees whose skills or motivation were no better than average. In orthodox settings, where employers lived up to the letter of scientific management, only inferior performers had to worry. And in firms that were also committed to personnel management, even that threat was minimal. But many employers were less scrupulous or less patient. In their minds faster work meant faster, more diligent workers, not better planning and coordination, improved communications, and systematic maintenance. They gave lip service to Taylor's idea of an interrelated whole, but they looked to the employees for immediate gains. Even among the 181 firms there was some tendency to use time study to cut rates. That was the prospect that sparked the famous Watertown Arsenal strike of 1912. It was apparently also the cause of strikes at Joseph & Feiss and at three American Locomotive Company plants where Emerson worked.[24] Outside the Taylor circle the tendency was far more pronounced. In early 1913, for example, Firestone Tire & Rubber Company managers assigned an employee named Robert Holmes to conduct time studies of tire workers to learn why earnings were so high. Holmes had had no contact with the Taylor group or experience in time study, but he spent a day timing the workers with a stopwatch and concluded, predictably, that piece rates were too high. The managers then cut the rates and the workers struck, precipitating the industry's most serious labor conflict before the 1930s.[25]

Considering the experiences of firms that have left records (including those like Firestone) several conclusions about the impact of scientific management on factory work seem warranted: (1) First-line supervisors lost much of their authority to higher-level managers and their staffs. (2) The proportion of the work day devoted to production increased due to the elimination of delays. (3) Fewer decisions depended on personal judgments, biases, and subjective evaluations. (4) The individual worker exercised less discretion, particularly in plants where time studies were used to schedule production and/or set piece rates; in the small minority of plants where individual instruction cards were also used, the area of discretion was reduced even more. (5) In most cases earnings rose, but there were enough exceptions to blur the effect. (6) The level of skill required in production did not change as a result of scientific management though the most highly skilled employees, like the foremen, lost some of their de facto managerial functions. (7) Some unskilled jobs disappeared as improved scheduling and routing reduced the need for gangs of laborers and encouraged the introduction of materials handling machinery. (8) The "great fear" of skill and job losses that David Montgomery has documented among craft workers in the early 1910s quickly waned and scientific management ceased to be associated with labor turmoil until the spread of the Bedaux system in the 1920s.[26]

Only in recent years has it become apparent that the traditional preoccupation of contemporary analysts with factory conditions was far too narrow. Scientific management was also applicable to the operations of stores and offices, as a handful of illuminating studies have emphasized.[27] There were parallels with manufacturing plants: large establishments were most likely to introduce scientific management techniques and the managers' overriding motivation was a desire to increase the speed of operations. But there were also differences. Because clerical work was labor intensive and dependent on small, hand-operated machines, reorganization efforts focused on the individual employee to a greater degree and at an earlier stage than in most factories. Indeed, the approach that Taylor and his orthodox followers scorned became the standard in white-collar settings and evoked little controversy. Efforts to improve scheduling and routing, to employ time and motion study to reduce wasteful effort, and to introduce economic incentives were most effective where large volume, repetitive operations were the rule. In other settings, employers paid less attention to industrial engineering techniques reminiscent of factories, and concentrated on improving employees' skills and morale. In either case, scientific management was associated with the mechanization of clerical operations and the growth of a largely female labor force. The impact on the individual worker is harder to gauge. Judging from the experiences of factory workers, it varied considerably and defies easy summary.[28]

In the meantime the "efficiency craze" that followed the publication of the *Principles* overshadowed everything Taylor's associates had accomplished or failed to accomplish in American factories. As a result, Taylor, Gilbreth, Emerson and other associates became celebrities; organizations and publications devoted to efficiency proliferated; professional societies recognized the importance of management as well as of technical knowledge; universities began to teach management, and virtually every organization gave lip service to the goal of enhanced efficiency.

This activity, together with Taylor's death in 1915, marked the beginning of a new phase in the history of the management movement. Though the picture is far from complete, a series of dramatic changes in the character and imagery of scientific management between 1915 and 1920 suggest the outlines of this new era. The best known of these changes was the reconciliation of Taylor's followers and union leaders that followed the engineers' formal endorsement of collective bargaining.[29] The practical importance of this concession is unclear but it removed a major source of misunderstanding and demonstrated the appeal of scientific management among union leaders once its anti-union implications were muted. Nearly as important was the gradual merger of the scientific management and personnel management movements. Thanks to labor market conditions during the war period, scientific management by 1920 embraced the full panoply of personnel reforms, including personnel departments that performed the foreman's traditional functions of hiring, firing, and training as well as new activities associated with industrial psychology.[30]

A third unanticipated development was the growing role of scientific management in the federal government. Taylor had had extremely poor relations with the Taft administration and his followers had little contact with Wilson and his advisors. Though virtually every member of the Taylor Society was a government employee during 1917–1918, they had no demonstrable effect on mobilization policy.[31] The war experience nevertheless had important indirect effects, not the least of which was the rise of Herbert Hoover to the forefront of American politics. Hoover quickly developed close and cordial relations with the scientific management movement and superseded Taylor as the nation's foremost apostle of efficiency. His influence was apparent in *Waste In Industry*, a report that soon rivaled the *Principles* as the most widely read manifesto of the scientific management movement. In subsequent years Hoover would lead an American rationalization effort that depended, even more than comparable efforts in Europe, on the ideas and techniques of scientific management.[32]

## Scientific Management in Europe and Japan

Before the 1970s most histories of scientific management gave the impression that it was an American phenomenon that had its greatest impact on American institutions. Authors either disregarded Paul Devinat's *Scientific Management in Europe* (1927) or relegated it to a footnote. In recent years, however, a new emphasis on scientific management has accompanied the study of twentieth-century political and economic institutions in European history. Taylor's popularity, for example, was "one of the first tangible signs of the Americanization of French society."[33] After World War I, scientific management became a potent force for economic and political renewal.[34] Above all, perhaps, it was a gauge of the growth of large organizations and bureaucratic cultures, a development that transcended national boundaries.

Before World War I, the diffusion of scientific management in most European countries and in Japan resembled the American experience. It depended on engineers and industrialists who had some exposure to systematic management and who were eager to realize the potential of the large and complex organizations they worked for or consulted. In most countries charismatic individuals within this group provided the intellectual and organizational impetus that converted the technicians' interest into a more broadly based movement. Initially, their focus was factory reform, which proved to be as difficult and contentious as it was in the United States. The most common conflicts pitted company executives, sensitive to costs and short-term results, like their American counterparts, against engineers and technicians who adopted the broader perspective of Taylor and his followers. Nearly as important before the war was the division between these groups and the labor unions, which strongly opposed any change in the industrial status quo.

Systematic management began to make inroads in Europe and Japan after 1900. As in the United States, the rise of the engineering profession and the enhanced role of the engineer in manufacturing were major underlying forces. The appearance of books and articles promoting coordination through management systems signaled a new sensitivity to the limits of empiricism and tradition. Yet change was gradual and uncoordinated. In Germany, for example, systematic management seemed to grow naturally out of "bureaucratic traditions."[35] As a result, German industrialists introduced "various scientific management techniques before they ever heard of the American movement."[36] On the other hand, Japanese railroad executives decided to introduce western managerial methods after they purchased American rolling stock.[37] The majority of European executives fell between these extremes. A crude measure of the spread of systematic management was the popularity of incentive wage plans. In Britain and France nearly half of all engineering employees worked under some form of incentive by 1914.[38] In Russia, the largest employers followed the lead of their western counterparts. St. Petersburg, with many large metal working factories, became a hotbed of experimentation. In state plants and then in private operations, engineers and managers debated ways to increase throughput and productivity. They installed cost accounting and incentive wage plans and, in some cases, made time studies. By 1908, at least sixteen of the largest plants in the St. Petersburg area had introduced "American" bonus plans.[39] Union leaders viewed the wage plans as another effort to undercut the powers of skilled workers and reduce wages, but were unable to prevent their introduction or extension.

Taylor first became known to European industrialists and engineers for his invention of high-speed tool steel. At the Paris Exposition of 1900, where high-speed steel attracted much attention, he had contacts with leading German and French technicians, including Henri Le Chatelier, who would soon emerge as his best-known European follower. Le Chatelier published Taylor's "The Art of Cutting Metals" in his prestigious *Revue de Métallurgie* in 1907 and "Shop Management" a few months later. In the meantime, *Zeitschrift des Vereins Deutscher Ingenieure*, the journal of the Association of German Engineers, published a long report on Taylor's work in 1901, stimulating widespread experimentation by German engineering firms. One of the participants in this activity, Professor Georg Schlesinger, of the Royal Institute of Physics at Charlottenburg, soon emerged as an expert on high-speed steel and Taylor's managerial ideas. A German translation of "Shop Management" appeared in 1904.[40] From this point, Taylor's international contacts increased and his influence grew. After hearing Taylor's lecture on the potential of scientific management, André Michelin, the French tire manufacturer, supposedly rushed out to buy a stopwatch. Japanese technicians were no less enthusiastic. Koichi Kanda, author of the first Japanese manual on factory management, published in 1911, included an extensive discussion of Taylor's work. Yoichi Ueno, a university professor and consultant, translated Gilbreth's *Motion Study* in 1911 and the *Principles* in 1913.[41]

Still, there were limits to Taylor's personal influence. Despite considerable effort, only a handful of European and Japanese engineers and managers spent extended periods in Philadelphia, and his associates worked almost exclusively in the United States. The notable exception was Gilbreth, who spent much of 1913 and 1914 at the Auergesellschaft company, which was allied with Allgemeine Elektrizitäts-Gesellschaft (AEG), the largest German engineering firm.[42] The exact nature of Gilbreth's work and his relations with his client remain a mystery, but Walther Rathenau, the head of AEG, and Wichard von Moellendorff, one of its key manufacturing executives, were among the most influential promoters of scientific management in Germany during the following decade.

Of the European pioneers, Le Chatelier was unquestionably the most important. After 1904 he became the "driving force" that insured the spread of Taylor's ideas "in France and over large parts of continental Europe."[43] As a distinguished chemist and professor at the Ecole des mines and the College de France, his prestige insured that Taylor's ideas received a respectful hearing in the highest circles of French society. Together with Charles de Fréminville, an engineer who held a succession of high positions in large industrial firms, Le Chatelier made France the center of the European scientific management movement.

After Le Chatelier, de Fréminville, and Schlesinger, no follower of Taylor had a greater impact than Alexsei Gastev, a Russian revolutionary who helped introduce scientific management to the new Soviet state. Trained as a teacher, Gastev became a metal worker in 1908 and began a lifelong fascination with western technology. Exiled in 1910 for political activity, he went to Paris, worked in several large plants, and became familiar with the contemporary debate over scientific management. He returned to St. Petersburg in 1913 and was employed at the large Aivaz plant when workers there struck against managerial innovations, including an ill-conceived effort to introduce time studies. Gastev, nevertheless, was intrigued with the potential of scientific management. Like Lenin, who began to write positively about Taylor's ideas in 1914, he saw scientific management as a method for achieving a "cultural revolution" and "making every man a manager."[44]

Only in Great Britain, among the larger European countries, was there no influential advocate or group of advocates before World War I. The major engineering publications either disregarded Taylor's work or criticized it. Industrialists such as Edward Cadbury and B. Seebohm Rowntree, closely identified with managerial reform, wrote generally hostile analyses. Socialist critics of the status quo were also unfriendly. The consensus of economic historians is that Taylor's work had no immediate impact in Britain due to the hidebound conservatism of British executives.[45] Their indictment may be overdrawn. As Judith Merkle has noted, the problem in British industry may have been the absence of a "self-propagating class of merchandisers," not lack of interest.[46] Michael Rowlinson has recently shown that Cadbury introduced many of Taylor's methods despite his public disclaimers.[47] Additional investigations would likely show that Cadbury and the few industrialists, such as Hans Renold, who publicly endorsed scientific management, were not alone. An American engineer who surveyed European industry in 1920 found in England "the most complete installations of scientific management I have ever seen."[48]

Why were British executives so reticent? The answer may have been their preoccupation with industrial relations and labor unrest. In Britain, as in other countries, the years after 1900 saw a sharp increase in labor militancy and union activity. Among craft workers, particularly those in technologically backward trades, changes in manufacturing operations were at least as threatening as wage cuts or attacks on unions.[49] Union leaders in Britain, France, and Germany carefully monitored the Watertown arsenal incident and the ensuing conflict between Taylor and the AFL, and were ready to react whenever a stopwatch appeared.

If European workers had any doubts about the malign intentions of Taylor and his European allies, Louis Renault soon eliminated them. A brilliant autocrat who created Europe's largest automobile firm, Renault was typical of the French manufacturers who were attracted to scientific management. In 1907, one of his subordinates, Georges de Ram, introduced a planning department, time study, instruction cards, and other measures in two shops. Production soon doubled. Renault was impressed but refused to extend de Ram's reforms because of their cost.[50] Four years later, after visiting Taylor in Philadelphia, touring several plants and publicly announcing his "conversion," he decided to proceed with his own version of scientific management, and abruptly introduced time studies into his factory. His workers, fearful of what would follow, struck. Renault was conciliatory. He blamed de Ram for the trouble, agreed to the election of shop stewards, and promised to consult the workers before revising their rates. The strikers returned to their jobs but remained suspicious. After reading exaggerated accounts of conditions in American plants and failing to gain new concessions, they struck again in February 1913. The second strike lasted six weeks and initially commanded the support of most Renault workers. Like the Firestone strike in the United States, which occurred at the same time, and a strike at the Bosch Company in Germany several months later, it collapsed when the strikers exhausted their savings and became disenchanted with their leaders.[51]

The Renault strike was a turning point in the diffusion of scientific management. From Britain to Russia, workers and unions became alert to the dangers of uncontrolled time study.[52] Yet they also became aware of the possibilities of scientific management. Le Chatelier argued that once workers learned about scientific management, they would distinguish between Taylor's promises of affluence and harmony and the foolish actions of a Renault. He considered the strike a public relations coup.[53] In any event, Taylor's writings became more popular after 1913. If the new enthusiasm did not match the American "efficiency craze," it did mark the beginning of a proliferation of nonindustrial applications of Taylor's ideas. And, as in the United States, one measure of this broader conception of scientific management was the reconciliation of many unionists and working-class political leaders who, like Gastev, were more impressed with the promise of order, planning, and security from capricious rule-of-thumb management than with the dangers of time study.

Though there were important similarities between the American and European experiences in the mid 1910s, there was one crucial difference—the First World War. Beginning in the fall of

1914, European executives and government leaders had to cope with mounting pressures for industrial expansion, coordinated activity, class and interest group cooperation, and efficient use of scarce resources, pressures that American executives and employees would not experience until 1918. As government expanded it became more dependent on individuals with managerial and technical expertise. As factories grew, their managers became more dependent on management systems. After 1914 the exigencies of war, more than the work of Taylor, Le Chatelier or others, shaped the scientific management movement.

In three areas this effect was especially noticeable. First, the disruption of the economy and the labor force created powerful pressures for effective resource utilization. Unlike the American firms that produced arms and munitions for the Allies, European manufacturers had to increase production without commensurate increases in materials and labor. Their responses inevitably were to reduce waste, reorganize production for volume operations, and recruit women, handicapped workers, and other heretofore unconventional employees. Second, the labor shortage and the demand for uninterrupted production forced manufacturers to introduce labor reforms and to work more closely and cooperatively with unions.[54] The result was an amalgamation of scientific and personnel management and a new emphasis on the compatibility of time study, incentive wage plans, and collective bargaining. Third, the substitution of political controls for market forces in many sectors required an unprecedented degree of production planning and coordination.

While there was growing reliance on scientific management in all countries, the French experience is particularly well documented.[55] Even before the war, French military officers had recognized the potential of scientific management for arsenal operations and had introduced Taylor's methods in at least one plant. After 1914, as they struggled to increase production, they increasingly relied on scientific management for the manufacture of shells, arms, explosives, motor vehicles, and airplanes.[56] At the Penhöet navy yard at Saint-Nazaire, for example, they gave Léon Guillet, Le Chatelier's close friend and associate, a "free hand." Guillet organized a planning department, introduced time studies and a bonus wage, and installed other managerial innovations. When he left in late 1915, de Fréminville succeeded him and completed his work. Guillet and de Fréminville treated the employees well and "won" their support.[57] Most private employers were less enthusiastic and less scrupulous. Yet an American expert wrote in 1918 that he found in France "a better grasp of the essentials . . . than in the United States." Interest in scientific management was "more widespread."[58] Aimée Moutet concludes that scientific management made substantial inroads in French industry during the war, that engineers substituted a "scientific spirit" for the "ruling empiricism," and that the war experience "integrated the Taylor system in the general organization of the enterprise."[59]

No less dramatic was the change in union attitudes. Organized labor's reaction to the Renault strike had suggested unyielding hostility. Yet the reformers who controlled the largest unions and the largest union federation were pragmatists who embraced the war effort and the campaign to increase production and productivity, provided they were accompanied by labor reforms. Under Alphonse Merrheim and Léon Jouhaux, the French labor movement shifted from hostility to qualified support for scientific management. The attitudes of rank-and-file workers are more difficult to ascertain, though there were apparently no strikes against scientific management during the war period.[60]

Most dramatic of all was the conversion of high government officials, notably the individuals responsible for directing the war economy and planning the postwar reconstruction. Neither Albert Thomas, the socialist who directed munitions production until late 1917, nor Etienne Clémental, the Minister of Commerce, had had more than a superficial knowledge of Taylor's writings. Yet by 1916 they were advocates of scientific management, promoters of industrial modernization, and champions of labor-management cooperation. Thomas, in particular, pushed scientific management in conjunction with collective bargaining and labor reform. His outspoken advocacy of scientific management won him the enmity of conservative industrialists and far-left political colleagues, but he persisted. His rival and successor, Louis Locheur, was no less aggressive in promoting scientific management. Clémental, who became the central figure in the reconstruction effort, saw in wartime experiences the basis of a new postwar order, which would feature larger, more modern, and more sophisticated industrial operations, scientific management, labor-management cooperation, and government coordination of the economy.[61]

The American role in the war, coupled with the collapse of living standards in the last months of the war and the first months of peace, created enormous interest in scientific management. In Germany more than one thousand books and articles on scientific management or "Taylorismus" appeared in the postwar period.[62] *Waste in Industry* had a galvanizing effect in Eastern Europe; it "contributed very largely to the promotion of scientific management in Czechoslovakia."[63] Karol Adamiecki, an engineering professor who had developed a series of charts and graphs similar to Gantt's, played a similar role in Poland.[64] Professional groups devoted to aspects of scientific management emerged in Britain, though an effort to form an English branch of the Taylor Society did not fare as well.[65] In industry, scientific management techniques became widespread. Corporations with at least some mass production operations, such as Renault, Siemens, and Fiat, were leaders, but smaller firms in the textile, food processing, and mining industries were also active. By the mid 1920s, banks, insurance companies, department stores, and a variety of government agencies were using scientific management to increase the quality and quantity of their services.[66]

Three developments of the 1920s illustrated the appeal of scientific management. First, the German Rationalization movement embraced a variety of objectives and causes. Yet the works of Schlesinger, Rathenau, Moellendorff, and other theorists, the operations of such firms as AEG and Siemens, and the activity of quasi-public agencies such as the Reichskuratorium für Wirtschaftlichkeit did not compartmentalize factory operations, economic planning, cartel negotiations, and corporatist political arrangements. Rationalization was a seamless web, a measure of the larger implications of Taylor's ideas.[67] Second, during the same period, enthusiasts in other nations formed a variety of promotional associations analogous to the Taylor Society: the Masaryk Labor Academy in Czechoslovakia, E.N.I.O.S. in Italy, the Oxford Management Conference in Britain, the French Conference on Scientific Management (which after its 1925 merger with Henry Fayol's Center for Administrative Studies became the French National Management Council). These groups organized international congresses in Prague (1924), Brussels (1925), Rome

(1927), and Paris (1929). They also persuaded the American phi-
lanthropist Edward A. Filene and the International Labor Organization to establish an International Management Institute in
Geneva in 1927. Headed by Albert Thomas and later Lyndall
Urwick, the Institute symbolized the acceptance of scientific
management in postwar, pre-Depression Europe. Third, the rapid spread of scientific management was also related to a new
tolerance among organized workers and union leaders similar to
the position of the French labor movement after 1915. This change
of attitude reflected greater care in the use of time study, but also
the new link between scientific management and labor reform, the
desire for American living standards, and the unions' declining
fortunes.[68]

The most striking example of the allure of scientific management in the 1920s was its popularity in the Soviet Union. Lenin
and Gastev found few allies until 1920. Then the desperate state of
the Soviet economy, the Bolshevik commitment to industrialization, and the attractions of western technology led Soviet leaders
to embrace scientific management in much the same way that their
successors in the 1930s would embrace a similar panacea, the
importation of American and German technology. At the height
of his influence, Gastev preached a "Soviet Americanism" and a
"new, flowering America" based on scientific management.[69]

Gastev's first victory came in 1920 when he obtained official
support for an Institute of Labor (TsIT) to conduct managerial
research and promote scientific management. In the following
months he outmaneuvered rivals and won additional patrons in
the Soviet government. With the advent of the New Economic
Policy, Gastev's cause flourished. In early 1921 there were twenty
groups conducting research under his auspices; by mid 1923 there
were fifty-eight. Most of them focused on raising industrial
productivity but "rationalizing education, combating excessive
lines at stores, improving the sorting of mail, reorganizing the
harvesting of potatoes and even curing syphilis were all subjects of
experimentation and research, . . ."[70] Gastev soon attracted critics and rivals. His opponents attacked his preoccupation with time
study and his technocratic approach, his slogan, for example, that
"mankind learned how to process things; the time has come to
thoroughly process man."[71] Gastev's most serious challenger was
Pavel Kerzhentsev, a journalist who promoted a popular, non-

technical approach to scientific management. Kerzhentsev's Time League, devoted to reducing waste in all areas of daily life, enjoyed a brief vogue in 1923–1924 and temporarily eclipsed Gastev's operations. Yet Kerzhentsev was no match for Gastev in the arena of bureaucratic combat. By 1925 he had lost official favor; together with the Time League he soon faded from view. Gastev, however, had little opportunity to savor his victory. The death of his chief patron, Felix Dzerzhinski, in 1926, made him vulnerable to attack and the triumph of Stalin in the late 1920s abruptly ended the Soviet commitment to scientific management. Some of Gastev's followers were purged as early as 1929; he persisted, with declining influence until his arrest and imprisonment in 1938. By that time nearly all his allies and associates had been killed or imprisoned.[72]

What did Gastev accomplish, if anything? The reports of American engineers who visited the Soviet Union provide one measure of his impact. Royal R. Keely, a peripheral member of Taylor's coterie who made an extended survey in 1920, was contemptuous of Soviet industry.[73] Walter Polakov, a prominent consultant of leftist sympathies who spent a year and half in the Soviet Union a decade later, reported only modest progress. "All of the vital details of scheduling, dispatching, production control, progress records, etc. are left mainly to chance." Time and motion study, he added, "is a thing little known in the U.S.S.R."[74] While Polakov probably missed subtle changes of approach and attitude as well as applications outside manufacturing, his judgment was a commentary on the corrosive effects of political infighting and the intensity of grassroots opposition. Despite official support for nearly a decade, scientific management had few friends in mines or factories. The management expert was "the most hated man in industry." As Gastev himself acknowledged in 1927, "he is opposed by the director; he is opposed by the chief engineer; to a large degree he is opposed by the foreman; he clashes with the opposition of the workers."[75] Donald Filtzer's recent examination of Soviet time study data attests to the enormity of the challenge.[76] As Gastev and his allies fell out of favor, the resistance grew increasingly violent. The Stakhanovite movement of the mid 1930s was a rebellion against time and motion study and the managerial authority that it enhanced.[77] By the end of the decade few engineers or managers were sufficiently bold or foolish to hold out.

The remarkable rise and fall of scientific management in the Soviet Union had no western parallel. The Depression of the 1930s diminished the attraction of American ideas and such European surrogates as rationalization, but apparently did not affect the progress of scientific management in industry. The best example was the success of the Bedaux firm in the 1930s. European affiliates of the American consulting company began to operate in Britain, France, Italy, Germany, and other countries in the late 1920s. Hard times were good for business, despite renewed labor opposition. Bedaux's promise to save more than his fee, primarily through increased labor productivity, suited the thinking of industrialists in the 1930s.[78] But Bedaux was not the only consulting firm that thrived. Urwick, Orr & Partners, and Wallace Clark & Co., for example, did well despite their fidelity to the Taylor approach. And though the international scientific management movement (including the International Management Institute) fell victim to hard times and rising political tensions, most of the institutions that impressed Paul Devinat in the 1920s continued to uphold the heritage of Taylor and his associates in the 1930s.

The Japanese experience was similar. In the late 1920s and 1920s three groups promoted scientific management in Japanese industry: consultants such as Yoichi Ueno and Araki Toichiro, who had personal contacts with Taylor, Gilbreth, and Emerson; mechanical engineers such as Takuo Godo of the naval arsenal at Kure and Shigeo Kato of Niigata Iron Works, who wanted to improve the operation of their plants; and engineering employees of Japanese firms allied with General Electric, Westinghouse, and other American multinationals, who borrowed technique as well as technology. Takeo Kato of Mitsubishi Electric, for example, brought back the Westinghouse factory manual and time study guide from a 1925 visit and used them to modernize operating procedures in his firm. The Japanese government encouraged this activity, creating committees on rationalization that served as forums for proponents of scientific management.[79]

Though the history of scientific management in Europe and Japan in the 1930s and 1940s is hardly more complete than the history of scientific management in the United States, it is clear that the post–World War II leaders who argued that American management techniques would save wartorn countries from economic backwardness greatly exaggerated the novelty of their proposals. Like Americans who saw in Stalin's Five Year plans the ultimate expression of scientific management planning, they confused superficial appearances with reality. The mental revolution was not and had never been an American monopoly.

## Scientific Management in America, 1915 to the 1950s

What happened to scientific management in the United States after 1915? The following essays examine the fates of the scientific management pioneers, the diffusion of scientific management in society and industry, and the criticisms of a later generation of analysts who had no firsthand knowledge of Taylor or his work. More important, they show that in the United States, as in Europe, scientific management continued to be a stimulus to thinking about the functions of organizations and a series of techniques for improving short-run economic performance. Because of this dual role, the study of scientific management provides an avenue for understanding the American interest in economic and technical rationalization as well as the evolution of production management and the changing character of industrial work in the middle decades of the century.

At the time of Taylor's death, none of the men close to him could match the fame or influence of two outsiders, Richard A. Feiss and Frank B. Gilbreth. Feiss was an innovative executive whose Joseph & Feiss Company had recently emerged as the most attractive and promising expression of the promise of scientific management. Feiss's operation was not only large and successful; it also was a compelling example of the logical links between Taylor-inspired industrial engineering and advanced personnel work. Feiss and his influential assistant, Mary Barnett Gilson, soon embraced a form of social engineering commensurate with the company's commitment to industrial efficiency but far exceeding anything Taylor or his immediate disciples ever imagined. Scientific management and a large female labor force proved to be a potent combination. David Goldberg's essay (chapter 2) is the most complete description to date of the Feiss operation and the ironic fate of Feiss and his colleagues in the 1920s.

Gilbreth's career is better known. His ebullient personality, innovations in job analysis, conflicts with Taylor, and unconventional family life made him a celebrity. Yet, as Brian Price explains in chapter 3, public visibility did not translate into professional or material success. Despite his fame, Gilbreth made little progress in establishing the superiority of his innovations to conventional time study or in satisfying his clients. At the time of his death in 1924, his career was at low ebb, his reputation sullied by repeated failures. He escaped the fate of Feiss, however, because of the potential of motion study and because of the efforts of his wife and partner, Lillian Gilbreth. During the 1930s, as motion study reemerged as an important feature of work analysis and Lillian became a celebrity in her own right, the Gilbreths of the early 1920s gave way to the more enduring and attractive Gilbreths of *Cheaper by the Dozen* (1948) — happy, successful, and respected.

In the meantime the ideas or principles of scientific management had attracted wide interest in American intellectual circles. Some writers and scholars became critics; others saw potential benefits for themselves and society. The spectrum of possibilities is evident in chapters 4 and 5, which examine the reactions of several groups of academics and the prominent social investigator, Mary Van Kleeck. Professors saw scientific management primarily in terms of academic politics; yet their effort to exploit it for their benefit created a powerful and wholly unanticipated mechanism for the spread of Taylor's ideas. It was no coincidence that a large proportion of active participants in the management movement of the 1920s and 1930s were university faculty members or that Taylor's work became an important feature of the education of engineers and managers. Van Kleeck, on the other hand, began her career as a prominent social worker, not unlike Mary Barnett Gilson. She became interested in industrial issues, saw scientific management as an answer to the disorganization and anarchic individualism of laissez-faire capitalism, and viewed its success as proof of the efficacy of production planning in society as a whole. As Guy Alchon explains, these views also led her to admire the Soviet experiment and ultimately to become an apologist for the Soviet state.

Although scientific management had implications for all institutions, it is most closely identified with industrial production. Supporters and critics alike assumed that its greatest impact was in the factory. But they have had more trouble specifying the nature of that impact. During Taylor's lifetime, when relatively small numbers of firms and workers were involved, it was possible to physically inspect most of the important sites, as C. Bertrand Thompson and Robert Hoxie did. By the late 1910s that type of evaluation was impossible; a small group of practitioners no longer controlled access to Taylor's techniques, and the number of applications exceeded the investigative capabilities of any individual. Nevertheless, several indirect measures are possible.[80] They suggest that by the 1930s scientific management in the workplace no longer implied revolutionary change or had special appeal for avant garde executives like Richard A. Feiss. In most cases managers viewed it in narrow, utilitarian terms and introduced or extended it to help achieve the potential of mass production technologies and to manage semiskilled workers. These trends probably accelerated in the 1930s, when economic decline spurred a renewed search for lower costs.

Three papers examine the application of scientific management in industry. Kathy Burgess's subject in chapter 6 is the Link–Belt Company, which had been one of Taylor's original demonstration firms. She reports a pattern of activity that was consistent over a long period but which differed markedly from that of Joseph & Feiss and presumably the mass production and service firms that embraced scientific management in the 1920s. Link–Belt depended on highly skilled workers. Scientific management improved their work and generally won their applause, but it could not insure that they would not join unions or strike. To Link–Belt managers, this was a serious shortcoming, which they addressed through traditional union avoidance measures: labor spies, black lists, and arbitrary discharges. Thus the mental revolution at Link–Belt was never complete; despite the introduction of modern personnel work and other refinements of scientific management in the 1920s, Link–Belt managers continued to rely on draconian anti–union tactics as long as it was legally feasible to do so.

During the same period, the enigmatic Charles Bedaux demonstrated that the techniques of scientific management could be successfully applied without a broader commitment, or a liberal vision like that of the Taylor Society insiders. In the 1920s and 1930s, Bedaux became the best-known industrial consultant, with a large clientele in the United States and Europe. A latecomer to scientific management, he prospered while Feiss, Gilbreth, and many of the pioneers stumbled. Yet the ingredients of his success are obscure because of his deliberately secretive approach. The discovery of the records of his British operations has finally raised the veil on Bedaux's activities. In chapter 7, Steven Kreis discusses Bedaux's tactics and their effects.

Most big businesses, however, did not employ outsiders or employed them only briefly and sporadically. John Rumm's study of Du Pont (chapter 8) is the first detailed account of an industrial engineering department over a long period. Like Kreis's study, it illustrates the narrow, practical focus of most scientific management applications. Du Pont executives had created a sophisticated organization based on principles of scientific management long before they established an industrial engineering department. Only when the Depression required extensive cost cutting did they extend scientific management to the shop floor. Still, their effort provides a detailed view of Taylor's techniques in action and an illuminating contrast with the experiences of Joseph & Feiss, Link-Belt, and other pioneers.

During Taylor's lifetime, the focus of most assessments of the impact of scientific management was its effect on work and workers. In the 1920s and 1930s this emphasis gradually faded, though Bedaux's work continued to elicit controversy. In part, this change was political; union policy changed and personalities like Taylor and Gilbreth no longer served as lightning rods for opposition to managerial change. In the 1930s, when labor militancy revived, organizing efforts and economic issues overshadowed the concerns of a more prosperous and confident era. Equally important, however, was the ambiguous effect of scientific management on industrial work. By the 1920s, it was clear that scientific management had not fulfilled its critics' apocalyptic forecasts. If Link-Belt and Du Pont were representative, most effects of scientific management were the results of changes in the operation of the firm as a whole, of changes in production processes, and of often diverse and inconsistent applications of time and motion study. The relationship between scientific management and work remained complex and variable.

Nevertheless, in the 1940s scientific management attracted a new generation of critics who focused on the worker. Two stimuli probably accounted for this development: the wide acceptance of managerial principles that were directly or indirectly associated with Taylor and a growing tendency to use Taylor as a straw man in order to emphasize revisionist ideas.[81] The result was a perception of scientific management as both influential and defective. Of the postwar critics, the best known was Peter F. Drucker, an Austrian-born scholar and management theorist whose works attracted a wide popular and academic audience. While professing admiration for Taylor's ideas, Drucker had reservations about their application in the large private bureaucracies that dominated the postwar economy. As an antidote to excessive specialization, organizational fragmentation, and professional isolation, Drucker proposed a procedure that he called Management By Objective (MBO). As Stephen Waring explains in chapter 9, MBO was a natural outgrowth of Drucker's earlier philosophical studies and ideological perspective. In practice it was highly controversial. Waring finds it flawed in conception and poorly or incompletely applied. Among other problems, Drucker, like Taylor, was afflicted by a legion of followers whose activities were half hearted or uninspired and whose principal interest was immediate financial gain.

Waring concludes that Taylor's ideas continued to influence managers in the 1950s and 1960s. To rephrase his point, Taylor's ideas, modified and expanded upon by Richard A. Feiss, Mary Gilson, Frank and Lillian Gilbreth, Mary Van Kleeck, Charles Bedaux, a host of academic proponents and critics, executives at Link-Belt, Du Pont, and other firms, and many others influenced the operation of American institutions in the 1950s, 1960s, and after. The precise nature of that influence has not been adequately gauged or appreciated. This collection of essays is a step toward that end.

NOTES

1. Frederick Winslow Taylor, *Scientific Management* (New York, 1947), pp. 26–27.

2. See Thomas P. Hughes, *American Genesis: A Century of Invention and Technological Enthusiasm, 1870–1970* (New York, 1989), pp. 184–87; Samuel Haber, *Efficiency and Uplift: Scientific Management in the Progressive Era* (Chicago, 1964), pp. 58–66.

3. See Frank Barkley Copley, *Frederick W. Taylor: Father of Scientific Management*, 2 volumes (New York, 1923); Daniel Nelson, *Frederick W. Taylor and the Rise of Scientific Management* (Madison, WI, 1980); Sudhir Kakar, *Frederick Taylor: A Study in Personality and Innovation* (Cambridge, MA, 1970).

4. See Monte Calvert, *The Mechanical Engineer in America, 1830–1910* (Baltimore, 1967); Bruce Sinclair, *A Centennial History of the American Society of*

*Mechanical Engineers, 1880–1980* (Toronto, 1980); Edwin T. Layton, Jr., *The Revolt of the Engineers* (Cleveland, 1971); Edwin T. Layton, Jr., "American Ideologies of Science and Engineering," *Technology and Culture* 17 (October 1976), pp. 688–701; Peter Meiksins, "The Revolt of the Engineers Reconsidered," *Technology and Culture* 29 (April 1988), pp. 219–46; Peter Meiksins, "Scientific Management and Class Relations: A Dissenting View," *Theory and Society* 13 (March 1984), pp. 177–209.

5. See Joseph A. Litterer, "Systematic Management: The Search for Order and Integration," *Business History Review* 35 (Winter 1961), pp. 461–76; Litterer, "Systematic Management: Design for Organizational Recoupling in American Manufacturing Firms," *Business History Review* 37 (Winter 1963), pp. 369–91; JoAnne Yates, *Control Through Communication: The Rise of System in American Management* (Baltimore, 1989), pp. 1–20. For the impetus to systematic management see Anthony Patrick O'Brien, "Factory Size, Economics of Scale, and the Great Merger Wave of 1898–1902," *Journal of Economic History* 48 (September 1988), pp. 639–49; Alfred D. Chandler, *The Visible Hand: The Managerial Revolution in American Business* (Cambridge, MA, 1977), pp. 240–83.

6. In addition to the Litterer articles cited in note 5, see Mariann Jelinek, "Toward Systematic Management: Alexander Hamilton Church," *Business History Review* 54 (Spring 1980), pp. 63–79; Daniel Nelson, *Managers and Workers: Origins of the New Factory System in the United States, 1880–1920* (Madison, WI, 1975), pp. 48–54.

7. The best account of Taylor's refinements of systematic management is the seldom-cited C. Bertrand Thompson, *The Taylor System of Scientific Management* (New York, 1917).

8. Frederick W. Taylor, "Shop Management," *Transactions of the American Society of Mechanical Engineers* 24 (1903), pp. 1337–1456.

9. See Milton Nadworny, *Scientific Management and the Unions, 1900–1932* (Cambridge, MA, 1955).

10. Charles D. Wrege and Amedeo G. Perroni, "Taylor's Pig-Tale: A Historical Analysis of Frederick W. Taylor's Pig Iron Experiments," *Academy of Management Journal* 17 (March 1974), pp. 6–27.

11. Charles D. Wrege and Anne Marie Stotka, "Cooke Creates a Classic: The Story behind F. W. Taylor's *Principles of Scientific Management*," *Academy of Management Review* 3 (October 1978), pp. 736–49. See also Frederick W. Taylor, *The Principles of Scientific Management* (New York, 1911); U.S. House of Representatives, *Hearings before the Special Committee of the House of Representatives to Investigate the Taylor and Other Systems of Shop Management under the Authority of H. Res. 90,* vol. 11 (Washington, DC, 1912), pp. 1377–1508.

12. See Samuel P. Hays, *Conservation and the Gospel of Efficiency* (Cambridge, MA, 1959); Haber, *Efficiency and Uplift,* pp. 58–66; Martin Schiesl, *The Politics of Efficiency: Municipal Administration and Reform in America, 1880–1920* (Berkeley, 1970; John F. McClymer, *War and Welfare: Social Engineering in America, 1890–1925* (Westport, CN, 1980); Bradley Robert Rise, *Progressive Cities: The Commission Government Movement in America, 1901–1920* (Austin, TX, 1977).

13. See Nelson, *Frederick W. Taylor*, pp. 101–3, 115–36; Milton J. Nadworny, "Frederick Taylor and Frank Gilbreth: Competition in Scientific Management," *Business History Review* 31 (1957), pp. 23–24; Nadworny, *Scientific Management and the Unions*, pp. 14–47.

14. See L. P. Alford, *Henry Lawrence Gantt, Leader in Industry* (New York, 1934); H. L. Gantt, *Work, Wages, and Profits* (New York, 1919); Gantt, *Industrial Leadership* (New York, 1921); Wallace Clark, *The Gantt Chart: A Working Tool of Management* (New York, 1922).

15. Kenneth E. Trombley, *The Life and Times of a Happy Liberal* (New York, 1954), pp. 15–46; Nadworny, *Scientific Management and the Unions*, pp. 114–17, 128–34; Layton, *Revolt of the Engineers*, pp. 154–78; Jean Christie, *Morris Llewellyn Cooke, Progressive Engineer* (New York, 1983), pp. 24–32.

16. For the original indictment and defense see Robert F. Hoxie, *Scientific Management and Labor* (New York, 1918). There are numerous recent works that subscribe to part or all of the indictment. Defenses of Taylor include Hindy Lauer Schachter, *Frederick Taylor and the Public Administration Community: A Reevaluation* (Albany, 1989); Edwin Locke, "The Ideas of Frederick Taylor: An Evaluation," *Academy of Management Review* 7 (1982), pp. 14–24; Louis W. Fry, "The Maligned F. W. Taylor: A Reply to His Many Critics," *Academy of Management Review* 1 (1976), pp. 124–29.

17. C. B. Thompson, *The Theory and Practice of Scientific Management* (Boston, 1917), pp. 36–104. Thompson was an instructor at the Harvard Business School who was given released time to visit plants and interview industrialists and consultants. He visited approximately 60 firms that Taylor's closest associates had worked at and approximately 20 (of perhaps 55) that Emerson and his staff had assisted. C. B. Thompson to Edwin F. Gay, August 17, 1914, Dean's Office File, Baker Library, Harvard Business School.

18. See Daniel Nelson, "Le Taylorisme dans l'industrie américaine, 1900–1930," in Maurice de Montmollin and Olivier Pastré, *Le Taylorisme* (Paris, 1984), pp. 56–57.

19. Nelson, *Managers and Workers*, pp. 71, 116.

20. See Nelson, *Frederick W. Taylor*, pp. 149–54.

21. Nadworny, *Scientific Management and the Unions*, pp. 48–67, 87–96; Hugh G. J. Aitken, *Taylorism at Watertown Arsenal* (Cambridge, MA, 1960), pp. 42–45, 150–57.

22. Frank B. Gilbreth, *Primer of Scientific Management* (New York, 1914), pp. 51–61. See also Gilbreth's clash with Charles S. Myers, the prominent British psychologist in Charles S. Myers, "The Efficiency Engineer and the Industrial Psychologist," *Journal of the National Institute of Industrial Psychology* 1 (1923), pp. 168–172; Frank and Lillian Gilbreth, "The Efficiency Engineer and the Industrial Psychologist," *Journal of the National Institute of Industrial Psychology* 2 (1924), pp. 40–45.

23. Schachter, *Taylor and the Public Administration Community*, pp. 111–23; Harry Braverman, *Labor and Monopoly Capitalism* (New York, 1974), pp. 85–168. For the avalanche of sociological writing that followed Braverman's work see Paul Thompson, *The Nature of Work: An Introduction to Debates on the Labour Process* (London, 1983), pp. 19–23; 74–77; 126–33; Stephen Wood,

ed., *The Degradation of Work: Skill, Deskilling, and the Labour Process* (London, 1982). For historical accounts see David Montgomery, *The Fall of the House of Labor: The Workplace, the State, and American Labor Activism, 1865–1925* (Cambridge, England, 1987), pp. 214–56; Dan Clawson, *Bureaucracy and the Labor Process: the Transformation of U.S. Industry, 1860–1920* (New York, 1980), pp. 222–43.

24. Aitken, *Taylorism at Watertown Arsenal*, pp. 147–53; Nadworny, *Scientific Management and the Unions*, p. 28.

25. Daniel Nelson, *American Rubber Workers and Organized Labor, 1900–1941* (Princeton, 1988), pp. 23–24.

26. Montgomery, *Fall of the House of Labor*, p. 247.

27. See Margery W. Davies, *Woman's Place Is at the Typewriter: Office Work and Office Workers, 1870–1930* (Philadelphia, 1982), pp. 97–128; Sharon Hartman Strom; "Light Manufacturing: The Feminization of American Office Work, 1900–1930," *Industrial and Labor Relations Review* 43 (October 1989), pp. 64–69; Elyce J. Rotella, "The Transformation of the American Office: Changes in Employment and Technology," *Journal of Economic History* 41 (March 1981), pp. 51–58; Yates, *Control Through Communication*, pp. 21–64.

28. Strom, "Light Manufacturing," pp. 68–69. See also Susan Porter Benson, *Counter Cultures: Saleswomen, Managers and Customers in American Department Stores, 1890–1940* (Urbana, 1986), pp. 38–47.

29. Nadworny, *Scientific Management and the Unions*, pp. 97–121.

30. Sanford M. Jacoby, *Employing Bureaucracy: Managers, Unions, and the Transformation of Work in American Industry, 1900–1945* (New York, 1985), pp. 100–104. See also Morris S. Viteles, *Industrial Psychology* (New York, 1932), pp. 40–56.

31. See Alford, *Gantt*, pp. 185–206, and Trombley, *Happy Liberal*, pp. 71–86 for the activities of two key members of the Taylor circle. For industrial mobilization in general, see Robert Cuff, *The War Industries Board; Business–Government Relations during World War I* (Baltimore, 1973).

32. Ellis Hawley, "Secretary Hoover and the Bituminous Coal Problem, 1921–1928," *Business History Review* 42 (1968), pp. 247–70; Robert H. Zieger, "Herbert Hoover, the Wage Earner, and the 'New Economic System,' 1919–1929," *Business History Review* 51 (1977), pp. 161–89; William J. Barber, *From New Era to New Deal Herbert Hoover, the Economists, and American Economic Policy, 1921–1933* (Cambridge, 1985), pp. 13–16; Guy Alchon, *The Invisible Hand of Planning: Capitalism, Social Science, and the State in the 1920s* (Princeton, 1985); Layton, *Revolt of the Engineers*, pp. 179–224; Donald R. Stabile, "Herbert Hoover, the FAES, and the AF of L," *Technology and Culture* 27 (October 1986), pp. 819–27.

33. Patrick Fridenson, "Un Tournant taylorien de la Société française (1904–1918)," *Annales Economies, Sociétés, Civilisations* 42 (September–October 1987), p. 1032.

34. Charles S. Maier, "Between Taylorism and Technocracy: European Ideologies and the Vision of Industrial Productivity in the 1920s," *Journal of Contemporary History* 5 (1970), pp. 27–61.

35. Jürgen Kocka, "The Rise of the Modern Industrial Enterprise in Germany," in Alfred D. Chandler, Jr. and Herman Daems, eds., *Managerial Hierarchies:*

*Comparative Perspectives on the Rise of the Modern Industrial Enterprise* (Cambridge, MA, 1980), p. 97.

36. Robert A. Brady, *The Rationalization Movement in German Industry: A Study in the Evolution of Economic Planning* (New York, 1974), p. 34. For Taylor's impact, see Lothar Burchardt, "Technischer Fortschritt und sozialer Wandel, Das Beispiel der Taylorismus-Rezeption," in W. Treue, *Deutsche Technikgeschichte* (1977), pp. 71–73; Heidrun Homburg, "Anfänge des Taylorsystems in Deutschland vor dem Ersten Weltkrieg," *Geschichte und Gesellschaft* 4 (1978), pp. 174–80.

37. Eisuke Daito, "Railways and Scientific Management in Japan 1907–30," *Business History* 31 (January 1989), p. 10. See also Koji Taira, "Factory Legislation and Management Modernization during Japan's Industrialization, 1886–1916," *Business History Review* 44 (1970), pp. 84–109.

38. Wayne Lewchuk, "The Role of the British Government in the Spread of Scientific Management and Fordism in the Interwar Years," *Journal of Economic History* 44 (June 1984), p. 356; John Child, *British Management Thought: A Critical Analysis* (London, 1969), pp. 38–39. Also see L. Urwick and E. F. L. Brech, *The Making of Scientific Management:* vol. 2, *Management in British Industry* (London, 1946), pp. 90–91.

39. Heather Hogan, "Scientific Management and the Changing Nature of Work in the St. Petersburg Metalworking Industry, 1900–1914," in Leopold H. Haimson and Charles Tilly, *Strikes, Wars, and Revolutions in an International Perspective* (Cambridge, England, 1989), pp. 365–73; S. A. Smith, *Red Petrograd, Revolution in the Factories, 1917–18* (Cambridge, England, 1983), p. 39.

40. Aimée Moutet, "Les Origines du système de Taylor en France, Le point de vue patronal (1907–1914)," *Le Mouvement Social* 93 (October–Décember 1973), pp. 17–21; George C. Humphreys, *Taylorism in France 1904–1920: The Impact of the Scientific Management Movement on Factory Relations and Society* (New York, 1986), p. 56; Judith A. Merkle, *Management and Ideology: The Legacy of the International Scientific Management Movement* (Berkeley, 1980), p. 178. See also *Zeitschrift des Vereins Deutscher Ingenieure* 45 (1901), pp. 462–64, 1377–86.

41. L. Urwick, ed., *The Golden Book of Management* (London, 1956), p. 56; Eisuke Daito, "Memorandum on the History of Scientific Management in Japan," July 1991. In author's possession.

42. Frank B. Gilbreth to Lillian M. Gilbreth, 1913, Frank B. Gilbreth Papers, Purdue University. See also Homburg, "Anfange des Taylorsystems in Deutschland," pp. 174–79.

43. Urwick and Brech, *The Making of Scientific Management*, vol. 1, *Thirteen Pioneers*, p. 95.

44. Mark R. Beissinger, *Scientific Management, Socialist Discipline, and Soviet Power* (Cambridge, MA, 1988), pp. 21–24. See also Kendall E. Bailes, "Alexei Gastev and the Controversy over Taylorism, 1918–1924," *Soviet Studies* 29 (July 1977), pp. 373–94; Richard Stites, *Revolutionary Dreams: Utopian Vision and Experimental Life in the Russian Revolution* (New York, 1989), pp. 149–52.

45. A. L. Levine, *Industrial Retardation in Britain, 1880–1914* (New York, 1967), pp. 60–68; Child, *British Management Thought*, p. 38; Craig R. Littler, *The Development of the Labour Process in Capitalist Societies* (London, 1982), pp. 89–90, 94–95; Wayne Lewchuk, *American Technology and the British Vehicle Industry* (Cambridge, 1987), pp. 89–92; Jonathan Zeitlin, "Between Flexibility and Mass Production: Product Production and Labour Strategies in British Engineering, 1880–1939," (unpublished paper), 1988, pp. 19–20. See also Bernard Elbaum and William Lazonick, *The Decline of the British Economy* (Oxford, 1986), pp. 7–8.
46. Merkle, *Management and Ideology*, p. 213.
47. Michael Rowlinson, "The Early Application of Scientific Management by Cadbury," *Business History* 30 (October 1988), pp. 377–95.
48. Dwight T. Farnham, *America vs. Europe in Industry: A Comparison of Industrial Policies and Methods in Management* (New York, 1921), p. 8. For suggestive examples see R. J. Overy, *William Morris, Viscount Nuffield* (London, 1976), pp. 28–31, 84–91.
49. See D. C. Coleman and Christine Macleod, "Attitudes to New Techniques: British Businessmen, 1800–1950," *Economic History Review* 39 (November 1986), pp. 605, 609. See also Peter N. Stearns, *Lives of Labor Work in a Maturing Industrial Society* (New York, 1975), pp. 121–47, 193–228; James Hinton, *The First Shop Stewards Movement* (London, 1973), pp. 98–99, 332–33; Edward H. Lorenz, "Two Patterns of Development: The Labour Process in the British and French Shipbuilding Industries 1880 to 1930," *The Journal of European Economic History* 13 (September–December 1984), p. 629.
50. Fridenson, "Un Tournant taylorien de la Société française," pp. 1042, 1053; Fridenson, *Histoire des usines Renault*, I, *Naissance de la Grande Enterprise, 1898–1939* (Paris, 1972), pp. 71–72; Moutet, "Les Origines du système de Taylor," pp. 29–30.
51. Fridenson, *Histoire des usines Renault*, pp. 73–75; Moutet, "Les Origines du systeme de Taylor," pp. 38–41; James M. Laux, *In First Gear, The French Automobile Industry to 1914* (Montreal, 1976), pp. 192–93; Homburg, "Anfänge das Taylorsystems in Deutschland," pp. 182–90. Gary Cross argues that the Renault strike was a turning point for the French labor movement, marking the beginning of a more positive approach to scientific management. Gary Cross, "Redefining Workers' Control: Rationalization, Labor Time, and Union Politics in France, 1900–1928," in James E. Cronin and Carmen Sirianni, *Work, Community, and Power: The Experience of Labor in Europe and America, 1900–1925* (Philadelphia, 1983), pp. 149–50. See also Patrick Fridenson, "Les premiers ouvriers français de l'automobile, 1890–1914," *Sociologie du Travail* (July–September 1979), pp. 297–325.
52. See Fridenson, "Un Tournant Taylorien de la Société francaise," pp. 1044–45; Laux, *In First Gear*, pp. 193–94; Moutet, "Les Origines du Système de Taylor," pp. 43–45; Homburg, "Anfänge des Taylorsystems in Deutschland," pp. 180, 182–83. For statements by Renault militants see H. Dubreuil, *Robots or Men? A French Workman's Experience in American Industry* (New York, 1930), pp. 65–66; Georges Friedmann, *Industrial Society, The Emergence of the Human Problems of Automation* (New York, 1955), pp. 265–67.

53. Fridenson, "Un Tournant taylorien de la Société française," p. 1044.
54. Professor Heidrun Homburg objects that this description oversimplifies the changes that occurred in Germany, particularly in industrial relations practices. Government intervention was as important as market forces in promoting cooperation. I am indebted to her for her careful critique. See also Gerald D. Feldman, *Army, Industry and Labor in Germany 1914–1918* (Princeton, 1966), pp. 89–92.
55. For other countries, see Merkle, *Management and Ideology*, pp. 183–92; Feldman, *Army, Industry and Labor in Germany*, pp. 46–49; Maier, "Between Taylorism and Technocracy," pp. 45–49; Jürgen Kocka, *Facing Total War, German Society, 1914–1918* (Cambridge, MA, 1984), pp. 33–34; Bailes, "Alexei Gastev," p. 383; Charles S. Myers, *Mind and Work: The Psychological Factors in Industry and Commerce* (New York, 1921) pp. 8–13.
56. Aimée Moutet, "Ingenieurs et rationalisation en France de la guerre a la crise (1914–1929)," in André Thépot, ed., *L'ingenieur dans la Société Française* (Paris, 1985), pp. 72–89; Moutet, "La Premiere Guerre mondiale et la taylorisme," in *Le Taylorisme*, pp. 67–81; Humphreys, *Taylorism in France* pp. 175–77; Devinat, *Scientific Management in Europe*, pp. 233–38; John F. Godfrey, *Capitalism at War: Industrial Policy and Bureaucracy in France 1914–1918* (Leamington Spa, 1987), pp. 56–63, 85–88, 181–97.
57. Humphreys, *Taylorism in France*, pp. 161–63.
58. C. Bertrand Thompson to Edwin Gay, August 13, 1918, Edwin Gay Papers, Dean's Office File, Harvard Business School.
59. Moutet, "La Première guerre mondiale et le taylorisme," pp. 73–74, 80.
60. Ibid., pp. 77–79; Fridenson, "Un Tournant Taylorien de la Société Française," pp. 1044–46; Maier, "The Two Postwar Eras and the Conditions for Stability in Twentieth Century Western Europe," *American Historical Review* 86 (April 1981), p. 335.
61. Godfrey, *Capitalism at War*; Richard F. Kuisel, *Capitalism and the State in Modern France, Renovation and Economic Management in the Twentieth Century* (Cambridge, 1981), pp. 35–57; Humphreys, *Taylorism in France*, pp. 151–76, 197–207, 226–28; Fridenson, "Un Tournant Taylorien de la Société Française," pp. 1051–52; Martin Fine, "Albert Thomas: A Reformer's Vision of Modernization," *Journal of Contemporary History* 12 (July 1977), pp. 545–49; Madelaine Reberioux and Patrick Fridenson, "Albert Thomas, pivot du reformisme Francaise," *Le Mouvement Social* 87 (April–June 1974), pp. 85–97.
62. Burchardt, "Technischer Fortschritt und sozialer Wandel," pp. 75–79; Heidrun Homburg, "Scientific Management and Personnel Policy in the Modern German Enterprise, 1918–1939: the case of Siemens," in Howard F. Gospel and Craig R. Littler, *Managerial Strategies and Industrial Relations* (London, 1983) pp. 100–102. For a contemporary overview see Gustav Winter, *Der Taylorismus Handbuch der Wissenschaftlichen Betriebs und Arbeitsweise für die Arbeitenden aller Klassen, Stande and Berufe* (Leipzig, 1920).
63. Devinat, *Scientific Management in Europe*, p. 13.
64. Zdzislaw P. Wesolowski, "The Polish Contribution to the Development of Scientific Management," *Proceedings, Academy of Management, 38th Annual Meeting of the Academy of Management, 1978*, pp. 12–13.

65. L. Urwick, *The Meaning of Rationalisation* (London, 1929), p. 60.

66. See Devinat, *Scientific Management in Europe*, pp. 111–14; Sylvie Van de Casteele-Schweitzer, "Management and Labour in France 1914–39," in Steven Tolliday and Jonathan Zeitlin, eds., *The Automobile Industry and Its Workers Between Fordism and Flexability* (New York, 1987), pp. 66–69; E. S. A. Bloemen, *Scientific Management in Nederland, 1900–1930* (Amsterdam, 1988).

67. Robert Brady, "The Meaning of Rationlization: An Analysis of the Literature," *Quarterly Journal of Economics* 46 (1932), pp. 527–35; Burchardt, "Technischer Fortschritt und sozialer Wandel," pp. 72–73, 87–89; Joan Campbell, *Joy in Work, German Work; The National Debate, 1800–1945* (Princeton, 1989), pp. 133–38; Ralph H. Bowen, *German Theories of the Corporate State with Special Reference to the Period 1870–1919* (New York, 1947), pp. 160–63, 183–209; Devinat, *Scientific Management in Europe*, pp. 225–27; Robert R. Locke, *Management and Higher Education Since 1940: The Influence of America and Japan on West Germany, Great Britain, and France* (Cambridge, 1989), pp. 94–95.

68. Maier, "Between Taylorism and Technocracy," p. 54; Moutet, "Ingénieurs et rationalisation en France," pp. 100–102; Urwich and Brech, The Making of Scientific Management, I, p. 95; Urwick *Meaning of Rationalisation*, pp. 75–76; Fine, "Albert Thomas," 552–56; Devinat *Scientific Management in Europe*, pp. 149–55, 216–22. Brady, *The Rationlization Movement*, pp. 330–34.

69. Bailes, "Alexei Gastev," p. 385. See also R. W. Davies, *The Soviet Economy in Turmoil, 1929–1930, the Industrialisation of Soviet Russia*, Vol. III (London, 1989), pp. 46–57.

70. Beissinger, *Scientific Management, Socialist Discipline*, p. 84.

71. Ibid., p. 51; Stites, *Revolutionary Dreams*, pp. 153–54.

72. Beissinger, *Scientific Management, Socialist Discipline, and Soviet Power*, pp. 95–98, 120–31; Stites, *Revolutionary Dreams*, pp. 155–58, 244.

73. Royal R. Keely, "An American Engineer's Experiences in Russia," *American Machinist* 55 (November 17, 1921), pp. 787–88; "The Deplorable Condition of Russian Industry," *American Machinist* 55 (November 24, 1921), pp. 840–42; "The Effect of Bolshevism on Russia," *American Machinist* 55 (December 1, 1921), pp. 879–80; "General Stagnation of Russian Manufacture," *American Machinist* 55 (December 8, 1921), pp. 919–21; "The Future of Bolshevik Russia," *American Machinist* 55 (December 15, 1921), pp. 947–49. I am indebted to Daniel Wren for these sources.

74. Walter N. Polakov, "Myths and Realities About Soviet Russia," *Harvard Business Review* 11 (October 1932), pp. 11–12. See also Daniel A. Wren, "Scientific Management in the U.S.S.R. with Particular Reference to the Contribution of Walter N. Polakov," *The Academy of Management Review* 5 (January 1980), pp. 1–11; Walter N. Polakov, "The Gantt Chart in Russia," *American Machinist* 65 (August 13, 1931), pp. 261–64.

75. Beissinger, *Scientific Management, Socialist Discipline, and Soviet Power*, p. 88.

76. Donald Filtzer, *Soviet Workers and Stalinist Industrialization: The Formation of Modern Soviet Production Relations, 1928–1941* (Armonk, 1986), pp. 157–61.

77. Beissinger, *Scientific Management, Socialist Discipline, and Soviet Power*, p. 135; and Lewis H. Siegelbaum, *Stakhanovism and the Politics of Productivity in the USSR, 1935–1941* (New York, 1988), pp. 16–65.

78. Littler, *Development of the Labour Process*, pp. 107–9, 114–15; Aimée Moutet, "Rationalisation du travail dan L'Industrie Française des Anness Trente," *Annales, Economies, Sociétés, Civilisations* 42 (Septembre–Octobre 1987), pp. 1070–74; Stefano Musso, *La Gestione Della Forze Lavoro Sotto il Fascismo* (Milan, 1987), pp. 38–80; Duccio Bigazzi, "Management and Labour in Italy, 1906–45," in Tolliday and Zeitlin, *The Automobile Industry and Its Workers*, pp. 84–88.

79. Daito, "Memorandum"; Andrew Gordon, "Araki Toichiro and the Shaping of Labor Management," and Kenji Okuda, "comment," in Tsunehiko Yui and Keiichiro Nakagawa, *Japanese Management in Historical Perspective* (Tokyo, 1989), pp. 173–97. See also Satoshi Sasaki, "On Materials of Scientific Management in Japan in Meiji-Taisho Era," *Japan Business History Review* 21 (April 1986), pp. 28–47; Sasaki, "The Introduction of Time Study Method into Mitsubishi Electric Co. at Kobe Works," *Japan Business History Review* 21 (January 1987), pp. 29–60. Both articles are in Japanese. I am indebted to Hitoshi Imai for these references.

80. See Daniel Nelson, "Scientific Management and the Workplace, 1920–1935," in Sanford Jacoby, ed., *Masters and Managers* (New York, 1990), pp. 74–89.

81. Schachter, *Frederick Taylor and the Public Administration Community*, pp. 111–23.

DAVID J. GOLDBERG

2  Richard A. Feiss, Mary Barnett Gilson, and
Scientific Management at Joseph & Feiss,
1909–1925

From the early 1910s to the mid-1920s, the premier example of the application of scientific management in industry was the
factory of the Joseph & Feiss Company, a Cleveland, Ohio,
manufacturer of men's suits. The architects of this remarkable
effort were the company's vice president, Richard A. Feiss, and its
pioneering personnel manager, Mary Barnett Gilson. Feiss and
Gilson demonstrated that scientific management was as appropriate to the comparatively labor-intensive production of suits as it
was to the more capital- and energy-intensive operations that
Taylor had reorganized. But they also grasped, better than Taylor,
the larger implications of scientific management for the worker
and society. Sensing the limitations of the engineers' approach,
they combined Taylor's industrial engineering techniques with
contemporary welfare practices to create a synthesis that anticipated the trend of the post–World War I years. In the process they
challenged conventional ideas about the relations of employer and
employee and the roles of women in industry. For a decade, Joseph
& Feiss was as famous for its social engineering as it was for its
suits.

Founded by German-Jewish immigrants in the 1840s, Joseph &
Feiss grew slowly until the 1890s when it became one of the first
clothing manufacturers to dispense with outside contractors and
to produce suits and clothing entirely within its own plant. This
change meant that the small contractors, primarily Czech immigrants, who had been doing the skilled tailoring and pressing
work for the firm could no longer maintain their own shops.

Many of these displaced craftsmen found employment at Joseph & Feiss Company as inspectors and foremen.

These changes occurred at a time when new technology and new managerial techniques were transforming the manufacture of men's clothing. Making use of semiautomatic machinery driven by electric power, employers thoroughly divided and subdivided operations so that the manufacture of a suit involved as many as 189 separate steps. Female employees performed most of the repetitive tasks, such as sewing on pockets, collars, and sleeves, and men worked primarily as cutters and tailors.

The men's clothing industry proved suitable for the use of high-volume production techniques since it did not have the constant changes of style that characterized the women's clothing industry. In addition, since Joseph & Feiss concentrated on the production of medium-priced suits (sold mainly through outlets in small towns of the middle west), its product lines proved relatively easy to standardize. Indeed, the firm's staple, the blue serge suit, came to be known as the "Model T" of the men's clothing industry. In peak years the company sold over 200,000 garments of this type.

Good salesmanship as well as mastery of mass-production techniques accounted for the firm's success. Capitalizing on the popularization of the craft ideal by the book publisher and editor Elbert Hubbard, the company in the 1890s began to market its goods under the "Clothcraft" label. Sales shot up immediately even though this bit of advertising gimmickry disguised the fact that changes initiated by Joseph & Feiss had eliminated the jobs of the custom tailors, which had been the basis of the craft.[1]

A turning point in the firm's history came in 1905 when Richard A. Feiss, the son of one of the company's owners, became vice president in charge of organization and manufacturing. Feiss graduated from Harvard in 1901 and received a law degree from Harvard Law School, but found the practice of law too "routine." While living in Boston, Feiss became a devotee of Frederick W. Taylor's theories of scientific management. Feiss hung Taylor's portrait in his office, acquired an extensive collection of pamphlets and books on Taylorism, and eventually became president of the Taylor Society. A person so compulsive and methodical that he measured the exact distance between his dormitory and his classrooms and later numbered each paragraph of his articles, Feiss set out to prove Taylor's theories could be applied to the notoriously seasonal and changeable clothing industry.[2]

Supremely confident in his own abilities, Feiss wanted to make the Clothcraft Company the most efficient clothing firm in the country. In keeping with Taylor's recommendations, engineers and time and motion study technicians scrutinized each task performed by operatives and placed them in eight separate grades. Each task was subdivided to the "last possible degree" and piece rates were reviewed four times annually to see if any readjustments were necessary. The greatest care was taken not to set the initial rate too high so that if reclassification proved necessary it would be in an "upward direction only." Operatives generally began at the lowest grade so they would have an opportunity to work their way up. Production clerks kept careful records and employees always had a slip informing them of their earnings.[3] The piece rate system was so detailed that John R. Commons considered it "as highly refined" as any in the country. Nowhere had he seen "such minute measurement."[4]

To spur on its workers and to reduce turnover and absenteeism, the Clothcraft Company developed an interlocking system of six separate bonuses. A daily production bonus was paid to each operative who maintained his or her standard rate; a daily quality bonus was paid to operatives who avoided rejections for defective workmanship; a daily attendance bonus of 50 cents per day rewarded those who came to work on time; an excuse bonus (which reduced the penalty for not reporting to work) rewarded those who explained their absence; a service bonus of 5 cents per day for every year of service rewarded long-term employees; and an advance notice bonus encouraged employees to forewarn the company about their intention to leave.[5]

No aspect of factory organization escaped scrutiny. The arrangement and placement of machinery was "scientifically" worked out to minimize lost time. An orthopedic surgeon designed new chairs for employees, and special tables made it possible for garments to be "handled as quickly and with as few motions as possible." To reduce monotony and fatigue the company allowed female operatives to get new batches of garments rather than have them delivered to their work stations.[6]

In keeping with Taylor's emphasis on the importance of the smooth flow of production, Feiss greatly enlarged the planning department, which developed a system by which trousers, vests, and coats were sent through the plant simultaneously. Pressing operations were also integrated into each step of production. A centrally located tally board served as the plant's "pulse" and foremen knew "at a glance" where "pressure" needed to be applied. Operatives were usually trained to perform more than one task and moved from one work station to another to remove bottlenecks. Since practically all of the sewing operations were carried out in a mammoth, well-lit, well-ventilated workroom in a state-of-the-art factory building (located in a westside residential neighborhood), supervisors did not even have to go from room to room to check on the production process.[7]

Speed became the firm's hallmark. A visitor to the plant in 1914 noted: "At the Clothcraft shops all workers are at full speed within a minute after the first bell rings and they keep up the drive until the last bell." Another outside observer commented: "Speed— lightning speed—is probably the first impression that forces itself upon the visitor in the factory. The operatives work with a smoothness, rapidity and precision that are astonishing."[8] According to Feiss, these methods enabled the firm to produce medium-grade clothing at one-half the cost of its competitors. They also meant that the company needed 20 percent fewer workers to produce the same amount of clothing as previously, although the firm's workforce continued to grow between 1910 and 1920 (when it reached a peak of 1,500) because of greatly expanded output.[9]

The company's initial efforts to implement this system led to one of the earliest walkouts against scientific management. In January, 1909, skilled pressers struck to protest wage cuts that they said would reduce their earnings from 25 to 50 percent, work rules that they considered onerous, and fines that penalized workers for damages. Ethnic solidarity also played a role in the strike. The Czech pressers protested against Feiss's efforts to eliminate the independent tailors, who were also Czech immigrants.[10]

One object of the workers' anger was a book of twenty-three rules that the firm issued in early 1909. The regulations mandated fines for tardiness and for failing to report a change of address and required all employees to obtain buttons when they arrived for work (instead of punching a clock) which meant that even those who were just a few minutes late had to go through the humiliating procedure of reporting to the supervisor's office. The rules also prohibited anyone from leaving the plant at lunch time.

It is hardly surprising that skilled, veteran, male workers led the protest against regulations that workers termed "penitentiary rules." Yet over 600 female workers joined the men on the picket lines, actively participated in the walkout, and insisted that they be included as officers in a branch of the AFL's United Garment Workers that was established during the month-long strike.

Despite demonstrations, parades, and picket lines, the company retained the loyalty of enough workers and hired enough strike-breakers to defeat the walkout. Those who were not fired returned to a factory that not only retained the twenty-three rules but that remained so regimented that male and female employees had to line up in "fire drill formation" before marching to separate lunchrooms at the noon hour.[11]

Clearly, the strike failed to halt or even to slow down the implementation of scientific management at the Clothcraft Company. On the other hand, the firm soon adopted a wide variety of welfare programs, despite Taylor's strictures against welfare work. By 1916 the firm had gone further in combining Taylorism and welfarism than any other company in the country.[12] Several factors in addition to the strike led Feiss to choose this course of action. Always concerned with improving productivity, he believed a more contented workforce would be more productive. He was also influenced by a wave of walkouts that hit the clothing industry between 1909 and 1911. In addition, Cleveland provided a sympathetic milieu, serving as home to a number of welfare-minded firms.[13] Lastly, Richard Feiss's personal motivations played a major role; in the manner of Henry Ford, he set out to uplift, Americanize, and remold his workforce. Feiss sincerely believed that industry had the responsibility for the "mental, moral and spiritual advancement" of its employees and desired that his factory perform functions that one normally associated with parenting or the public school.[14]

To Feiss, these endeavors had to become an integral rather than a peripheral part of management. To insure that the firm recognized their importance, he created a new department called Employment and Service (rejecting Welfare because it smacked too much of "philanthropy"). In 1913, he invited Mary Barnett Gilson, a Wellesley College graduate, to become its head.[15]

Gilson was an example of a Progressive era reformer who cast her lot with industry rather than with settlement houses or trade unions. Upon graduating from college she helped train department store clerks but had come to dislike the "artificiality" of that environment. She subsequently worked as a vocational counselor at a trade school for girls, where she gained her experience making home visits. Sympathetic to the needs of working women, she had even walked a picket line in support of striking textile workers. In 1912, she heard Taylor speak and became a convert to his theories, in particular because of the stress he put on the "responsibilities" of management. Thus when Feiss offered her a position with the Clothcraft Company, she jumped at the opportunity to integrate personnel work with factory management.[16]

Assuming the position of superintendent of the Employment and Service Department in 1913, Gilson remained with the firm for twelve years and became the nation's best-known welfare secretary.[17] Since Feiss and Gilson both shared a commitment to Taylorism and to service work (the term they preferred), they made an ideal team.

Many of the programs that Feiss and Gilson introduced resembled those in existence at other industrial plants. For example, they sponsored dances, picnics, choral societies, clubs, an orchestra, and an extensive athletic program.[18] On the other hand, no employer made a more determined effort to alter the values and behavior of the Czech, Italian, Hungarian, Slovak, and Lithuanian women who comprised the bulk of its workforce. In the process of trying to create more productive workers and an achievement-oriented business culture, the firm left little to chance. As Gilson later admitted, "There was no facet of life we did not touch."[19]

Gilson's role began when the prospective employee appeared at the plant. During the hiring process the Employment and Service Department administered a battery of psychological, intelligence, and dexterity tests. Upon being hired, a new employee had her "duties" explained to her by a company representative who emphasized "the unfairness of trying to work in the factory and at home."[20] This issue particularly concerned Gilson, who believed that fatigue caused by overwork in the home reduced the productivity and increased the absenteeism of female workers. For this reason, she used systematic home visits and in-plant talks with women workers and their mothers to convince them to be more assertive within their families. This could involve getting "foreign-born men" to share the cooking rather than treating their wives as "beasts of burden;" convincing parents to allow their daughters to attend wholesome evening entertainments in the plant rather than making them "practically" prisoners in their own homes; or suggesting to a "fat, comfortable and tradition-worshiping woman" that her six sons could pack their own lunches and do their own mending rather than leaving such chores exclusively to the sole daughter who worked at the Clothcraft Company. But as a realist, Gilson knew that most men wished to avoid "effeminating themselves" and thus advocated the five-day workweek so that women would have Saturday to work in the home.[21] Since Feiss also believed Saturday work to be inefficient, the plant in 1919 went on an eight-and-one-half hour day, five-day week, fulfilling Taylor's prediction that implementation of his system would lead to a reduction in hours.[22]

Assaults on traditionalism concerned "even the most intimate matters." A well-equipped medical department offered birth control information, gave instruction on diet and hygiene, and discouraged employees from patronizing quacks. Other members of the Employment and Service Department visited "every absentee" in order to investigate home conditions. At such times, they might give advice on how to make more "practical" use of parlors and how to ventilate homes in order to prevent headaches. The firm also began a savings program since it believed young, female operatives lacked incentives when, as occurred in "an astonishing number of cases," they had to hand unopened pay envelopes over to "avaricious parents."[23]

Feiss and Gilson, who both frowned upon any form of ostentation, also made a concerted effort to control the conduct and dress of their employees. On various occasions, Feiss berated workers for smoking, for wearing rolled-down stockings, makeup, or jewelry, and for chewing gum, which he considered "unhealthy" and "disgusting."[24] Gilson later admitted that the company became overly "authoritarian" and "obsessed" with personal habits, but in 1916 she claimed that "it is no longer a debatable question that elaborate clothes and jewelry and powder and paint have a demoralizing effect on the character and ability of a working girl."[25] Articles in the *Clothcraft* magazine, such as "What Shall I

Wear to Work Today," aimed at instructing young women on the proper way to dress. Foremen (who frequently objected to being given such petty tasks) were responsible for enforcing the personal standards set by Feiss and Gilson.[26]

Disturbed by their employees' patronage of "cheap amusements" and attendance at "cheap dance halls and movies," the company instituted a series of choral performances, entertainments, and dances that aimed at providing a wholesome alternative to the coarser forms of amusement. Company programs ended promptly at 9 P.M., "thereby setting a standard of proper hours." Another opportunity to control behavior came at the noon hour when employees sat at tables with assigned "heads" who monitored conversations and forbade the use of foreign languages.[27]

Gilson also sought to ensure that women had opportunities for promotion. Wishing to discourage hasty marriage, she urged female employees to think of their jobs as more than a way station to matrimony. In general, the firm preferred to promote from within and, far more than most firms, encouraged women to seek "positions of responsibility." By 1920, twenty-one of the firm's forty-six supervisors were female and a number of the women managed men—an uncommon occurrence in American industry.[28] Gilson also hoped to "bridge the gulf between office and factory" and tried to discourage clerical employees from regarding themselves as superior to factory hands. However, she had less success in this endeavor since the firm's executives refused to submit their "blond twinkle toes secretary(s)" to the same discipline as other employees.[29]

In keeping with Taylor's recommendations, the firm also reduced the foremen's authority. This meant that foremen and forewomen no longer had the power to hire and fire and that all planning was now done by management. To avoid any possible favoritism on the part of supervisors, all batches were assigned to sewing room operatives in numerical sequence. And as a sign of the firm's solicitousness of employees, Employment and Service personnel elicited complaints about foremen and forewomen during home visits.[30] Indeed, the firm tried so hard to remove the "old style bosses with their petty tyrannies" that Richard Feiss claimed "one of the words we never permit used in our factory is 'authority.' Foremen are employed for responsibility alone."[31]

By the early 1920s, Gilson and Feiss could claim considerable success in their efforts to join scientific management with welfare capitalism. As one of the many laudatory articles written about the company put it, this truly was "a shop where science and humanity combine[d]."[32] Morris Cooke, Carl Barth, Lillian Gilbreth, and many other luminaries of the management movement visited the plant and many journalists wrote favorable articles about working conditions, which the company reprinted in its advertising campaigns. Through the use of home visits, bonuses, the five-day week and other means, the turnover rate was reduced from 150.3 percent per year in 1910 to 41.3 percent in 1923. Feiss even claimed that his firm had "the steadiest payroll force in the city of Cleveland." Despite all of his denials of philanthropic intent, Feiss believed that employers had a "duty" and a "moral responsibility" to provide steady employment under "all possible conditions." This goal was achieved through the firm's practice of producing its staple—blue serge suits—during slack seasons rather than laying off large numbers of employees.[33]

It is difficult to assess the impact these programs had on the company's employees. By paying higher wages, reducing the hours of labor, promoting on the basis of performance, providing instruction on health and hygiene and encouraging women to think in terms of self-advancement, the Employment and Service Department contributed to the employees' well-being. On the other hand, the Clothcraft Company also demanded loyalty to the corporation. Whatever benefits workers realized from the company's programs came at the expense of privacy. By requiring yearly physical exams, by forbidding workers from leaving the plant at lunchtime, by exercising the right to visit a worker's home after each and every absence, by inspecting lockers and by regulating employees' dress and conduct, the Clothcraft Company exercised authority over all aspects of workers' lives.[34] Defending management's right "to interest itself in the lives of workers outside as well as inside the factory," Gilson claimed it as not just a "right" but as a "duty" that was "a natural outgrowth of executive responsibility."[35] Significantly, a report prepared for the firm suggested that "husky and oftentimes obstreperous men" might have raised more objections to these programs than young female operatives.[36] More recently, historians have suggested that women might have proven more amenable to social control than men because they had already been socialized to accept authority.[37]

From the firm's perspective, one measure of the success of welfare capitalism was the fact that after 1909 the company remained free of labor unrest. Most notably, between 1922 and 1925, Joseph & Feiss withstood a well-financed organizing drive conducted by the Amalgamated Clothing Workers of America (ACWA). The ACWA had been founded in 1914 when Sidney Hillman and other members of the AFL's United Garment Workers decided to leave that organization. Immediately upon its formation, the ACWA successfully organized thousands of immigrant and female workers. It scored even greater gains between 1916 and 1919 when it took advantage of war-induced prosperity and the immediate postwar boom to secure contracts from all of the large firms in such men's clothing centers as Baltimore, Rochester, and Chicago.[38]

The ACWA's first victories in Cleveland came in March 1919 when a concerted drive led to the unionization of a number of the city's smaller shops.[39] At this time, the ACWA made little effort to organize Joseph & Feiss or Richman Brothers, the city's other large nonunion firm.[40] Upon the onset of the 1920–1921 depression, the ACWA was forced to assume a defensive posture, but when prosperity returned in late 1922, the ACWA decided to take on the Clothcraft Company.

Given Sidney Hillman's open support for scientific management, it may seem surprising that the Joseph & Feiss Company did not welcome the ACWA. However, Joseph & Feiss was not one of the "elite" firms that believed unions had a role to play in establishing standards and bringing stability to the industry.[41] Feiss may have been an admirer of Hillman but he definitely believed the firm would be better off without the interference of local Cleveland ACWA leaders, whom he deemed less capable and more militant than Hillman. Though Gilson in her memoirs claimed the company did not interfere with the organizing drive, the firm fired one ACWA organizer, and management convened a special meeting of foremen and forewomen to discuss inroads made by the union.[42]

The ACWA launched its campaign in October 1922. Led by a female organizer, Hortense Powdermaker, the union opened an office near the Joseph & Feiss plant and began to distribute leaflets to employees. By November 1922, the ACWA had enrolled 236 male and 122 female Clothcraft employees. Confident that it was on the road to victory, the ACWA formed a local for the plant's employees in February 1923, and began the second phase of its drive. During the next six months, the union sponsored a number of meetings for various ethnic groups and held numerous educational and social gatherings. During the entire period it said little about welfarism and focused its demands on wages, union recognition, and abolition of the "hated blue marks," which reduced employees' bonus earnings.[43]

In late 1923 the ACWA concluded that it lacked the support to carry out a successful organizing strike and dropped the entire effort. During the next year local leaders ceased open activity, but in December 1924 the ACWA launched a second campaign, led by a male organizer, Beryl Peppercorn. This time the ACWA challenged the company's welfare policies more directly, urging workers, "Demand to be let alone." Challenging notions that the factory could be thought of as a "charitable institution," the ACWA mocked the "hypocritical smile of the uplifter who gets paid to smile" and ridiculed the handing out of gifts at Christmastime. In questioning the level of regimentation inside the plant, the union asked workers: "Are you free men and women?"

This drive proved even less successful than the first one. In early 1925 the union began to issue sarcastic leaflets that asked: "How much longer are you going to sleep and have them keep a veil over your eyes"; "Don't stand still, you are blocking the traffic"; and most tellingly of all, "Play bridge girls, it is a very good game if you have no other troubles." The union ended its campaign in May 1925.[44]

A number of factors accounted for the failure of the two organizing drives. Undoubtedly, Feiss and Gilson had created a "family" atmosphere that the union threatened.[45] The ACWA itself blamed "continuity of work," which had largely eliminated layoffs.[46] The company also screened out potential organizers or militants during the hiring process, dismissed those whose views ran counter to the "spirit" of the organization and followed a policy of hiring friends and relatives of current employees.[47] The smooth flow of work did much to remove bottlenecks that often irked pieceworkers; an employee representation plan established in 1919 provided a means of presenting grievances; and the curbs on foremen and forewomen removed other problems.[48]

Ironically, the ACWA's campaign collapsed at a time when tensions that had been brewing within the firm for a number of years finally came to a head. The company's problems began with a sales slump during the postwar depression. That decline coincided with the opening of a new factory building that after 1921 housed all of the company's operations and imposed a considerable burden on the firm. Even after the depression lifted, the company's position did not improve much. Its major difficulty was that "the farmer, the coal miner and the factory worker," who were the company's best customers, now had automobiles and no longer had to shop in their own immediate localities. By 1925, many clothing stores in small midwestern towns that had previously served as outlets for the firm's goods had closed entirely. Compounding the difficulty, many of the company's old customers began to buy more stylish suits and overcoats. The firm was poorly situated to cope with changing fashions since it had only a small design department, and Feiss was indifferent to if not contemptuous of trends in clothing styles.[49]

Given its large overhead costs, the firm could ill afford a slump in sales. By 1925, the new plant, with a capacity of 750,000 suits per year, was only producing 350,000 per year. The company's net earnings dropped from $375,006 in 1923 to $138,422 in 1924, and it failed to pay its preferred dividend for the first time.[50] Not very surprisingly, given the dire economic situation, some of the firm's executives began to view the work of the Employment and Service Department as "frills." Facing deep cuts in the welfare program and the end of her influence, Gilson chose to resign at the end of 1924.[51]

Feiss's troubles were far worse. His father and brother (both of whom held high executive positions in the firm) had come to believe that scientific management was too costly and no longer provided the "efficiencies or economies" it had in better times.[52] As part of their revaluation of the firm's commitment to Taylorism, Feiss's relatives also began to question the "'big' salaries" paid to engineers and other scientific management experts in the manufacturing department. Feiss made every effort to defend the application of Taylor's principles and blamed the firm's difficulties on its failure to apply scientific management to the merchandising and selling departments. But his father and brother gained the support of all of the firm's other executives and he had little choice but to resign in mid 1925. According to Kepple Hall, the firm's superintendent of planning and a nationally known management expert whose own "big" salary was being questioned, Feiss was "crushed" by this series of events.[53]

From Hall's perspective, the "unenlightened members" of the firm had gained control and were about to dismantle key aspects of scientific management, including the bonus system, the routing plan, and the cost system.[54] Nothing this drastic seems to have occurred, although in June 1926 Feiss complained about "changes" that had been made in "some of the control methods which mean a step away from the fundamental principles of coordination and control."[55] In reality, the firm appears to have maintained many of the essential features of Taylorism but "dropped many of the refinements" and simplified controls so as to require a smaller supervisory force.[56]

Regardless of how many changes the firm actually made, the business difficulties encountered by the Joseph & Feiss Company and the subsequent revaluation of its commitment to Taylorism were a major embarrassment to the scientific management movement. Richard A. Feiss had served as president of the Taylor Society, and as late as October 1924 had published an article on "Personal Relationship as a Basis of Scientific Management" in the *Bulletin of the Taylor Society.* Kepple Hall, who also lost his job, probably spoke for many in the Taylor Society when he insisted that the problem was not scientific management but a "temperamental Jew losing his head because he does not see a profit."[57]

The reorganization of Joseph & Feiss was thus a blow to the progress of scientific management. After 1925 the company was no longer a showcase for industrial and social engineering; proponents no longer could point to it as proof of the power of scientific management to overcome the vicissitudes of the marketplace; and Feiss and Gilson no longer played the practical and symbolic roles they had performed so convincingly in earlier years. Yet it would be wrong to exaggerate these changes. Joseph & Feiss recovered quickly and resumed its growth with most of its managerial infrastructure and many of its welfare programs intact.[58] The management movement also became more, not less, prominent in the late 1920s. Gilson went on to a distinguished career in university teaching and most Joseph & Feiss employees were reemployed by 1926. Only Richard A. Feiss did not fare well. His dismissal marked the beginning of a personal and professional decline that effectively ended his career. His brother later wrote that he was poorly qualified for the clothing business, which depended on financial and merchandising expertise more than on production management.[59] But it appears that his inflexibility and obsessiveness, which had helped make him and Joseph & Feiss stars in the scientific management firmament, also made it difficult for him to work for anyone in any industry.

In the meantime Feiss, Gilson and their subordinates had demonstrated what a commitment to scientific management could mean. Starting with Taylor's technical and organizational reforms, they pursued the logic of scientific management to the factory door and beyond, challenging convention at every step. Their initiatives obliterated the distinction between contemporary Taylorism and welfare work; exposed the artificiality of customary notions of women's abilities and motivations; redefined the boundaries of employer-employee relations; and challenged a host of other orthodoxies, for example that supervisors were the best judges of current or potential employees, that turnover was inevitable, and that shorter hours increased production costs. Their approach was not the only way to interpret Taylor's message and it was not the choice of most executives. But for a decade it enabled them to explore, as well as anyone, the possibilities that Taylor had in mind when he spoke of "a mental revolution."

NOTES

1. For a history of the firm, see "The Joseph & Feiss Company: History and Outline of Its Operation," The Joseph & Feiss Papers (hereafter cited as J & F Papers), Western Reserve Historical Society, Cleveland, Ohio, Container 1, Folder 1; and O. D. Foster, "He Found 'Short Cuts' to Long Steps of Progress," J & F Papers, Container 5, Folder 8. For a description of the "elite" men's clothing manufacturers, see Steve Fraser, "Combined and Uneven Development in the Men's Clothing Industry," *Business History Review* 57 (Winter 1983), pp. 522–47.

2. Foster, "'Short Cuts' to Long Steps of Progress."

3. Boyd Fisher, "Clothcraft Shops," J & F Papers, Container 4, Folder 9; Louis Lux, "A Perfect Machine is a Systematic Assemblage of Details, Second Report of Apprenticeship Course with H. Black Company," November 22, 1911, J & F Papers, Container 5, Folder 8 (hereafter cited as Lux Report); Frank J. Becvar, "A Method of Grading and Valuing Operations," J & F Papers, Container 5, Folder 9.

4.  John R. Commons, "Lizzie Likes Her Job," *The Independent* 104 (November 6, 1920), pp. 184–204.

5.  Kepple Hall, "Wage Systems," J & F Papers, Container 5, Folder 9; Becvar, "A Method of Grading and Valuing Operations."

6.  "A Clothing Plant of High Efficiency," J & F Papers, Container 5, Folder 8; Becvar, "A Method of Grading and Valuing Operations"; Foster, "'Short Cuts' to Long Steps of Progress"; Commons, "Lizzie Likes Her Job," pp. 184–204.

7.  Kepple Hall, "The Planning Department as an Instrument of Executive Control," J & F Papers, Container 5, Folder 8; Lux Report. For the use of similar methods in the automobile industry, see Stephen Meyer, *The Five Dollar Day: Labor Management and Social Control in the Ford Motor Company, 1908–1921* (Albany, NY, 1981), chap. 3.

8.  Fisher, "Clothcraft Shops"; "A Shop Where Science and Humanity Combine," J & F Papers, Container 5, Folder 12.

9.  "A Shop Where Science and Humanity Combine"; Ida M. Tarbell, *New Ideas in Business: An Account of Their Effects Upon Men and Profits* (New York, 1917), p. 254.

10. The strike events can be followed in *Cleveland Citizen,* January 16, 23, 30; February 6, 13, 20, 1909; *Cleveland Press,* January 6, 10, 11, 14, 1909; *Cleveland Plain Dealer,* January 6, 10, 14, 17, 28, 1909.

11. Foster, "'Short Cuts' to Long Steps of Progress."

12. Joseph Bancroft (a cotton textile firm) had somewhat earlier attempted to combine scientific management and welfarism but had dropped aspects of Taylorism that it viewed as incompatible with welfare work. See Daniel Nelson and Steward Campbell, "Taylorism Versus Welfare Work in American Industry: H. L. Gantt and the Bancrofts," *Business History Review* 46 (Spring 1972), pp. 1–16.

13. For welfarism in Cleveland, see Richard Ely, "Industrial Betterment," *Harpers Monthly Magazine* 105 (September 1902), pp. 548–53; Daniel Nelson, *Managers and Workers: Origins of the New Factory System in the United States, 1880–1920* (Madison, WI, 1975), p. 110.

14. M. O. Truesdale, "Personal Relations in Scientific Management," J & F Papers, Container 5, Folder 8. For the "reform impulse" that often motivated welfare work, see Sanford M. Jacoby, *Employing Bureaucracy; Managers, Unions and the Transformation of Work in American Industry, 1900–1945* (New York, 1985), pp. 59–60.

15. Gilson replaced Emma S. Brittin, who had implemented the company's earliest welfare programs. See Emma S. Brittin, "Two Years of Successful Welfare Work in a Factory Employing One Thousand People," *Human Engineering* 1 (April 1911), pp. 80–86; Richard A. Feiss, "Personal Relations in Business Administration," Richard Feiss Papers, Labor-Management Documentation Center, Cornell University.

16. Mary Barnett Gilson, *What's Past is Prologue* (New York, 1940), pp. 1–57.

17. Nelson, *Managers and Workers,* p. 219 n. 86.

18. For a listing of the company's programs, see Richard A. Feiss, "Personal Relationship as a Basis of Management," J & F Papers, Container 5, Folder 8.

19. Gilson, *What's Past is Prologue*, p. 138. For the ethnic composition of the company's workforce, see Lux Report; *Advance*, July 13, 1923.

20. Fisher, "Clothcraft Shops." See also William M. Leiserson, *Adjusting Immigrants and Industry* (New York, 1924), pp. 90–91.

21. Mary Barnett Gilson, "The Relation of Home Conditions to Industrial Efficiency," J & F Papers, Container 5, Folder 9; Gilson, "What Women Workers Mean to Industry," U.S. Department of Labor Women's Bureau, *Bulletin Number 23* (Washington, DC, 1923), pp. 69–70.

22. For the workweek, see Benjamin Kline Hunnicutt, *Work Without End, Abandoning Shorter Hours for the Right to Work* (Philadelphia, 1988), chap. 1; David Roediger and Phillip S. Foner, *Our Own Time: A History of American Labor and Working Day* (Westport, CT, 1989), p. 240; Robert Whaples, "Winning the Eight-Hour Day, 1909–1919," *Journal of Economic History* 50 (June 1990), pp. 393–406.

23. Gilson, "The Relationship of Home Conditions to Industrial Efficiency"; Foremen's Council Minutes, November 11, 1921, J & F Papers, Container 4, Folder 6; Untitled document, October 7, 1914, J & F Papers, Container 4, Folder 9; Feiss, "Personal Relationship in Business Administration."

24. For Feiss's concerns, see Foremen's Council Minutes, J & F Papers, Container 4, Folder 6.

25. Gilson, "The Relationship of Home Conditions to Industrial Efficiency." For Gilson's regret over the firm's zealousness in this matter, see Gilson, *What's Past is Prologue*, p. 134.

26. See in particular, "Personal Standards Recommended by a Committee Composed of Members of the Operatives Council and Foremen's Council," J & F Papers, Container 4, Folder 7; Foremen's Council Minutes, March 1, 1922, November 23, 1923, December 14, 1923, J & F Papers, Container 4, Folder 7.

27. Gilson, "The Relationship of Home Conditions to Industrial Efficiency"; Foremen's Council Minutes, February 2, 1920, November 11, 1921, J & F Papers, Container 4, Folder 6; Untitled document, October 7, 1914, J & F Papers, Container 4, Folder 9.

28. Untitled document, June 11, 1914, J & F Papers, Container 4, Folder 9; *Sunday News*, November 14, 1922, J & F Papers, Container 5, Folder 12; Mary B. Gilson, "Women's Place in the Factory," *Clothcraft Bulletin*, November 1920, J & F Papers, Container 5, Folder 10; Gilson, *What's Past is Prologue*, pp. 98–100.

29. Gilson, *What's Past is Prologue*, pp. 75–76, 113–114; "Work of the Employment and Service Department of the Clothcraft Shops," J & F Papers, Container 5, Folder 8.

30. Lux Report; Mary B. Gilson, "Taking Stock in an Employment Department," J & F Papers, Container 5, Folder 8; Gilson, "Work of the Employment and Service Department of the Clothcraft Shops," J & F Papers, Container 5, Folder 8; Gilson, *What's Past is Prologue*, pp. 152–56. For rules and regulations that applied to the foremen and forewomen and for their objections to assuming some of these responsibilities, see Foremen's Council Minutes, J & F Papers, Container 4, Folder 6.

31. Richard A. Feiss, "The Spirit of Scientific Management," January 17, 1917, J & F Papers, Container 5, Folder 8; Feiss, "Personal Relationships in a Business Administration."

32. "A Shop Where Science and Humanity Combine."

33. Richard Feiss, "The Engineering Approach to the Problem of Continuous Employment," J & F Papers, January 31, 1921, Container 5, Folder 8; Richard S. Feiss, "Personal Relationship as a Basis of Scientific Management," J & F Papers, Container 5, Folder 9.

34. See, for example, Foremen's Council Minutes, July 6, 1920, July 11, 1921, J & F Papers, Container 4, Folder 6.

35. Gilson, "The Relationship of Home Conditions to Industrial Efficiency."

36. See Fisher, "Clothcraft Shops."

37. See France S. G. Couvares, *The Remaking of Pittsburgh, Class and Culture in an Industrializing City, 1877–1919* (Albany, NY, 1984), p. 117; Alice Kessler-Harris, *Cut to Work; A History of Wage Earning Women in the United States* (New York, 1982), 239; Gilson, "The Relationship of Home Conditions to Industrial Efficiency."

38. Joel Seidman, *The Needles Trades* (New York, 1942), pp. 127–42; Leiberson, *Adjusting Immigrant and Industry*, pp. 209–11.

39. *Report of the General Executive Board to the Fourth Biennial Convention of the Amalgamated Clothing Workers of America, May 10–15, 1920* (Boston, 1920), pp. 84–85; *Cleveland Citizen*, March 22, 1919.

40. Richman Brothers avoided unionization largely through the use of an extensive employees' stock subscription program. See Charles Elliot Zaretz, *The Amalgamated Clothing Workers of America — A Study in Progressive Trades Unionism* (New York, 1934), pp. 147–48.

41. For firms that did welcome the union role, see Steve Fraser, "Dress Rehearsal for the New Deal: Shop Floor Insurgents, Political Elites and Industrial Democracy in the Amalgamated Clothing Workers," in Michael M. Frisch and Daniel J. Walkowitz, eds., *Working Class America: Essays on labor, Community and American Society* (Urbana, IL, 1983), pp. 219–55.

42. Gilson, *What's Past is Prologue*, pp. 108–12. For the special meeting to discuss the union question, see Foremen's Council Minutes, December 18, 1922, J & F Papers, Container 4, Folder 7.

43. *Advance*, October 20, 27, November 3, 24, December 1, 15, 22, 1922; January 19, February 2, 16, March 2, 30, April 16, May 15, June 15, 29, August 10, 1923.

44. Beryl Peppercorn Papers, Western Reserve Historical Society, Folder 1.

45. For the ability of welfarism to create a "family" atmosphere, see Gerald Zahavi, *Workers, Managers and Welfare Capitalism: The Shoeworkers and Tanners of Endicott Johnson, 1890–1950* (Urbana, IL, 1988).

46. *Report of the General Executive Board and Proceedings of the Seventh Biennial Convention of the Amalgamated Clothing Workers of America, May 10–15, 1926* (Montreal, 1926), pp. 122–23.

47. See Lux Report; Feiss, "Personal Relationship as a Basis of Scientific Management"; Stuart D. Brandes, *American Welfare Capitalism, 1880–1940* (Chicago, 1970), p. 118.

48. For these aspects, see Gilson, *What's Past is Prologue*, pp. 91, 105–7; Truesdale, "Personal Relations in Scientific Management."

49. For the best analysis of the firm's difficulties, see Paul L. Feiss to Mary Gilson, June 3, 1940, J & F Papers, Container 1, Folder 12. See also Gilson, *What's Past is Prologue*, pp. 206–8. For the more general shift from the approach that Joseph & Feiss relied on to a "segmented" marketing strategy, see Richard S. Tedlow, *New and Improved, The Story of Mass Marketing in America* (New York, 1990).

50. Kepple Hall to Morris Cooke, November 1, 1924, Kepple Hall Papers, Labor-Management Documentation Center; *Moody's Manual of Investment and Security Rating Service* (New York, 1927).

51. Gilson, *What's Past is Prologue*, p. 210.

52. Paul L. Feiss to Mary Gilson, June 3, 1940, J & F Papers, Container 1, Folder 12.

53. Kepple Hall to Morris Cooke, November 1, 1924, October 5, 1925, Hall Papers; Minutes of the Board of Directors, November 19, 1924, and July 3, 1925, J & F Papers, Container 1, Folder 2. For another account that also stresses that business differences preceded family divisions, see Paul L. Feiss to Mary Gilson, June 3, 1940, J & F Papers, Container 1, Folder 12.

54. Kepple Hall to Morris Cooke, October 5, 1926, Kepple Hall Papers.

55. Richard Feiss to William O. Stillman, June 6, 1926, J & F Papers, Container 2, Folder 2. Feiss had managed to obtain a position with the Denison Manufacturing Company in Framingham, Massachusetts, a firm that remained committed to scientific management. See Richard Feiss to Emma Stark, July 7, 1925, J & F Papers, Container 2, Folder 1.

56. Paul L. Feiss to Mary Gilson, June 3, 1940, J & F Papers, Container 1, Folder 12.

57. Kepple Hall to Morris Cooke, November 1, 1924, October 5, 1925, Kepple Hall Papers; Emma Stark to Richard Feiss, March 3, 1926; John Younger to Emma Stark, April 27, 1926, J & F Papers, Container 2, Folder 1.

58. The firm was unionized in 1934. See "The J and F Company: History and Outline of Its Operation," J & F Papers, Container 1, Folder 1.

59. Paul L. Feiss to Mary Gilson, June 3, 1940, J & F Papers, Container 1, Folder 12.

BRIAN PRICE

3   Frank and Lillian Gilbreth and the Motion
    Study Controversy, 1907–1930

$F$rank and Lillian Gilbreth were promoters of Taylor and
his circle and, at the same time, competitors with them, as Milton
Nadworny has noted.[1] The causes of the conflict between Taylor
and the Gilbreths included professional jealousies, disputes over
clients and fees, and the Gilbreths' remarkable facility as publicists. The immediate results were personal hostility and the fragmentation of the Taylor circle. The longer term consequences,
however, were more positive and important, and provide a useful
guidepost to the evolution of scientific management technique
and to the application of that technique on the shop floor. Competition in scientific management encouraged innovation as well as
bickering and criticism. In the decade and a half after Taylor's
death, competitive pressures forced the Gilbreths to strengthen
the time and motion study methods that were their trademark. By
1930, when their struggle with the more orthodox practitioners of
scientific management ended, time and motion study had become
a more formidable but no less controversial managerial resource.

Unlike most of Taylor's followers, Frank Gilbreth did not learn
his efficiency techniques at the master's feet. For twelve years
prior to his first meeting with Taylor in 1907, he was an innovative
building contractor, whose specialty was speed work achieved by
mechanical innovations and systematic management. Gilbreth
developed improved cement mixers, techniques for driving con-

The author gratefully acknowledges the assistance of Lindsey Wharton Bolger
and Mrs. Patricia Price.

crete foundation piles swiftly, and an adjustable scaffold, which could be raised to keep the masons level with the wall they were building. His *Field System, Concrete System*, and "Office System" outlined standardized procedures for organizing building sites, facilitating the flow of work on the ground, and enabling managers to keep the company current on building progress and costs through a series of detailed forms. To increase the worker's efficiency, he organized runways for concrete and brick delivery, advocated competition between gangs of workers (often divided by ethnicity), and designed a "white list" to reward reliable workers with more regular work.[2]

Gilbreth did not approach Taylor as a beginner, therefore, but rather as one who had as much to teach as to learn.[3] He soon demonstrated his usefulness to the nascent scientific management movement. While employing Stanford Thompson, Taylor's time study expert, to introduce time study for piece rate setting on his building sites, Gilbreth undertook systematic motion study experiments on bricklayers and soon claimed to have reduced their motions from as many as eighteen to as few as four.[4] He impressed Taylor, who incorporated Gilbreth's work in *The Principles of Scientific Management* (1911), and used Gilbreth's bricklaying achievements to illustrate the efficacy of the stopwatch technique he called the "keystone" of scientific management.[5]

Even at this time, however, occasional differences arose between the men. The most serious problem occurred when bricklayers at Gardner, Massachusetts in May, 1908, and at Glen Falls, New York in March, 1911, successfully struck Gilbreth's sites.[6] Taylor, feeling that Gilbreth had provoked the Gardner strike by rushing the installation process, ordered Sanford Thompson not to undertake any other work for Gilbreth.[7]

When Gilbreth faced bankruptcy during the 1911–1912 building industry depression and decided to dedicate himself full time to Taylorism and motion study, he regained some favor with Taylor. Louis Brandeis's promotion of scientific management in the 1910 Eastern Rates Case, and the Watertown Arsenal strike of 1911, raised Taylorism's public profile and galvanized trade union antagonism.[8] In defense of his mentor Gilbreth participated in debates against union leaders and organized the Society for the Promotion of the Science of Management (SPSM).[9] His wife Lillian, who was completing a Ph.D. in psychology, became his active partner at that time. Lillian wrote the *Primer of Scientific Management* (printed under Frank's name), and *Psychology of Management*, both of which argued that Taylorism was the only management method consistent with the health and development of workers.[10]

Gilbreth began his scientific management career in 1912 at the New England Butt Company, of Providence, Rhode Island, a firm of 300 employees that produced braiding machines used in the manufacture of shoe laces, dress trimmings, and electrical wire insulation. Gilbreth viewed New England Butt as his version of the Tabor Company of Philadelphia, where Taylor had demonstrated and promoted scientific management. Indeed, he and Lillian went to Providence to out-Taylor Taylor.[11]

The history of the Butt Company installation reveals the seriousness with which the Gilbreths took their task. The foundation of the installation was orthodox scientific management: improvements in the routing of work and the organization of tool and store rooms, introduction of a planning department and functional foremen, task setting, and cost accounting. Appropriately, Gilbreth hired Taylor's disciple, Horace K. Hathaway, to plan and guide these changes.[12] In addition, the Gilbreths added two kinds of innovations. First, they responded to the trade unionists' argument that scientific management was merely a dictatorial driving system by inaugurating industrial betterment programs. They organized a series of weekly meetings of managers, foremen, and workers, during which the progress of the installation was openly debated; a lecture series to allow employees to enhance their knowledge of scientific management and motion study; a suggestion system offering monthly prizes for the best ideas for factory improvement; and a promotion plan that increased upward mobility within the firm.[13]

Second, Frank Gilbreth developed a new motion study technique, which he called micromotion study. It involved filming a worker's operations against a cross-sectioned background while a chronometer recorded the time. By examining the film through a magnifying glass, Gilbreth could determine the times of each of the worker's motions to one-thousandth of a second. He could then compare methods and working conditions and synthesize the best elements into a method that would become standard for that job.

Gilbreth saw micromotion study as a potent antidote to labor hostility, as well as a major advance over stopwatch time study. When the unions charged that time study was a management tool designed to speed up the pace of production, he would show that micromotion study, by replacing the human observer and the stopwatch with the camera and the chronometer, provided scientific accuracy in timing work operations. Furthermore, his films would demonstrate that motion study increased output through more effective use of time rather than through faster speed.[14] To forestall the type of problems he had experienced on his building sites at Gardner and Glen Falls, Gilbreth installed his micromotion equipment in a "betterment room" at a remove from the factory floor, paying workers bonuses for allowing him to study them in isolation from their peers.[15]

Even as the Butt Company installation progressed, Gilbreth sought to publicize micromotion study as an advance over time study and as a benefit to workers. He first summarized his work at the December, 1912 meeting of the American Society of Mechanical Engineers (ASME), claiming that his new technique revolutionized braider machine assembly processes and increased output per assembler from 11–12 to 60 machines per day. The commentator, Robert T. Kent, called micromotion study "as revolutionary in the art of time study as was the invention of the power loom in the art of weaving."[16] In the following months, Gilbreth pressed home his image as an innovator, popularizing his new technique by using it to time the speeds of baseball pitchers and inaugurating a series of Summer Schools of Scientific Management for college professors in Providence, beginning in 1913.[17]

Taylor was impressed. In his own presentation to the ASME meeting he redefined time study to incorporate Gilbreth's motion study ideas, though not his specific techniques. Dividing time study into "analytical" and "constructive" categories, he argued that time study "analysis" involved dividing a worker's job into its "simple elementary movements," discarding the "useless" ones, timing the quickest and best motions, and making their times the standard for the job. "Constructive" time study involved grouping combinations of elementary movements commonly repeated in any trade, and recording and indexing them so that the records could be of use in determining appropriate times in other, parallel kinds of work. Though motion study remained subordinate to time study, the attention Taylor paid to it demonstrated the seriousness with which he took the Gilbreths' versions of his "keystone."[18]

Still, Taylor knew only part of the story. What he did not know, and what Gilbreth did not admit, was that Gilbreth had completed most of his work at the Butt Company by straightforward observation before the micromotion laboratory had been completed, that the greatly increased output per assembler had been achieved by assigning time-consuming elements of the process to other workers, and that Gilbreth continued to be almost totally reliant on stopwatch time study for piece rate setting because he could not arrange artificial lighting powerful enough to overcome the factory gloom. In short, at the time that Gilbreth announced its virtues, micromotion study had not yet lived up to a single one of them.[19] Moreover industrial betterment had not cured the workers of their misgivings about the Gilbreths. In the late summer of 1912, at a time when trade union militancy against scientific management was at a peak, Frank Gilbreth had narrowly averted a strike at the Butt Company by workers influenced both by the Industrial Workers of the World and the AFL.[20] Taylor, wary of Gilbreth's hubris in undertaking a major installation without prior experience, and alarmed by the possibility of another strike, grew increasingly anxious about his work.[21]

Matters between the two came to a head in 1913–1914, when Gilbreth undertook a major reorganization of the Herrmann-Aukam Company, a manufacturer of handkerchiefs. To aid him in studying the motions of handkerchief folders, Gilbreth invented additional motion study techniques, which he dubbed cyclegraphs, chronocyclegraphs, and stereochronocyclegraphs. The cyclegraph method involved mounting a miniature electric light on a ring that could be slipped onto a worker's finger, showing on the back of his or her hand. The movement of the light created a bright line on a single time-exposed photograph. A line full of twists and turns bespoke inefficient movement. The worker's tools, equipment, and motions could then be altered until the shortest, smoothest line was developed. Gilbreth improved on the cyclegraph technique by interrupting the flow of current to the light in order to obtain, in the resulting sequence of flashes, a record of the time and direction of the motions. The resulting image was a chronocyclegraph. A stereochronocyclegraph created a three-dimensional image of motion by using time exposed photographs from two slightly offset cameras, the positives from which could be viewed through a stereopticon or stereoscope. With his customary eye for publicity, Gilbreth arranged for Fred Colvin of the *American Machinist* to break the news of his latest advances to the engineering world.[22]

Despite his apparent progress, Gilbreth interrupted his work at Herrmann-Aukam to accept a contract to install scientific management at the giant Auergesellschaft electric light and gas mantel manufacturing company in Berlin, Germany. In Gilbreth's absence, the Herrmann-Aukam owners broached Taylor with complaints about the pace and quality of Gilbreth's work. Convinced that Gilbreth was unreliable, Taylor arranged for his orthodox disciple, Hathaway, to finish Gilbreth's job.[23]

An outraged Gilbreth viewed Taylor's action as a declaration of war. From Germany he wrote Lillian: "*We must have our own organization and we must have our own writings so made that the worker thinks we are the good exception* (emphasis Gilbreth's)."[24] To deal with the negative comments of Taylor and his disciples, Gilbreth immediately decided to keep all information about his present and future installation work secret, sacrificing potential publicity for security against claims of incompetency.[25] He also began to rewrite his autobiography. Having earlier emphasized his debt to Taylor, Gilbreth now sought to show that he had invented motion study, independent of, and prior to, his contact with Taylor.[26] By the time Frank returned from Germany, Lillian had completed two booklength manuscripts that emphasized both Gilbreth's concern with the "human factor" and his scientific outlook.

The first manuscript, published as a series of articles in *Iron Age* under both of their names, addressed the problem of the troublesome "human element." Its primary contention was that motion study was less a series of mechanical devices for improving output than a systematic program for the betterment of the worker. It argued that motion study would train workers and make them valuable aids to management, not mere specialists in a craft or humdrum machine tenders. Such workers could then be individually rewarded by higher wages and promotion.[27]

In the second work, *Fatigue Study*, Lillian Gilbreth argued that the aim of motion study was to eliminate unnecessary fatigue by designing convenient workbenches and chairs, providing regular rest periods, and introducing other salutary measures. This approach also had strategic and psychological value. By performing a fatigue survey on first entering a factory and providing immediate antidotes to obvious fatigue-producing activities, such as standing and stretching, the motion study engineer bettered his chances of acceptance by workers more than by announcing that his intention was to speed up production. Together with related activities such as weekly open meetings to discuss fatigue elimination, a suggestion system, and a promotion plan, the motion study engineer added a new dimension to the industrial welfare movement.[28]

To aid in their effort Gilbreth devised a final motion study innovation. By 1915 he had formulated a basic alphabet of work motions, naming them *therbligs* ("Gilbreth" reversed, with a small concession to euphony). All work motions, he contended, could be reduced to sixteen categories: search, find, select, grasp, position, transport loaded, assemble, use, disassemble, inspect, preposition (for next operation), release load, transport empty, wait (unavoidable delay), wait (avoidable delay), and rest (for overcoming fatigue). By analyzing micromotion film or chronocyclegraphs, the therbligs could be identified and plotted on "simultaneous cycle motion" or "simo" charts. The simo chart listed horizontally the parts of the body — arms, legs, trunk, and head — with subdivisions (for example, the upper and lower arm, wrist, thumb, fingers, and palm). The vertical axis displayed elapsed time. By assigning each therblig a color and symbol, Gilbreth could chart each body part's motion over time, producing a clear visualization of the relationships between the therbligs. Simo charts enabled Gilbreth to discern whether, for instance, one arm was actively working while the other was merely passively holding an object during the motion cycle. If so, he could redesign the operation to employ each arm simultaneously, while shortening the times for movements made by placing tools and parts closer to the worker's grasp. Therbligs provided Gilbreth with a new analytical tool and bolstered his confidence in the validity of his pursuit of a science of motions. Gilbreth nevertheless took the precaution of making his discovery public in a 1915 paper entitled "Motion Study for the Crippled Soldier," whose ostensible subject, the treatment of handicapped war veterans, reduced the likelihood of a substantial critique.[29]

To complete their work, the Gilbreths devised a slogan that underlined their concern with the human element and the scientific analysis of work processes. They were, they intoned, devoted to "*The quest of the one best way to do work* (emphasis Gilbreths')."[30]

The Gilbreths' efforts to distinguish themselves from Taylor and his immediate circle had mixed results. Frank organized a Committee for the Elimination of Unnecessary Fatigue within the new Society of Industrial Engineers, hosted regular fatigue luncheons at the Society's quarterly meetings, and worked with the National Safety Council, the American Posture League, and the Eyesight Conservation Committee, stressing motion study's health benefits.[31] These activities promoted the Gilbreth name and suggested the breadth of their interests. But their assertion that they were the humane alternative to orthodox scientific management was less persuasive. In the aftermath of World War I, the AFL and the Taylor Society (as the SPSM was renamed) reached a new understanding that ended organized opposition to scientific management and paved the way for the identification of the Taylor Society with the liberal wing of the business community. Thus, in regard to the "human factor," the perceived distance between the Gilbreths and their opponents rapidly shrank.[32]

Similarly, their attempt to portray motion study as the central element in a broader management system was unrewarding. While motion study in isolation attracted wide interest, few executives were willing to authorize the more sweeping changes the Gilbreths advocated. This problem elicited two very different responses from the Gilbreths. First, Frank tried to employ motion study as a Trojan horse to gain both entrance to a company and an opportunity to win incremental extensions of his work until he had implementated his entire revisionist system. Second, because the Gilbreths were forced to rely primarily on motion study for income, they felt compelled to defend the scientific efficacy of motion study against the more conservative defenders of stopwatch time study. Accordingly, they pushed for a decisive showdown with their critics in an attempt to establish, once and for all, motion study's scientific superiority.

A single example of Frank Gilbreth's Trojan horse strategy will suffice. In January, 1919, the Pierce-Arrow automobile company of Buffalo, New York, hired Gilbreth to use motion study to improve assembly procedures for its five-ton truck. Given offices, laboratory space for micromotion experiments, and the right to bring in four assistants, Gilbreth initiated changes, not in truck assembly, but in the office system that monitored and directed the assembly procedures. Only later did his assistants begin the systematic examination of carburetor subassembly methods. When they had reduced assembly times from seven and two-tenths hours to one hour under experimental conditions, Gilbreth felt confident in pushing for the extension of his contract to enable him to modernize the company's toolroom, tool sharpening methods, and storeroom procedures. The company rejected all of these requests except his proposal to revamp its storeroom, and then allowed him to make changes only on a limited, experimental basis. Somewhat disheartened, Gilbreth nevertheless urged the establishment of a messenger service in the drill department, a salvage department to clean up the company yards, and a planning department to coordinate work in the rooms where workers were trained in new assembly methods. The Pierce-Arrow managers turn him down flatly, advising him to keep his nose to the motion study grindstone, eschewing interest in all else. Though this forced concentration soon produced more promising results, the election of a new company president resulted in the revocation of Gilbreth's contract just when he began demonstrations of revised methods for the final assembly of trucks.[33]

The Gilbreths' push for a final confrontation with the orthodox scientific managers also produced unexpected results. The Gilbreths' position on motion study had been clear since 1912: time study was unscientific, fraught with human error, and dependent on obsolete equipment that had been superseded by cinematographic micromotion study apparatus. Now, thanks to therbligs, the Gilbreths argued additionally that micromotion study could measure objectively the *correct* elements of worker motions. They elaborated on this position at length in their 1917 book of essays, *Applied Motion Study.*[34] In December 1920, the Gilbreths arranged for a decisive confrontation with their opposition before the Taylor Society.

In their presentation, the Gilbreths assailed the validity of stopwatch data, arguing that "the inevitable interference of the human element, when the stop-watch is read while it is running or pressed to stop or start, prevents accurate observations and records."[35] Because micromotion study recorded the surrounding conditions and behavior of the workers, measured motions in therblig units, and provided absolutely accurate times, it constitutes a "science" that enabled work to be developed, taught, and perpetuated at the highest standard—the "one best way."[36]

The Taylorites' response was surprisingly restrained. Dwight Merrick admitted that for detailed operations he had often wished for something more accurate than a stopwatch.[37] Robert Kent observed that micromotion study devices were less significant than the methods on which they were based.[38] Carl Barth contended that micromotion study was good for detailed work, but that, after all, if the magnifying glass was still useful after the invention of microscopes and telescopes, the stopwatch still had a place in scientific management.[39]

If the Taylorites' response was mild, it was in part because they increasingly endorsed the Gilbreths' approach while ignoring their precise techniques and language.[40] Sanford Thompson summarized their position in a preface to a book on time study by his partner, William Lichtner:

> Our modern engineers, like Mr. Lichtner, realize that the men who work in the mills are not machines, . . . and that the increase in production that we need is one that will benefit, not exploit the workers. Time and job analysis achieves that increased production through saving waste in time and material, by determining the simplest and easiest way. . . .[41]

Lichtner's technique consisted of comparing various methods to find the best way of performing the operation under the best conditions, eliminating waste and making allowances for necessary delays and fatigue, and then setting standards and instructing employees in these methods. "The exact and systematic character of time and job analysis," he claimed, "merits for it the term 'science.' The 'laws' which it formulates take into consideration the necessary energy . . . to produce with the minimum of machine time and the minimum of human labor the maximum of quantity that is at the same time of the maximum quality."[42] Substitute "motion study" for "job analysis" and the Gilbreths could not have said it better. Lichtner went on to revise Taylor's statement on the importance of time study to read "job standardization is sometimes called the cornerstone of scientific management."[43]

The Gilbreths' attempt to position themselves as the humane and scientific alternative to orthodox scientific management was no more successful abroad than at home. In England, where a government-created Health of Munition Workers Committee (later renamed the Industrial Fatigue Research Board) and a private National Institute of Industrial Psychology used motion study to investigate fatigue and develop improved work methods, the Gilbreths fared badly.[44] The prominent psychologist Charles S. Myers, who headed the Institute, and several colleagues published articles arguing that incentives for increased output were irrelevant to motion and fatigue study.[45] Myers was more explicit and personal in attacking a paper the Gilbreths had prepared for the First International Conference on Applied Psychology and Vocational Guidance in 1921.[46] To their assertions that "the Quest of the One Best Way is the crux of the present-day industrial problem," and that psychologists must "cooperate" with engineers "so that the latter could discover the One Best Way,"[47] Myers responded bluntly:

> To this the adequately trained psychologist retorts — "there is no One Best Way." On the contrary, physiological and psychological differences between individual workers prevented them from adhering to one method.
>
> By nature, the efficiency engineer is prone to regard human workers as machines. Rather than understand them, he would mold them to a common type. Instead of trying to appreciate the various emotional influences and incentives which affect the worker's efficiency, the efficiency engineer is led by his mechanistic interests . . . [to] devise some elaborate scheme of payment.[48]

The Gilbreths' response, published in January 1924, attempted to defend the One Best Way and the supremacy of the efficiency engineer. Though they conceded that they had never seen any two workers with exactly the same motions, they insisted that this "in no wise belittles the fundamental importance of 'the One Best Way to Do Work,' as an ideal, or makes it less necessary." They insisted that all workers be taught the One Best Way first and allowed to deviate from the standard method only with the approval of the efficiency engineer. To Myers's concern that the task system could produce unwarranted stress, they argued that the worker received from thirty to one hundred percent more wages and worked under conditions that were highly educational. Finally, they insisted "that psychology will progress faster in industry through the cooperation of, and usually under the direction of the INDUSTRIAL ENGINEER."[49]

Frank Gilbreth's installation work was another source of frustration. At the Auergesellschaft company, for example, workers at first watched Gilbreth's activities suspiciously as he renovated the company's office system, then demanded that he be prevented from extending his work to the shop floor. They were so successful that only after many of them had been drafted into the armed forces did Gilbreth make any progress in their domain.[50] In 1919, messenger boys at the Pierce-Arrow company threatened to strike unless Gilbreth fulfilled his promises of promotion, a problem he solved by disbanding the messenger system.[51] In 1924, workers at the American Radiator Company in Buffalo refused to be time studied by Gilbreth's assistants, provoking the management to revoke Gilbreth's contract and remove him from the plant.[52]

If anything, Gilbreth found foremen, superintendents, and managers even more recalcitrant than workers. At Auergesellschaft in 1914–1915, Cluett-Peabody in 1916, U.S. Rubber in 1917, Pierce-Arrow in 1919, and American Radiator in 1923–1924, they stalled, failed to respond to his directives, and questioned the quality of his work.[53]

Owners could be equally recalcitrant, as Gilbreth discovered at Herrmann-Aukam and American Radiator. In addition, the owners of the Erie Forge Steel Company, financially straightened by the postwar depression, sued Gilbreth to revoke his expensive contract and locked him out of the plant.[54] Of the seventeen contracts Gilbreth signed between 1918 and 1924, he completed five requiring limited work and three more that required only written recommendations. Five of his six most important contracts were cancelled prematurely. Gilbreth was working on three contracts when he died in June, 1924.[55]

Thus, the Gilbreths' record in the decade after their break with Taylor fell far short of their goal. They had failed to distance themselves from their former colleagues, had invited ridicule with such slogans as the One Best Way, and had little success in persuading clients of the primacy of motion study or the necessity of their services. Frank had influenced technicians such as Thompson and Lichtner but had received little recognition for his contributions. Contemporaries could justifiably dismiss the Gilbreths as colorful but inconsequential imitators of Taylor, not unlike other self-proclaimed management experts of that era.

In fact, however, Frank's death marked the nadir of the Gilbreths' troubles; in the following years their reputations grew steadily. Two factors accounted for this change. One was the inherent value of motion study, as even the critics had acknowledged by 1920. The potential of motion study for extending scientific management, for combining the "science" and the "scientifically trained worker," as Taylor had proclaimed in the *Principles*, increased as the technical obstacles that made it expensive and unweildy declined. In 1923, Eastman Kodak introduced new spring-driven cameras, 16-millimeter safety film, and simple 500-watt lights. Simpler, easier to set up, and practical to use without a chronometer (spring-driven cameras ran steadily at one thousand frames per minute, making the timing of motions simple), the new cameras greatly increased the flexibility and quality of micromotion study while reducing its cost.[56]

The second factor was Lillian Gilbreth, who not only continued her husband's practice, but gave it the distinctive character that it lacked during Frank's lifetime. Technically, she relied on the methods that he had devised in the 1910s. She also sought industrial clients, though she was far more diligent and systematic in cultivating them than Frank had been. From 1925 to 1927 she ran a series of motion study courses from her house, training motion study engineers, among them her husband's last installation assistant, Joseph Piacitelli, and participants from Johnson & Johnson, R. H. Macy, General Electric, and Cadbury, the British chocolate manufacturer. She retained close relations with these students after the courses ended.[57] Beginning in 1927, she also aggressively sought work with such major companies as R. H. Macy, Johnson & Johnson, Sears Roebuck, and Green Line Cafeteria. Her own work, and that of her students, insured the continued identification of the Gilbreth name with motion study.[58]

But Lillian also recognized her unique position in an all-male profession and used it effectively. Her apparent success in raising a large family and competing with the country's top engineers made it easy for her to publicize her work. As a consultant she shrewdly exploited the fact that many businesses were run exclusively by men but sold almost exclusively to women. While she continued to offer the kinds of services that her male counterparts provided, she specialized in advice on women's work in the home, office, or store, and on methods for reaching a female clientele. Her efforts to streamline kitchens for the Brooklyn Gas Company and to evaluate feminine hygiene products for Johnson & Johnson were indicative of this approach.[59] Like Frank, she understood the possibilities of motion study outside the factory. Unlike him, she managed to convert that insight into a distinctive business.

Finally, Lillian made peace with the Taylor Society. In a brief paper for the *American Machinist*'s 1927 tribute to "Fifty Years of Mechanical Achievement," she announced that stopwatch time study, like motion study, had its place in scientific management. She noted the passing of the pioneers of both methods and the rapid diffusion of new manufacturing techniques, which had helped blur distinctions between the two.[60] The following year, before the Taylor Society, she declared that time and motion study were "fundamentally complementary."[61]

Her message was well received. In a swelling chorus, time study men insisted that their activities embraced not only accurate piece rate setting, but improvements in methods, and conditions of work, and labor processes. As Earl E. Watson declared, "Management must be made to see clearly that today reduced costs are to be expected, not so much as the result of any particular wage incentive plan, but rather, as a result of better methods. . . ."[62]

Ironically, it was Horace K. Hathaway who in 1930 rehabilitated the Gilbreths to a central place in the pantheon of scientific management giants. In an extraordinary paper, "Methods Study: The Principles and Technique of Analyzing Work Methods," Hathaway told the Taylor Society that the Gilbreths had done the most vital work in forwarding methods study.

> The scientific management movement is indebted to the Gilbreths not only for focusing attention on this feature of Taylor's philosophy and setting it forth in the light of its true importance but for refining and developing its technique along truly scientific lines, for reducing and codifying its fundamentals and setting, by years of persevering effort, a new standard which industry is just beginning to understand and make an effort to attain.[63]

He advocated further research into the determination and uses of therbligs, and quoted from the Gilbreths' writings to emphasize the need for cooperation among methods study investigators.[64]

The new consensus was apparent in the texts that appeared in the following years, such as Allan Mogensen's *Common Sense Applied to Motion and Time Study* (1932), and Ralph Barnes's *Industrial Engineering and Management: Problems and Policies* (1931).[65] However, Steward M. Lowry, Harold B. Maynard, and G. J. Stegmerten's widely used *Time and Motion Study and Formulas for Wage Incentives* best illustrated the trend. The 1927 edition treated motion study only briefly and insubstantially, while devoting many chapters to stopwatch methods and rate setting formulas. In 1932, the authors approached Lillian Gilbreth and her research group for more detailed information on their methods. By 1940 Lowry, Maynard, and Stegmerten had reduced their treatment of wage incentive formulas from nine chapters to three, and increased the number of chapters devoted to motion study to seven.[66] By that time motion study was no longer an incidental refinement of Taylor's time study techniques and the Gilbreths were no longer peripheral figures in the development and diffusion of scientific management.

While it is easy to portray midcentury scientific management practices as logical, even inevitable, outgrowths of earlier work, such a perspective distorts the Gilbreths' abrasive but constructive role and the impact of competition on the maturation of scientific management. The Gilbreths attacked the Taylor system at a vulnerable point and directly and indirectly accelerated the process of innovation. Both the timing and the character of the changes they influenced meant that a new, more attractive version of scientific management would be available to hard-pressed manufacturers during the troubled years of the 1930s.

NOTES

1.  Milton Nadworny, "Frederick Taylor and Frank Gilbreth: Competition in Scientific Management," *Business History Review* 31 (Spring 1957), pp. 23–34.
2.  F. B. Gilbreth, General Contractors, "Modern Concrete Machinery," (1903), Box 3, File 0030-18, Gilbreth Collection, Purdue University (hereafter cited as GC); "The Gilbreth Scaffold for the Rapid and Economical Construction of Masonry," (1906), Box 3, File 0030-18, GC; "Apparatus for Sinking Concrete Piles," patent, Box 140, File 0832-1, GC; Frank B. Gilbreth, *Field*

*System* (New York, 1908); *Concrete System* (New York, 1908); "General Rules and Office System," (1906), Box 33, File 180-4, GC.

3. For accounts of the Gilbreth-Taylor relationship see Samuel Haber, *Efficiency and Uplift: Scientific Management and the Unions, 1900–1932: A Historical Analysis* (Cambridge, 1955), pp. 19–20, 40–55; Nadworny, "Frederick Taylor and Frank Gilbreth" pp. 23–24; Daniel Nelson, *Managers and Workers: Origins of the New Factory System in the United States, 1880–1920* (Madison, WI, 1975), pp. 58, 64–65, 75–76; Nelson, *Frederick W. Taylor and the Rise of Scientific Management* (Madison, 1980), pp. 131–36, 171–75, 183–84, 190–91.

4. Frank B. Gilbreth to Frederick W. Taylor, March 19, 1908, File 59A, Frederick W. Taylor Papers, Stevens Institute of Technology (hereafter cited as TP); Frank B. Gilbreth, *Bricklaying System* (New York, 1909), pp. 148–51.

5. Frederick W. Taylor, "The Principles of Scientific Management," in *Scientific Management* (New York, 1947), pp. 117–18. On time study as the "keystone" of scientific management, see Taylor, "Shop Management," in *Scientific Management*, p. 148.

6. Sanford E. Thompson to Frank B. Gilbreth, May 20, 1908, File 59A, TP; "Refuse to Lay Bricks By Rule," *New York Times*, n.d., n.p., Box 3, File 0030-20A, GC; "Organized Labor and Scientific Management," *Harper's Weekly* 55 (April 8, 1911), p. 5.

7. Frederick W. Taylor to Frank B. Gilbreth, April 27, 1908, File 59A; Taylor to Sanford E. Thompson, May 25, 1908, File 126, TP.

8. U.S. Interstate Commerce Commission, *Evidence Taken By the Interstate Commerce Commission. Proposed Advances in Freight Rates By Carriers, August to December, 1910* (Washington, 1911); Hugh G. J. Aitken, *Scientific Management in Action: Taylorism at Watertown Arsenal, 1908–15* (Princeton, 1985), pp. 149–69.

9. *Boston Globe,* March 22, 1911, Box 4, File 0030-23, GC; *New York Times,* March 28, 1911; Frank B. Gilbreth, "The Theory at Work," *Journal of Accountancy* 12 (July 1911), pp. 195–200; Robert T. Kent, "The Taylor Society Twenty Years Ago," *Bulletin of the Taylor Society* 17 (February 1932), pp. 39–40.

10. Frank B. Gilbreth, *The Primer of Scientific Management* (New York, 1912); Lillian M. Gilbreth, *Psychology of Management: The Function of Mind in Determining, Teaching, and Installing Methods of Least Waste* (New York, 1914).

11. Charles B. Going to Margaret Hawley, October 30, 1927, Box 111, File 0812-1, GC.

12. Horace K. Hathaway, "Report to the New England Butt Co., Providence, R.I." June 8, 1912, Box 95, File 0702-6, GC.

13. *Providence Sunday Journal,* December 22, 1912, Box 4, File 0030-24, GC; S. E. Whitaker to Frank B. Gilbreth, July–October, 1912, Box 159, File 0952-2, GC; Lillian M. Gilbreth, *The Quest of the One Best Way: A Sketch of the Life of Frank Bunker Gilbreth* (Easton, PA, 1973), pp. 41–42; Edna Yost, *Frank and Lillian Gilbreth: Partners for Life* (New Brunswick, NJ, 1949), p. 237.

14. John Aldrich, "Discussion," *ASME Transactions* 34 (1912), pp. 1182–87; Robert T. Kent, "Discussion," *ASME Transactions* 34 (1912), pp. 1187–89.

15. S. E. Whitaker to Frank B. Gilbreth, July 1912, Box 159, File 0952-2, GC.

16. Frank B. Gilbreth, untitled lecture, April 28, 1912, Box 99, File 0721-2, GC; Kent, "Discussion," p. 1188.

17. *Providence Sunday Journal*, n.d., 1913, Box 5, File 0030-25, GC; *New York Tribune*, June 15, 1913, Box 5, File 0030-25, GC; Frank B. Gilbreth, "First Summer School of Scientific Management," August, 1913; "Second Summer School of Scientific Management," August, 1914; "Third Summer School of Scientific Management," August, 1915, Gilbreth Library, Purdue.

18. Frederick W. Taylor, "Discussion," *ASME Transactions* 34 (1912), p. 1199–1200.

19. S. E. Whitaker to Frank B. Gilbreth, July 1912–January 1913, Box 159, File 0952-2, GC.

20. S. E. Whitaker to Frank B. Gilbreth, August, 1912, Box 159, File 0952-2, GC.

21. Frederick W. Taylor to Horace K. Hathaway, September 2, 1912, File 122, TP; Taylor to Carl Barth, October 12, 1912, File 113, TP.

22. Fred H. Colvin, "The Latest Development in Motion Study," *American Machinist* 38 (June 5, 1913), pp. 937–39.

23. Frederick W. Taylor to Frank B. Gilbreth, March 11, 1914, File 59A; Taylor to Horace K. Hathaway, March 12, 1914, File 123, TP.

24. Frank B. Gilbreth to Lillian M. Gilbreth, May 9, 1914, Box 112, File 0813-6, GC.

25. Frank B. Gilbreth to C. B. Thompson, June 19, 1916, Box 122, File 0816-131, GC.

26. Frank B. Gilbreth to Lillian M. Gilbreth, May 6, 9, 13, 1915, Box 112, File 0813-5, GC.

27. Frank B. and Lillian M. Gilbreth, "Conserving the Worker's Health and Energy," *Iron Age* 97 (April 6, 1916), pp. 836–28; "The Co-operative Spirit and Industrial Peace," *Iron Age* 96 (September 2, 1915), pp. 528–30; "Educating the Workers for Higher Efficiency," *Iron Age* 96 (December 30, 1915), pp. 1530–33; "The Individual in Modern Management," *Iron Age* 96 (October 17, 1915), pp. 802–4; "The Three Position Plan for Promotion," *Iron Age* 96 (November 4, 1915), pp. 1057–59; "The Work, the Worker, and his Age," *Iron Age* 97 (March 9, 1916), pp. 602–4.

28. Frank B. and Lillian M. Gilbreth, *Fatigue Study: the Elimination of Humanity's Greatest Waste: A First Step in Motion Study* (New York, 1916); H. F. J. Porter, "Industrial Betterment," *Cassier's Magazine* 38 (August 1910), p. 311.

29. Frank B. and Lillian M. Gilbreth, "Motion Study for the Crippled Soldier," in *Applied Motion Study: A Collection of Papers on the Efficient Method to Industrial Preparedness* (New York, 1917), pp. 138–39.

30. Frank B. and Lillian M. Gilbreth, "The Engineer, the Cripple, and the New Education," in *Motion Study for the Handicapped* (London, 1920), pp. 96–97.

31. Frank B. Gilbreth, "Eye Conservation in the Industries," February, 1922, Box 153, File 0896-3, GC; Frank B. Gilbreth, "Fatigue Study: A First Step in Safety Work," *National Safety Council Proceedings* 10 (September 28, 1921), pp. 838–45; Frank B. and Lillian M. Gilbreth, "The Relation of Posture to Fatigue of Women in Industry," Address to American Posture League, March 12, 1921, Box 153, File 0896-4, GC; Frank B. Gilbreth, "Practical Methods of Fatigue Elimination," Report to the Committee on the Elimina-

tion of Unnecessary Fatigue, Society of Industrial Engineers, April 29, 1921, Box 153, File 0896-4 GC; and "Society of Industrial Engineers," *Industrial Management* 59 (January 1920), pp. 54–55.

32. Nadworny, *Scientific Management and the Unions*, pp. 104–21.

33. Frank B. Gilbreth to Lillian M. Gilbreth, January–August, 1919, Box 113, File 0813-9, GC; Nathaniel Major, "History of Frank B. Gilbreth's Work at Pierce-Arrow Motor Car Co.," September 26, 1919, Box 163, File 0972-7, GC; E. J. Terry to Frank B. Gilbreth, May–July, 1919, Box 122, File 0816-126, GC.

34. Frank B. and Lillian M. Gilbreth, *Applied Motion Study.*

35. Frank B. and Lillian M. Gilbreth, "An Indictment of Stop-Watch Time Study," *Bulletin of the Taylor Society* 6 (June 1921), p. 100.

36. Frank B. and Lillian M. Gilbreth, "Indictment," pp. 102–3.

37. Dwight V. Merrick, "A Defense of the Stop-Watch," *Bulletin of the Taylor Society* 6 (June 1921), pp. 111–12.

38. Robert T. Kent, "A Defense of the Stop-Watch," *Bulletin of the Taylor Society* 6 (June 1921), p. 112.

39. Carl Barth, "A Defense of the Stop-Watch," *Bulletin of the Taylor Society* 6 (June 1921), p. 110.

40. See William O. Lichtner, *Time Study and Job Analysis As Applied to Standardization of Methods and Operations* (New York, 1921).

41. Sanford E. Thompson, "Forward," to "Time and Job Analysis in Management, I" by William O. Lichtner, *Industrial Management* 59 (April 1920), p. 301.

42. William O. Lichtner, "Time and Job Analysis in Management, I" *Industrial Management* 59 (April 1920), p. 306.

43. Lichtner, *Time Study and Job Analysis*, p. 14.

44. H. J. Spooner, "Some Aspects of Industrial Fatigue," *Cassier's Engineering Monthly* (October 1917), p. 225; Morris S. Viteles, "Psychology in Business—in England, France, and Germany," *ASPSS Annals* 110 (November 1923), pp. 207–8.

45. See Eric Farmer, "Time and Motion Study—I–VI," *Engineering and Industrial Management* 7 (January 19–April 20, 1922), pp. 70–75, 95–98, 136–39, 221–23, 247–51, 361–65; Farmer, "Economy and Human Effort in Industry," *Engineering and Industrial Management* 6 (November 10, 1921), pp. 535–37.

46. Frank B. and Lillian M. Gilbreth, "The Place of the Psychologist in Industry," Paper to the International Conference on Applied Psychology and Vocation Guidance, Barcelona, 1921, Box 1532, File 0896-5. ...

47. Frank B. and Lillian M. Gilbreth, "The Place of the Psychologist in Industry," pp. 5, 8, 11.

48. Charles S. Myers, "The Efficiency Engineer and the Industrial Psychologist," *Journal of the National Institute of Industrial Psychology* 1 (January 1923), pp. 168, 170–71.

49. Frank B. and Lillian M. Gilbreth, "The Efficiency Engineer and the Industrial Psychologist," *Journal of the National Institute of Industrial Psychology* 2 (January 1924), pp. 41, 44, 45.

50. Frank B. Gilbreth to Lillian M. Gilbreth, April 23, 1914, Box 112, File 0813-6, GC.

51. Mayor, "History of Gilbreth's Work at Pierce-Arrow," p. 32.

52. John Gaillard to Frank B. Gilbreth, January–February, 1924, Box 173, File 0990-4, GC.

53. Frank B. Gilbreth to Lillian M. Gilbreth, April 15, 1914, Box 112, File 0813-6, GC; Frank B. Gilbreth, Report to R. O. Kennedy, Cluett-Peabody Company, May 1917, Box 97, File 714, GC; Frank B. Gilbreth, U.S. Rubber Company, notes, July 26, 1917, Box 170, File 0892-1, GC; John Gaillard to Frank B. Gilbreth, November–December, 1923, Box 173, File 0990-4, GC.

54. Frank B. Gilbreth to Lillian M. Gilbreth, July 12–17, 1921, Box 114, File 0813-14, GC.

55. For further details, see Brian Price, "One Best Way: Frank and Lillian Gilbreth's Transformation of Scientific Management, 1885–1940," vol. 2, chap. 9, (Ph.D. Diss., Purdue University, 1987).

56. Ralph M. Barnes, "Motion Picture Camera in Micromotion Study," *Iron Age* 128 (October 1931), pp. 866–67, 902.

57. M. K. Wisehard, "Making One Hour do the Work of Two," *American Magazine* 103 (March 1927), p. 43; Margaret E. Hawley, "The Life of Frank B. Gilbreth and His Contributions to the Science of Management (M.A. Thesis, University of California, Berkeley, 1929), p. 202; Yost, *Partners for Life*, pp. 320–321; Frank Gilbreth, Jr. and Ernestine Gilbreth Carey, *Belles on Their Toes* (New York, 1950), pp. 94–99.

58. On Gilbreth's consulting work, see R. H. Macy files, Box 95, File 0707, Box 134, File 0830-20; Johnson and Johnson files, Box 95, Files 0704-2; Sears, Roebuck files, Box 97, Files 0713-5 and 0713-6, Box 135, File 0830-26; Green Line Cafeteria files, Box 94, File 0701, Box 134, File 0830-14.

59. Gilbreth Papers, Boxes 88, 95.

60. Lillian M. Gilbreth, "Time and Motion Study Developments," *American Machinist* 66 (May 19, 1927), p. 872.

61. Lillian M. Gilbreth, "The Relations of Time Study and Motion Study," *Bulletin of the Taylor Society* 13 (June 1928), p. 126.

62. Earl E. Watson, "Unit Times Versus Overall Times," *Bulletin of the Taylor Society* 13 (June 1928), p. 117.

63. Horace King Hathaway, "Methods Study: The Principles and Technique of Analyzing Work Methods," *Bulletin of the Taylor Society* 15 (October 1930), p. 214.

64. Hathaway, "Methods Study," pp. 226, 240–42.

65. Allan Mogensen, *Common Sense Applied to Time and Motion Study* (New York, 1932); and Ralph E. Barnes, *Industrial Engineering and Management: Problems and Policies* (New York, 1931).

66. Stewart M. Lowry, Harold B. Maynard, and G. J. Stegmerten, *Time and Motion Study and Formulas for Wage Incentives* (New York, 1927, 1932, 1940).

DANIEL NELSON

4    Scientific Management and the
Transformation of University
Business Education

The public furor that followed the publication of *The Principles of Scientific Management* in 1911 underlined the appeal of Taylor's ideas and their applicability to nonindustrial settings, from social welfare agencies to public school systems. Among the educators who reacted positively to Taylor's message were faculty members at the burgeoning American universities of the second and third decades of the century. University professors, particularly those who prepared students for business careers, were attracted to scientific management because of its implications for the practical curriculum and for their relations with colleagues in more academically respectable and theoretically rigorous disciplines. Intrigued by time study, wage incentives, cost accounting, and other features of Taylor's work, but especially by the idea that management techniques were the building blocks of a larger edifice, a body of theory applicable to any institution, professors of business and engineering found scientific management highly useful.[1] In the decade after Taylor's death, they made it a notable feature of the practical curriculum. By 1930 they rivaled the consultants as promoters of scientific management. As the role of the university in business and society continued to grow, they became the leading interpreters of Taylor's legacy.

The author is indebted to Steven A. Sass and Guy Alchon for their comments and suggestions, and to the National Endowment for the Humanities for financial assistance.

The background to this development is one of the most dramatic chapters in the history of the multiversity.[2] College enrollments grew during the early decades of the century, spurred by the rise of technical and professional occupations and the spread of secondary education. During the most critical growth period, 1915 to the mid 1920s, the proportion of eighteen- to twenty-one-year-olds attending colleges rose from 8 to 12 percent.[3] An additional potent factor was the "entrepreneurial zeal" of administrators and professors, particularly at the less prestigious urban and state universities. Perceiving that middle-class parents would only pay college tuitions if they were confident that their sons (and some daughters) would qualify for well-paying jobs, they aggressively developed new curricula that satisfied the needs of employers and the demands of parents and students. As David O. Levine explains, the university curriculum "became inextricably tied to the nation's economic structure, particularly its white-collar, middle-class sector."[4]

The best example of this development was the growth of collegiate business education. The Wharton School of the University of Pennsylvania, founded in 1881, was the only university college of commerce for more than a decade. Six institutions added business programs between 1898 and 1900; thirty-three universities introduced business majors between 1900 and World War I; and thirty-seven others added business studies during the war period, expressions of the wartime emphasis on discipline and practicality. The postwar years saw a "veritable craze for business education," with 117 new programs by 1924, despite a decided reaction against the asceticism of the war era.[5] Many other schools also introduced business courses on a piecemeal basis. One observer estimated that at least 400 colleges offered some form of business training by 1924.[6] In 1915 there were 9000 business majors; by 1918, 17,000; by 1920, 37,000; and by 1926, 58,000. The number of degrees awarded rose from less than 1000 in 1918 to more than 6000 per year in the late 1920s.[7] Rapid expansion created tensions as well as opportunities. Administrators and professors discovered to their chagrin that many students were career-oriented and anti-intellectual. At such fast-growing urban universities as Northwestern and New York University, which had extensive night school programs and many parttime students, professors struggled against a pervasive trade school outlook. The

Northwestern faculty, for example, had to emphasize job training to maintain enrollments.[8] More surprising was the prevalence of narrowly utilitarian attitudes among fulltime residential students. Administrators found that many students stayed only for a year or two while they took technical courses that qualified them for entry-level jobs. The dean of the Wharton School confessed in 1913 that a two-year liberal arts requirement for admission to the professional program would decimate the school. As it was, Wharton's junior class was only one-third the size of its freshman class.[9]

The expansion of business studies also exacerbated tensions between the arts and sciences and business faculties. To the former, business education smacked of the clerical and secretarial courses offered by proprietary "business colleges." After thirty years, Wharton professors still suffered from the "sneers and suspicions" of their colleagues.[10] At many other universities, business professors were isolated and intimidated. A recent study of higher education concludes that business studies "had low prestige, a practical orientation and small scope for knowledge enhancement."[11] Even before the boom some administrators and professors had tried to raise the quality and reputation of their work. After 1915, as the pressures of the enrollment surge threatened career aspirations, professional recognition, and potentially the quality of the nation's business leadership, they redoubled their efforts. Their reactions gradually gave business education the aura of serious inquiry and professional respectability that had seemed so notably lacking.

One response grew out of the rise of accounting as a professional specialty and an area of academic concentration. In an era of industrial expansion and big business, the demand for accountants and accounting education seemed inexhaustible. In many universities the growth in accounting enrollments and course offerings was the immediate reason for separating business from economics departments. By all quantitative measures, accounting overshadowed other business disciplines before 1930. It was the *raison d'être* of university business education.[12] Because of close association with scientific management, it also had the potential to redefine the character and image of business education. Costs systems had been a staple of early systematic management and Taylor had been a prominent accountant before he achieved fame as an expert on production and labor issues. He and his followers, notably Harrington Emerson, pioneered in the extension of standards to cost data and in the analysis of variances between standard and real performance.[13] By the mid 1920s they had made accounting a powerful management tool, not just a technique for recording and presenting financial data. The link between accounting, the most popular business specialty, and scientific management, the most notable effort to integrate business operations, had potentially fruitful implications for the business curriculum and the role of business education within the university.

But these possibilities never materialized because of two contrary developments. First, the management accounting methods that Taylor, Emerson, and their allies developed were exceedingly cumbersome and costly in the era before the electronic computer. Executives concluded that costs outweighed potential benefits and abandoned them.[14] Second, the growth of external corporate financing and intrusive government, in the form of the income tax amendment, the Federal Reserve Act, the Federal Trade Commission Act, and other measures, overshadowed the link with scientific management.[15] The "demand for financial reports audited by independent public accountants" had a "profound and lasting influence."[16] In the universities, this pressure insured that financial accounting retained its central role in the accounting curriculum and that accounting education continued to focus on technical detail. Though critics within the profession often complained that universities offered "narrow technical training," neglected "basic principles of accounting," and only prepared students for the CPA exam, the move toward narrowly defined specialties, mastery of technical detail, and job training was irresistible.[17] Following the example of engineers in the late nineteenth century, accounting professors created a network of specialized professional groups and formulated canons of professional behavior that emphasized technical virtuosity and peer approval. A larger vision was not necessary.

Wharton was the acknowledged leader of this development. As it evolved from an elite institution into an urban university (night classes were introduced in 1904 and an extension night school that operated in other Pennsylvania cities was added in 1913) the accounting program flourished. Enrollments grew, the accounting faculty became large and distinguished, and course offerings became increasingly specialized. Moreover, under dean Emory R. Johnson (1919–1930) accounting became a model for the rest of the school. In the 1920s Wharton's specialized offerings proliferated. It became the "best place" to learn the "practical intricacies" of business.[18] The Wharton approach was a stimulus to other urban universities. In part this was due to Wharton's commanding size and influence. Its large graduate programs were a major source of faculty and precedents for other universities. Wharton graduates made the University of Pittsburgh business school a virtual clone of the Wharton operation.[19] In the 1930s a dean recruited from the Wharton faculty had a similar effect at Columbia.[20] But the Wharton influence transcended such associations. As one of the largest and most prestigious business schools, Wharton offered administrators at other urban universities a convenient rationale for doing what logic and the economics of a parttime student body dictated anyway. Northwestern, with no direct ties and a substantial reputation in its own right, embraced the Wharton approach in the late 1910s and 1920s. Courses proliferated and "the specialized, technical fields expanded enormously."[21] New York University, which had the largest business program of any university by the 1920s, exceeded even Wharton in its varied course offerings.[22]

The problem with the Wharton approach was that it looked suspiciously like a rationalization for inaction. The financial accounting model, which had many critics, often broke down when it was applied in fields with less explicit vocational connotations. Even the Wharton faculty had trouble creating professional specialties in transportation and marketing.[23] The other urban universities failed to escape the shadows of improvisation and opportunism. Their continued reliance on parttime faculty was a powerful indictment. Even more serious, was the narrow, technical character of many of their Wharton-type specialties. When the Massachusetts Institute of Technology considered the introduction of a business major in 1913, an alumni committee dismissed the urban universities as models because their programs were "largely devoted to accounting, and as such are little better than those given at the so-called 'commercial colleges,' whose principal province is to train clerks and amaneunses."[24] Clearly, the accountants' approach provided only a partial answer to the challenges of intellectual and academic legitimacy.

Other academics embraced scientific management with fewer inhibitions. During Taylor's lifetime several professors had become scientific management practitioners and others eagerly sought his advice. In the late 1910s, they and their colleagues joined the Taylor Society en masse, converting a narrowly conceived sanctuary for technicians into a center of the liberal avant garde. In the late 1910s and 1920s they became the most vigorous promoters of scientific management. Like many industrialists, they were interested in time study and other managerial techniques that enhanced day-to-day operations. But their principal concern was the broader principles, especially the notion of management as a feature of all business endeavor. Taylor's writings suggested to even the most naive reader that industrial management required some sense of the larger character of the enterprise. To the better informed, they underlined the essential principles of the management movement: the necessity of systematic organization and communications, the value of organized planning and research, and the importance of performance standards and managerial controls.[25] To the professors, they made sense of the experiences of successful big businesses and the disjointed prescriptions of management reformers and publicists. Above all, Taylor's message had the potential to bring coherence to the practical curriculum and greater professional standing to those who prepared students for business careers. It was a powerful and satisfying alternative to the accounting model.

Between 1910 and the 1920s these individuals introduced scientific management to most large American universities.[26] The process was irregular and haphazard, particularly in the early years, and had many dimensions. One indicator of it was the introduction of courses on management subjects in the curricula of engineering and business departments. The appearance of management courses was rarely an isolated occurence. In the vast majority of cases it was a proxy for the growth of professional consciousness among faculty members and contacts with Taylor and his followers, the Taylor Society, or other organizations devoted to the study and dissemination of scientific management. Table 4.1 includes information on twenty-one universities, chosen for their size, prestige, and regional importance.[27] The first two columns indicate when courses specifically devoted to management subjects appeared in engineering and business departments.

TABLE 4.1

Management Courses in American Universities

| Institution | Engineering | Business | Scientific Management | Personnel Management |
|---|---|---|---|---|
| **Technical** | | | | |
| Penn State | 1906 | *** | 1908 | 1915 |
| Cornell | 1905 | * | 1914 | 1920 |
| Purdue | 1908 | * | 1919 | 1932 |
| Carnegie | 1908 | * | 1910 | 1919 |
| MIT | 1899 | * | 1915 | 1920 |
| Drexel | 1919 | * | 1919 | 1926 |
| **Elite** | | | | |
| Harvard | 1914** | 1908 | 1908 | 1919 |
| Dartmouth | 1918 | 1904 | 1911 | 1915 |
| Chicago | * | 1913 | 1915 | 1916 |
| **State** | | | | |
| Ohio State | *** | 1911 | 1913 | 1923 |
| Wisconsin | 1909 | 1915 | 1910 | 1918 |
| Michigan | 1914 | 1914 | 1916 | 1918 |
| Iowa | 1905 | 1915 | 1915 | 1921 |
| **Urban** | | | | |
| Penn | *** | 1901 | 1914 | 1919 |
| NYU | 1914 | 1903 | 1915 | 1916 |
| Northwestern | * | 1908 | 1913 | 1912 |
| Pitt | 1920 | 1911 | 1911 | 1920 |
| **West/South** | | | | |
| California | * | 1913 | 1918 | 1921 |
| Washington | 1924 | 1917 | 1917 | 1917 |
| North Car. | 1921 | 1919 | 1919 | 1921 |
| Vanderbilt | 1921 | 1919 | 1920 | * |

*inappropriate or unavailable
**cooperative program with MIT
***cross-listed courses

The third column adds the date when references to "scientific management" or specific activities associated with Taylor first appeared in course descriptions. The table also dates the introduction of courses in employment and personnel management, which after Taylor's death became a hallmark of the new, broader approach of the second generation of theorists and practitioners.[28]

A significant effort to utilize scientific management in business education occurred in engineering schools, where a small number of influential professors responded to mounting evidence that engineering graduates became industrial managers as often as they became inventors and designers. Their efforts had an immediate impact on engineering education that persists to the present. Beyond that restricted area, however, their work had comparatively little effect. Engineering was based on esoteric skills that most students who aspired to business careers did not have and probably could not hope to attain. The professors' primary objective was to broaden the outlook of students who had chosen engineering as a course of study, not to recruit additional students whose principal interest was business. Within engineering departments there were other obstacles. By the early twentieth century, engineers had a clear conception of who they were and what they did. They conceded that management was becoming a common and appropriate activity for engineers, but they insisted that it was different from and probably subordinate to the technical activities that defined their profession. They were willing to add management to the engineer's function, but not to make it a central feature of that function.[29]

The experiences of the Pennsylvania State College engineering college made that institution a prototype for other engineering schools. In 1907 Hugo Diemer, an Ohio State graduate who had taught at the University of Kansas, became the head of the Penn State Mechanical Engineering department. While a faculty member at Kansas, Diemer had become a devotee of scientific management and a close acquaintance of Taylor's; his appointment at Penn State may have been due to Taylor's influence.[30] His goal was to make management studies an integral feature of the mechanical engineering program. Penn State already had a course, "Shop Economics," which covered many of the specific features of scientific management. In 1907 Diemer added "Factory Planning," and in 1908 introduced a concentration in "Industrial Engineering" within the mechanical engineering curriculum. In 1909 he won approval for an industrial engineering department, the first in any American university. Students took conventional engineering courses for their first two years. They studied "Shop Time Study" and "Manufacturing Accounts" as juniors, and "Shop Economics," "Labor Problems," and "Factory Planning" as seniors.[31] In 1913 Diemer added "Industrial Management," devoted to "departments and departmental reports, planning, scheduling, time study, labor and efficiency, wage system and welfare methods."[32] The following year he added an advanced course on "Scientific Management," which used Taylor's writings as texts.[33] Diemer left Penn State during World War I but his successors, E. G. Kunze and J. O. Keller, were sympathetic to his approach. By 1921 the industrial engineering department had 12 faculty members, six of professorial rank.

Diemer succeeded in creating a professional specialty, but not in making scientific management an integral feature of the engineering curriculum or the basis for a broader business curriculum. Though he wrote a popular, nontechnical management text, his preoccupation with machine shop activities strongly suggested that industrial engineering was factory management. To most engineers it was a peripheral vocational specialty; to most business students, an inaccessible and undesirably narrow option.

The experiences of Cornell and Purdue, two other leaders in industrial engineering, were similar. Dexter S. Kimball, a mechanical engineer who, like Taylor, had served a traditional apprenticeship and worked as a machinist before attending college, introduced a required junior-level course on the principles of manufacturing and an elective in works administration at Cornell in 1905.[34] The former covered manufacturing methods, cost accounting, and plant management; the latter, retitled "Industrial Organization" in 1910, focused on welfare work, wage systems, and labor legislation.[35] In 1914, when Kimball was appointed to head a new Department of Industrial Engineering, he revised "Industrial Organization" to include "modern industrial tendencies and the principles that underlie modern methods of production."[36] Kimball also introduced a senior course, "Industrial Administration," that covered "modern time-keeping and cost-finding systems, methods of planning work and of insuring production, administrative reports, time and motion study, purchasing, etc."[37] He thus insured that Cornell students became familiar with contemporary scientific management. Yet, even as dean of the College of Engineering (after 1921), he made no effort to make scientific management more than a specialty for students who anticipated careers as industrial managers. Industrial Engineering remained an unimportant major in a small and declining engineering program.[38]

Purdue introduced "Industrial Engineering" in 1908 as a senior requirement for mechanical engineering students. The two-semester course covered factory construction and power generation as well as "organization and management of shops; methods of paying wages; systems of cost accounting and shop bookkeeping. . . ."[39] Charles Henry Benjamin, the dean of the engineering school, taught the course until 1910, when L. W. Wallace joined the faculty. Under Wallace, who would later become a leader of the management movement, the introductory course increasingly reflected the popularity of scientific management. By 1919 it focused on the "fundamental principles of Management."[40] Wallace also added advanced courses on scientific management methods and, like many of his colleagues, embraced personnel management as a feature of industrial engineering. Wallace left during World War I, but the Purdue program continued to be closely connected to the scientific management movement. In the 1920s the faculty added courses on time study technique and in the early 1930s lured Lillian M. Gilbreth to help teach them.

Other universities followed the examples of Penn State, Cornell, and Purdue and created majors for students who had a strong interest in management or a weak interest in "pure" engineering. Several took an additional step and broke the implicit link between engineering and industrial management. In 1910 the Carnegie Institute of Technology responded to employer requests for technically educated sales representatives with a major in "Commercial Engineering."[41] A "special feature" of the program was "the attention given to the scientific methods of management and production. . . ."[42] Students took two years of conventional engineering courses, together with "Works Management," which the Mechanical Engineering department had introduced in 1908. During the next two years they studied various business subjects, taught by a small Commercial Engineering faculty and the university's social science departments.[43]

The Carnegie Tech program was the prototype for MIT's Course XV, the best known of the engineering and business curricula. By the turn of the century Davis R. Dewey, MIT's distinguished economist, and several colleagues offered courses in economics, law, and history, which Dewey wanted to expand into a social science major. He was unable to win the support of the university administration, in part because of an anticipated merger with Harvard.[44] When the merger failed, Dewey succeeded in introducing Course XV, which combined existing courses in engineering and social science with several new courses in business management. Dewey ran the program until 1930.[45] Although his interests in banking and corporate organization were reflected in the course requirements, he also insisted that management was an important feature of the curriculum. An unhappy alumnus recalled that Course XV was "really a course in 'scientific management' and Frederick Taylorism."[46]

Among business schools, scientific management first influenced the elite universities and then spread to the business departments of the midwestern and western state universities during the boom years of the late 1910s. At Harvard, Dartmouth, and a growing number of private and public business schools, scientific management became the basis of the practical curriculum. Each university introduced courses in factory operations, like the engineering schools, but also promoted a conception of executive activity based on the principles of scientific management that transcended production. Two factors were essential to this development. First, the elite universities were under no pressure to provide narrow vocational training; indeed, as the urban universities and their accounting-based curricula became more prominent, the selective schools had a powerful incentive to adopt a broader and more theoretical approach. Second, scientific management emerged as an appealing option during the formative period of university business education, before disciplinary lines had hardened and the majority of business professors identified with a professional specialty. As a result administrators and faculty had more flexibility than the engineers of that period or their successors of the 1920s and later.

The individual who had the greatest influence on this process was Edwin F. Gay, the distinguished economist who became the first dean of the Graduate School of Business at Harvard in 1908. Gay had no intention of presiding over a trade school or an urban university and was determined to make manufacturing and marketing, not accounting, the basis of his curriculum. Most important, he was "convinced there is a scientific method involved and underlying the art of business. . . ."[47] Initially, he had no idea how to proceed. At the suggestion of Dean Wallace C. Sabine of Harvard's engineering school he visited Taylor in May, 1908, listened to a lecture on scientific management, and toured the Tabor Company to see Taylor's approach in operation. Taylor encouraged him to incorporate scientific management in the business school curriculum.[48] Gay was receptive. That fall he introduced "Industrial Organization," a course designed to provide the kind of integrative experience, based on the study of modern manufacturing, that he wanted to make the core of the Harvard program. "The principles of organization, carefully elucidated in connection with the factory," he wrote, "will then be traced in their wide application to other forms of enterprise."[49]

"Industrial Organization" brought together the leading figures of the contemporary management movement. Though Gay himself was the nominal instructor, J. Newton Gunn, the prominent industrial consultant, did most of the work. The course began with a series of lectures by Charles B. Going, editor of *Engineering Magazine*, on management as an executive function. Other experts on factory operations followed. The course concluded with Taylor, who gave three lectures, and Carl G. Barth, who discussed scientific management techniques. Taylor gave his standard introductory speech, a talk on industrial discipline, and a lecture entitled "The Organization of a Manufacturing Establishment Under Modern Scientific or Task Management," his last original paper and his only effort to describe the responsibilities of top managers.[50] "Industrial Organization," and Taylor in particular, were extremely popular. Melvin T. Copeland, a Harvard faculty member, recalled that the course "was new and . . . newsworthy. It was concrete, dealing with specific factory problems. And to many it seemed to provide something of a formula for management."[51]

Scientific management became increasingly important in the Harvard curriculum in the following years. Taylor repeated his lectures every year until his death, and the roster of lecturers in "Industrial Organization" become virtually a list of his closest followers. Sanford E. Thompson, Taylor's time study expert, also gave lectures on time study methods in an advanced course.[52] In 1911, C. Bertrand Thompson, one of Gay's former economics students, took over his classroom duties. With Gay's support, Thompson also conducted extensive research on the application of scientific management and wrote the first scholarly analyses of Taylor's work.[53] By 1914 he was a successful practitioner and F. L. Coburn, a naval officer who had been involved in scientific management installations in government shipyards, took over his courses. In the meantime, Gay had approved an advanced course on "The Practice of Scientific Management," which featured both lectures by Barth, Sanford E. Thompson, Morris L. Cooke, and H. K. Hathaway and the installation of scientific management techniques, first at the Rindge Manual Training School and the Harvard University Press and later at other Boston-area plants.[54] H. L. Farquhar, a business school graduate who assisted and then succeeded Coburn, acknowledged that this approach "did not really teach the Taylor System as it should be taught."[55] Even this modest effort, however, exceeded the resources and patience of local manufacturers. In 1920, Wallace Donham, Gay's successor, complained that with fifty students in the advanced course, "we can no longer find sufficient factories on the Taylor System to give the instruction which we wish to offer. . . ."[56] Despite such obstacles, "The Taylor System" continued to be a notable feature of the Harvard curriculum until 1926, when it was absorbed into the burgeoning course offerings of a Department of Industrial Management.

Equally important were the indirect effects of scientific management on the Harvard program. Taylor's lectures and his followers' work provided a "formula for management" that fulfilled Gay's promise of a "scientific method . . . underlying the art of business." Their success spurred related efforts, particularly in marketing. Under Donham, Harvard turned decisively against the Wharton approach and emphasized broad executive functions and responsibilities. The Harvard program became a model for others who sensed the potential of Taylor's writings.

Harlow S. Person, who had received a Ph.D. in economics at the University of Michigan in 1902 and joined the faculty of Dartmouth College's Amos Tuck School of Business, introduced a course entitled "Business Management" in 1904.[57] Like many of his colleagues he was attracted to Taylor's work and became active in the scientific management movement. When Morris L. Cooke lectured at Dartmouth in early 1911, Person persuaded him to return in the fall to convene a national conference on scientific management. The Tuck School Conference, in October, attracted more than 300 executives, educators, and consultants and was an important stimulus to the diffusion of scientific management.[58] It was also a turning point in the evolution of the Tuck School. Person revised his introductory course to make scientific management its focus, added "Problems of Management," a course that emphasized the application of scientific management techniques and, in 1913, introduced a related course, "Principles and Mechanism of Scientific Management."[59] By that time he had also become the school's first professor of management.[60] His colleague Harry W. Shelton, who worked closely with him, introduced "Scientific Management in Distribution" and "Scientific Management in Manufacturing" in the mid 1910s. When Person left Dartmouth in 1919 to become the permanent secretary of the Taylor Society, Nathanial G. Burleigh and Harry Wellman, specialists in production and marketing respectively, took over his management courses. For many years they sustained the approach to business education that Person had pioneered.[61]

Despite their interest in scientific management, academics such as C. B. Thompson and Harlow Person objected to Taylor's derogatory references to workers like "Schmidt" and his contentious relations with trade union leaders. On such issues they were closer to the contemporary proponents of systematic welfare work than they were to Taylor and his closest disciples. As their presence in the movement grew, they helped erase the last vestiges of the conflict between the engineers and organized labor. In the 1920s they made the Taylor Society the most liberal business organization of the time.[62] On campus they promoted the discussion of labor issues and personnel management. From the beginning, Gay's "Industrial Organization" included lectures on labor problems. Person introduced a course, "The Employment Function in Management" in 1915, and his successors continued to teach it as a feature of their series of courses on scientific management.[63] By the early 1920s Harvard's introductory course, "Industrial Management" devoted almost as much attention to labor and personnel topics as it did to more conventional scientific management subjects. It is unlikely, however that the students noticed a marked change in perspective between the Taylor disciples and Ordway Tead, Ralph G. Wells, and Earl D. Howard, leaders of the nascent personnel management movement, or even Sidney Hillman, the president of the Amalgamated Clothing Workers, who discussed his efforts to use scientific management to stabilize employment and improve working conditions.[64]

The broader conception of scientific management was also apparent in the evolution of the business curriculum at another elite school, the University of Chicago. Despite earlier efforts, Chicago did not have a business program of any consequence until 1912, when new funds became available.[65] L. C. Marshall, a student of Gay's who had been dean at Chicago since 1909, then turned to his mentor for advice. In 1913 he introduced a course in industrial organization, emphasizing manufacturing problems and scientific management.[66] In 1916 he added a course in personnel management, which became another staple of the Chicago curriculum.[67] The Chicago program soon became almost indistinguishable from the Harvard and Tuck School curricula and Marshall, like Gay and Person, was satisfied that he had resolved the issue of the legitimacy of university business education. The Association of Collegiate Schools of Business, which he and Gay founded in 1916 to promote the professionalization of their enterprise, was a tangible expression of that confidence.[68]

The examples of the elite schools, coupled with the contemporary furor over Taylorism, had a profound impact on the hundreds of other schools that were introducing or expanding their business programs. Like Gay and Person, the academics of the 1910s and 1920s found in Taylor's writings a way to make sense of the vast organizational changes of the preceding decades and to pass on the essence of that experience to students who would work in the new hierarchies. As a result they introduced a series of courses on the techniques and details of scientific management, often in competition with their industrial engineering departments. They also created courses on management principles and the application of those principles to nonfactory activities, especially marketing, the fastest-growing specialty of the postwar era. By the time that the enrollment boom slowed in the late 1920s, they were committed to teaching management as well as technical detail.

The large midwestern universities provide the clearest examples of this process. In 1911 Mathew Hammond, a prominent figure in The Ohio State University economics department, introduced a course in industrial organization that emphasized factory operations and welfare work. In 1913 he added a section on scientific management. When business became a separate college in 1916, "Industrial Organization" became a senior requirement for students of manufacturing. In the following years Hammond and his colleagues introduced related courses in factory organization and management, office management, and time and motion studies, and an ever-growing host of specialized offerings. By the mid 1920s, parallel series of courses, emphasizing "principles" and "management," had evolved in marketing and finance.[69] The pattern at Illinois was similar.[70] At Michigan and Iowa the engineering departments first introduced courses in factory operations and scientific management, which were open to advanced business students. Beginning in the mid 1910s, however, the business colleges at both universities introduced courses in office, sales, store and employment management, and then, having preempted the field, added factory and production management. By the late 1920s they had comprehensive management programs, not unlike those at Ohio State and Illinois.[71]

The development of the business curriculum at Wisconsin differed slightly because of faculty opposition to rigid disciplinary barriers. In 1909, business professor Stephen W. Gilman introduced "Business Organization and Management," which examined "the fundamental principles and methods of modern business procedures." The following year the Department of Mechanical Engineering introduced a major in commercial mechanical engineering, which included lectures by business professors on "shop management, methods of remuneration of labor and the effects upon the cost of production."[72] Their collaboration continued in the following years. Gilman's course evolved into a series of courses on industrial and marketing management ("Factory and Office Administration" became "Fundamentals of Management" in 1919) and commercial mechanical engineering became an industrial engineering major. In 1918 the Economics Department added a program in employment management, which became the basis for a related series of courses. Students were encouraged and in some cases required to cross disciplinary boundaries.[73] With this exception, Wisconsin's business program was essentially indistinguishable from Ohio State's by the mid 1920s.

Universities in the West and the South soon caught up with the other schools. At California, Washington, North Carolina, and

Vanderbilt, the business faculty and curricula were extremely modest until the late 1910s, when the enrollment surge created pressures for more elaborate programs. By that time there was no need to improvise. Many of the newer faculty were graduates of the eastern and midwestern universities and introduced similar courses. By the mid 1920s, the business curricula of the western and southern universities, while still modest by the standards of other areas, bore many resemblances to the curricula of the midwestern universities, including courses in industrial, sales, and personnel management.[74]

The urban universities were equally vigorous in grafting the approach of the elite institutions onto their accounting-based programs. Wharton had offered courses in industrial management since 1900, but there is no evidence that they included instruction in scientific management or that it played more than a tangential role in the curriculum.[75] A major obstacle was J. Russell Smith, who headed the department of geography and industry for nearly a decade. A geographer, Smith made no effort to keep abreast of developments at Harvard or Dartmouth. Since several of his courses required field trips to Philadelphia factories, his students may have been exposed to the practice of scientific management but he, and the Wharton program, were wholly unaffected. In the late 1910s, Smith was succeeded by Richard Lansburgh and Joseph Willits, who were conversant with scientific management, active in the Taylor Society, and aware of the new emphasis in business education. Like their colleagues at the elite universities, they "saw themselves as involved in a much more grandiose enterprise" than teaching factory management.[76] Still, their influence was not substantially greater than Smith's. Lansburgh's courses on industrial management emphasized the techniques of scientific management and Willits's specialty, personnel management, flourished because it, like other popular fields at Wharton, prepared students for a specific vocation.[77] Lansburgh and Willits filled embarrassing gaps in the Wharton curriculum, but their "more grandiose enterprise" had to await another generation of administrators and professors.

New York University was characteristically bold and adaptable. It offered no courses in industrial management until 1914, when it introduced "Factory Organization" (in a new Industrial Engineering program) and "System and Organization in Commercial Business," which examined the implications of scientific management for office and service activities. In 1916, it created a Management department, headed by Lee Galloway, that taught a variety of management courses and a management seminar devoted to controversies over the application of scientific management.[78] No university responded more quickly to the opportunities of the moment. In the following years NYU introduced more specialized courses on industrial and labor management in response to the demands of the swelling student population. Yet courses disappeared as fast as they appeared, faculty turnover was high, and there was no evidence that the swollen curriculum was more than a reaction to the uproar over scientific management and the labor problems of the war period.[79] Accounting and finance remained the core of the ever-burgeoning business curriculum.

Northwestern and Pittsburgh were more typical of the urban universities. The former introduced a course in industrial organization in 1908 and a course on labor problems in 1912. In 1913 Professor Arthur E. Swanson introduced "Business Organization," which included a section on scientific management, and an advanced course on factory organization. Henry P. Dutton took over "Factory Organization" the following year and continued to teach it and related courses on personnel management for many years.[80] Swanson, Dutton, and the other instructors had distinguished careers but, like Lansburgh and Willits, only a slight effect on the college's curriculum. In 1920, only three of forty-two faculty taught courses on management; in 1923, only six of fifty-four.[81] The Pittsburgh faculty introduced a course, "Industrial Management," which emphasized scientific management, in 1911 and taught it every year for the rest of the decade.[82] Yet despite this early start, and the presence of several specialists in production and labor problems, there were few course offerings in management and factory operations, general or specialized, until 1922, when the Evening College introduced an Industrial Engineering major, and 1924, when the business college expanded its Industry department.[83] High faculty turnover and a large parttime student body probably insured that even these developments had little impact on the Pittsburgh program.

By the mid 1930s the first phase of the twentiety-century evolution of business education was largely complete. University business education was no longer a novelty to employers or the university community. University graduates occupied a growing percentage of entry-level jobs in large corporations, and business professors occupied more secure and prestigious niches in their institutions. But the quantitative changes — in enrollment, faculty positions, curricula, and professional activities — were only part of the story. University business education was also qualitatively different and this difference was an important measure of the diffusion of scientific management. More specifically, five important changes in university business education were apparent by 1930.

First, scientific management had become a central feature of the practical curriculum. Most obviously, it was the foundation for programs in industrial engineering and production management. It was also a decisive influence in the growth of other management specialties, notably employment and marketing management. Above all, it had become an important integrative factor in business education, an antidote to the centrifugal forces that undermined the integrity of university business studies. As a consequence, business education matured and business professors rapidly superseded the consultants and manufacturers as the disseminators of scientific management. Henceforth, the spread of the principles and techniques depended more on the developments within the universities than on "object lessons," the personalities of individuals, or contacts with the public.

Second, by the 1920s business professors enjoyed a more secure professional role in the university and the business community. By establishing their claims as heirs to the intellectual legacy of Taylor and his followers, they were able to answer the "sneers" of colleagues and the complaints of executives that they were preoccupied with technical detail. By the end of the decade they could confidently argue that their work was no less informed by theoretical insights than that of their counterparts in other utilitarian disciplines.

Third, professors became increasingly important as innovators of management theory and technique. Nearly all of the individuals mentioned above wrote texts that became authoritative works in their specialties. In the process they and their students refined and extended what they had learned, just as Taylor had revised and extended the ideas of an earlier group of theorists. None of their innovations rivaled Taylor's in influence but collectively their work had at least two major effects. It helped recast the image of scientific management as a progressive force, compatible with trade unionism, advanced personnel management, and an activist state, and it blurred the distinctions between orthodox and unorthodox ideas and methods that had been so important to Taylor's generation.

Fourth, training in factory management, including personnel work, became as widely available as training in accounting had been in 1910. Between industrial engineering and management programs, nearly every university that offered any type of business education provided some instruction in production management. Though the total number of students in accounting and in marketing continued to be substantially higher, the university graduate was no more an oddity in the factory of 1930 than in the sales or accounting office.[84]

Last, from the 1910s to at least the 1940s a large percentage of business students and a smaller but not inconsiderable proportion of engineering students were exposed to the tenets of scientific management, whether they realized it or not. At Harvard in the early 1910s and at other institutions at various times, they listened to Taylor, Taylor's closest followers, or professors who identified their information with the Taylor System. In many other cases, they listened to professors and read texts that encouraged them to think about management as Taylor had thought about it, as a rational, systematic endeavor based on attention to detail, and on the application of the scientist's perspective to economic activity.

By the eve of the Depression, then, collegiate business education was securely established, intellectually and institutionally. A blend of the accounting model and scientific management had become the basis of the practical curriculum in virtually all universities and professors enjoyed a more satisfying professional role. Anti-intellectual students and courses that emphasized technical minutiae had not disappeared, but they were no longer the threats they had been in the early 1910s, or so it seemed. The collapse of the economy in the early 1930s created compelling pressures for job-oriented training and effectively ended opportunities for curricular innovation.[85] The result was a new round of specialized course offerings that eventually provoked criticism reminiscent of the 1910s and demands for broader, more explicitly theoretical approaches.[86] The critics' ahistorical analyses captured only a part of the reality of business education and missed entirely the transforming effects of the scientific management movement.

NOTES

1. The appeal of scientific management was by no means confined to engineering and business professors. The argument here is simply that its impact was greatest among those groups. For suggestions of a similar effect in home economics, see Bettina Berch, "Scientific Management in the Home: The Empress's New Clothes," *Journal of American Culture* 3 (Fall, 1980), pp. 440–45. Taylor's education theories are summarized in Daniel Nelson, *Frederick W. Taylor and the Rise of Scientific Management* (Madison, 1980), pp. 186–88. See also Morris L. Cooke, *Academic and Industrial Efficiency: A Report to the Carnegie Foundation for the Advancement of Teaching* (New York, 1910).

2. Roger L. Geiger, *To Advance Knowledge: The Growth of American Research Universities, 1900–1940* (New York, 1986), p. 17. See also the essays in Alexander Oleson and John Voss, *The Organization of Knowledge in Modern America, 1860–1920* (Baltimore, 1979).

3. Geiger, *To Advance Knowledge*, p. 108.

4. David O. Levine, *The American College and the Culture of Aspiration, 1915–1940* (Ithaca, NY, 1986), p. 19.

5. James H. S. Bossard and J. Frederick Dewhurst, *University Education for Business, A Study of Existing Needs and Practices* (Philadelphia, 1931), p. 253. On the social atmosphere of the postwar years, see Paula S. Fass, *The Damned and the Beautiful: American Youth in the 1920's* (New York, 1977).

6. Bossard and Dewhurst, *University Education for Business*, p. 253; Levine, *The American College*, pp. 58–59.

7. Bossard and Dewhurst, *University Education for Business*, pp. 254–55.

8. Michael W. Sedlak and Harold F. Williamson, *The Evolution of Management Education: A History of the Northwestern University J. L. Kellogg Graduate School of Management, 1908–1983* (Urbana and Chicago, 1983), p. 31.

9. Roswell C. McCrea, "The Work of the Wharton School of Finance and Commerce," *Journal of Political Economy* 21 (February 1913), p. 114. See also William A. Scott, "Training for Business at the University of Wisconsin," Ibid., p. 133.

10. Steven A. Sass, *The Pragmatic Imagination: A History of the Wharton School, 1881–1981* (Philadelphia, 1982), p. 134. See also Merle Curti and Vernon Carstensen, *The University of Wisconsin, A History, 1848–1925*, vol. I (Madison, 1949), p. 631; Paul J. Miranti, Jr., *Accountancy Comes of Age: The Development of an American Profession, 1886–1940* (Chapel Hill, 1990), p. 80.

11. Geiger, *To Advance Knowledge*, p. 114.

12. Bossard and Dewhurst, *University Education for Business*, p. 43.

13. Mark Jay Epstein, *The Effect of Scientific Management on the Development of the Standard Cost System* (New York, 1978), pp. 108–18.

14. H. Thomas Johnson and Robert S. Kaplan, *Relevance Lost: The Rise and Fall of Management Accounting* (Boston, 1987), p. 128.

15. Paul J. Miranti, Jr., "Associationalism, Statism and Professional Regulation: Public Accountants and the Reform of Financial Markets, 1896–1940," *Business History Review* 60 (Autumn, 1986), pp. 438–68.

16. Johnson and Kaplan, *Relevance Lost*, p. 130.

17. Gary John Previts and Barbara Dubis Merino, *A History of Accounting in America: An Historical Interpretation of the Cultural Significance of Accounting* (New York, 1979), pp. 154–55, 213.

18. Sass, *Pragmatic Imagination*, pp. 167–69, 158; Miranti, *Accountancy Comes of Age*, p. 80.

19. Agnes Lynch Starret, *Through One Hundred and Fifty Years, the University of Pittsburgh* (Pittsburgh, 1937), pp. 408–10, 416–17.

20. Horace Coon, *Columbia, Colossus on the Hudson* (New York, 1947), pp. 235–36.

21. Sedlack and Williamson, *Evolution of Management Education*, p. 47.

22. Theodore Francis Jones, ed., *New York University, 1832–1932* (New York, 1933), pp. 357–62.

23. Sass, *Pragmatic Imagination*, pp. 172–74.

24. "Engineering and Business Administration," *The Technology Review* (1913), p. 391.

25. Nelson, *Frederick W. Taylor*, pp. 168–74; Charles D. Wrege and Anne Marie Stotka, "Cooke Creates a Classic: The Story Behind F. W. Taylor's *Principles of Scientific Management,*" *Academy of Management Review* 3 (October 1978), pp. 736–49.

26. Despite the popularity of scientific management in Europe, I have found little evidence of a parallel development in European institutions of higher education. The closest analogue was apparently in British education, where industrial engineering curricula appeared in the late 1910s and 1920s, and business courses with an emphasis on management emerged in the 1920s. See L. Urwick and E. F. L. Brech, *The Making of Scientific Management*, vol. 2 (London, 1949), pp. 128–29, 139–42. Robert R. Locke writes that by the 1930s German business economics "had become, with American, the most highly developed in the world." Robert R. Locke, *Management and Higher Education Since 1940: The Influence of America and Japan on West Germany, Great Britain, and France* (Cambridge, 1989), p. 91.

27. I am indebted to the following individuals who assisted with the case studies: Barbara Krieger (Dartmouth), Kevin Boyle (Michigan), Stephen P. Waring (Iowa), Donald L. Winters (Vanderbilt), Kathy Burgess (Penn), Laura O'Keefe (North Carolina), Daniel Meyer (Chicago), Kathy Marquis and Alan Taylor (MIT), Steve Sims (California), Angela Chin (New York University), Florence Bartoskesky (Harvard), Diane L. Bridgman (Washington). I was unable to find anyone to help with the University of Illinois material, which explains the near omission of that formidable program.

28. For background, see Sanford M. Jacoby, *Employing Bureaucracy: Managers, Unions, and the Transformation of Work in American Industry, 1900–1945* (New York, 1985), especially pp. 128–32.

29. For the emergence of the engineering profession, see Monte A. Calvert, *The Mechanical Engineer in America, 1830–1910* (Baltimore, 1967); Edwin T. Layton, Jr., *The Revolt of the Engineers* (Cleveland, 1971), pp. 1–78; Bruce Sinclair, *A Centennial History of the American Society of Mechanical Engineers, 1880–1980* (Toronto, 1980); Terry S. Reynolds, "Defining Professional Boundaries: Chemical Engineering in the Early 20th Century," *Technology and Culture* 27 (October 1986), pp. 694–716.

30. Michael Bezilla, *Engineering Education at Penn State: A Century in the Land Grant Tradition* (University Park, 1981), p. 58.
31. *Pennsylvania State College Bulletin* 3 (April 1909), p. 120.
32. Ibid. 7 (March 1913), p. 193.
33. Ibid. 8 (February 1914), pp. 206–8.
34. *The Register, Cornell University, 1905–1906*, p. 418; *1906–1907*, p. 412. Morris Bishop, in *A History of Cornell* (Ithaca, 1962), p. 400, dates Kimball's course from 1904.
35. *Official Publication of Cornell, 1910–1911*, p. 24.
36. Ibid., *1914–1915*, p. 30.
37. Ibid., *1915–1916*, p. 27.
38. Bishop, *History of Cornell*, p. 475.
39. *Annual Catalogue of Purdue University, 1908–1909*, p. 128.
40. Ibid., *1919–20*, p. 126.
41. *Bulletin of Carnegie Institute of Technology, 1909–1910*, p. 78.
42. Quoted in "Engineering and Business Administration," *The Technology Review* (1913), p. 391.
43. *Bulletin of Carnegie Institute of Technology*, years 1910 to 1920 inclusive.
44. James R. Killian, Jr., "The Origin and Rise of Programs in Management at MIT: A Personal Memoir," Massachusetts Institute of Technology, Sloan School of Management, *Annual Report, 1981–82* (Cambridge, 1982), p. 4.
45. Killian, "The Origin of Programs at MIT," pp. 4–7; "To Teach Engineering Administration," *The Technology Review* (1914), pp. 381–85; Massachusetts Institute of Technology, *Catalogue, 1915–16* (Cambridge, 1915), pp. 380–81; *Catalogue, 1920–21* (Cambridge, 1920), pp. 39, 104.
46. F. J. Roethlisberger, *The Elusive Phenomena* (Cambridge, 1977), p. 21.
47. Quoted in Jeffrey L. Cruikshank, *A Delicate Experiment: The Harvard Business School, 1908–1945* (Boston, 1987), p. 54.
48. Cruikshank, *A Delicate Experiment*, pp. 56–57.
49. Harvard University, *The Graduate School of Business Administration, 1908–1909* (Cambridge, 1908), p. 20.
50. Nelson, *Frederick W. Taylor*, pp. 188–89.
51. Melvin T. Copeland, *And Mark An Era, The Story of the Harvard Business School* (Boston, 1958), p. 26.
52. Harvard, *The Graduate School of Business Administration, 1910–11*, p. 21.
53. See the Thompson-Gay correspondence file, Dean's Office Files, Harvard Graduate School of Business Administration (Baker Library, Boston); C. Bertrand Thompson, ed., *Scientific Management; A Collection of the more Significant Articles Describing the Taylor System of Management* (Cambridge, 1914); C. Bertrand Thompson, *The Theory and Practice of Scientific Management* (Boston, 1917).
54. Harvard, *The Graduate School of Business Administration, 1911–1912*, p. 23.
55. H. H. Farquhar to G. Schultz, January 4, 1917, Dean's Office Files, Harvard Business School.
56. W. B. Donham to A. W. Shaw, June 15, 1920, Dean's Office Files, Harvard Business School.

57. Dartmouth College, *Announcement of the Amos Tuck School of Administration and Finance, 1904–1905* (Hanover, NH, 1904), p. 32.

58. H. S. Person to Frederick W. Taylor, March 7, 1911, Frederick W. Taylor Papers (Stevens Institute of Technology, Hoboken, New Jersey), File 116A. Cooke's plan was to make the Tuck School Conference "a reunion similar to the one in Washington" at the famous 1910 Eastern Rate Case hearings. Morris L. Cooke to Taylor, March 15, 1911, Taylor Papers, File 116A.

59. Dartmouth, *Announcement of the Amos Tuck School, 1913–1914*, p. 26.

60. H. S. Person to Frank B. Gilbreth, March 15, 1913, Frank B. Gilbreth Papers (Purdue University, West Lafayette, Indiana).

61. *Catalogue of Dartmouth College*, years 1919 to 1930 inclusive.

62. Nelson, *Frederick W. Taylor*, pp. 184–85; Jacoby, *Employing Bureaucracy*, pp. 102–4; Milton J. Nadworny, *Scientific Management and the Unions, 1900–1932* (Cambridge, MA, 1955), pp. 97–141.

63. *Catalogue of Dartmouth College, 1915–1916*, p. 244.

64. Harvard, *The Graduate School of Business Administration, 1921–22*, pp. 54, 57–58; Wallace B. Donham to F. C. Hood, Feb. 10, 1921, Dean's Office Files.

65. Thomas Wakefield Goodspeed, *A History of the University of Chicago* (Chicago, 1916), pp. 323–24; Leon C. Marshall, "The College of Commerce and Administration of the University of Chicago," *Journal of Political Economy* 21 (February 1913), pp. 97–100.

66. University of Chicago, *Annual Register, 1913–14* (Chicago, 1913). The Marshall-Gay correspondence file, Dean's Office Files, Harvard Business School, documents the close ties between the two men.

67. Chicago, *Annual Register, 1916–17*, p. 404. Robert Hoxie was scheduled to teach a course, "Scientific Management and Labor," during the 1915–1916 school year but died before the course was offered. *Annual Register, 1915–16*, p. 121.

68. Gay-Marshall correspondence, February, 1916–March, 1917, Dean's Office Files, Harvard Business School. Willard E. Hotchkiss, who became dean of the new Stanford Business School in 1925, shared their perspective. See Willard Eugene Hotchkiss, *Higher Education and Business Standards* (Boston, 1918), pp. 68–70.

69. Guy-Harold Smith, *The First Fifty Years of the College of Commerce and Administration* (Columbus, OH, 1966), pp. 21–31, 39; *Ohio State University Bulletin, 1911–1912* (Columbus, OH, 1911), p. 40; *1913–1914*, p. 43; *1923–1924*, pp. 209–11.

70. *Sixteen Years at the University of Illinois* (Urbana, 1920), pp. 215–16.

71. *University of Michigan Department of Engineering General Announcement, 1914–1925*, (Ann Arbor, 1914), p. 153; *1916–1917*, pp. 181–82; Michigan, *Literature, Science and the Arts Annual Announcement, 1913–1914*, p. 115; *1920–1921*, pp. 102–3; Michigan, *School of Business Administration Annual Announcement, 1924–1925*, pp. 22–23; *State University of Iowa Catalog, 1905–1906*, pp. 89, 126; Iowa, *School of Commerce Bulletin, 1916–1917*, pp. 24–25; *1922–1923*, pp. 14–15.

72. *University of Wisconsin Catalogue, 1909–1910* (Madison, 1910), p. 210; *1910–1911*, pp. 299, 313–14. For the origins of the business program see Curti and Carstensen, *The University of Wisconsin*, p. 644; Scott, "Training for Business," pp. 127–135.

73. See, for example, *Vanderbilt University Catalogue, 1919–1920* (Nashville, 1919), p. 83; *1920–1921*, p. 82; *1921–1922*, p. 118; *University of Washington Catalog, 1917–1918* (Seattle, 1917), p. 115; *1919–1920*, p. 193.

74. *Catalogue of the University of Pennsylvania, 1901–1902* (Philadelphia, 1901), p. 152; *1903–1904*, p. 144; *1904–1905*, p. 214; *1909–1910*, p. 278; *1914–1915*, p. 242.

75. Sass, *Pragmatic Imagination*, p. 175.

76. *Catalogue of the University of Pennsylvania, 1919–1920*, pp. 142–43; *University of Pennsylvania Bulletin: The Wharton School of Finance and Commerce Announcement, 1920–1921*, pp. 39–40; *1921–1922*, pp. 50–51; *1922–1923*, pp. 56–57.

77. Sass, *Pragmatic Imagination*, pp. 176–80.

78. *New York University Bulletin, School of Commerce, Accounts and Finance, Announcements for the Year, 1914–1915*, (New York, 1914), pp. 50–51; *1915–1916*, pp. 60, 82–83; *1916–1917*, pp. 83–84, 87.

79. Ibid., *1920–1921*, pp. 92, 95–96; *1921–1922*, pp. 114, 131–32; *1922–1923*, pp. 143–48; and New York University, *College of Engineering Announcements for the Year 1920–1921*, pp. 43–45.

80. *Northwestern University School of Commerce Announcement, 1908–1909* (Evanston, 1908), pp. 20–21; *1912–1913*, pp. 29–30; *1913–1914*, pp. 20, 23; *1914–1915*, pp. 29–30, 33–34, 36.

81. Ibid., *1920–1921*, pp. 16–29; *1923–1924*, pp. 17–30.

82. *University of Pittsburgh Bulletin, 1911–1912*, p. 18; *1912–1913*, p. 25; *1913–1914*, p. 25; *1914–1915*, p. 16; *1915–1916*, p. 18; *1919–1920*, p. 139.

83. Ibid., *1920–1921*, pp. 23–24; *1924–1925*, p. 30; Pittsburgh, *School of Engineering, 1922–1923*, p. 35.

84. See Bossard and Dewhurst, *University Education for Business*, pp. 285–87.

85. Geiger, *To Advance Knowledge*, pp. 247–48. Business and engineering curricula at the twenty-one universities were virtually unchanged in the 1930s.

86. See Frank C. Pierson et al., *The Education of American Businessmen* (New York, 1959); Richard Hofstadter and C. DeWitt Hardy, *The Development and Scope of Higher Education in the United States* (New York, 1952), pp. 92–94.

GUY ALCHON

# 5  Mary Van Kleeck and Scientific Management

The diffusion and political content of scientific management during the first half of the twentieth century has long interested scholars. Originally preoccupied with work processes and labor discipline, scientific management ultimately informed the international development of several fields. Education, public administration, industrial psychology, and personnel management, among others, absorbed in different ways the Taylorist ethos of organizational efficiency through expert research and functional prescription. As for its political thrust, most scholars have viewed Taylorism, for good or ill, as an important part of modern capitalist ideology, or as a vehicle for the promotion of new classes standing above or between capital and labor. More recently, the gender politics of Taylorism's spread have come under review, if often only implicitly, in studies of women's work and the home.[1]

Critical to both the appeal and the development of Taylorism were the "scientizing" and utopian impulses at its core. The "mental revolution" Taylor demanded of labor and management was to produce both a more rational and productive workplace and, by extension, a more abundant and harmonious society. This sensibility only increased after Taylor's death in 1915; his notoriety, the proselytizing of his associates, and wartime lessons in cooperative planning, would liberate scientific management from the shop floor. And during the postwar years, an international search for new mechanisms of social integration increasingly turned scientific management into an ideology of broad social transformation.[2]

Visions of a world made rational and abundant through the planning of technical elites now animated the thinking of novelists and revolutionaries, as well as engineers and businessmen. H. G. Wells, V. I. Lenin, and Herbert Hoover, in different ways, subscribed to the new faith, made plain its political ambitions, and thus helped to advance its pretensions and values. From approximately 1915 through the 1930s, then, serious people believed and promoted the view that scientific management's proven ability to raise productivity within the firm could become the basis for a new utopia. One of these was the Russell Sage Foundation executive, social worker, and industrial sociologist, Mary Abby Van Kleeck.[3]

"The archetypal social feminist," Van Kleeck (1883–1972) was one of the network of women reformers and social investigators active in New York's labor and social justice causes early in the century. Her studies of women workers led to her appointment as director of the Sage Foundation's Department of Industrial Studies, a post she would hold from 1916 to her retirement in 1948. In that capacity, she led the development of a program of labor and economic planning research, and almost singlehandedly turned the foundation into an institute for advanced social study. During the interwar period she emerged as the leader of the left wing of American social work, a radical defender of labor and civil rights. And there, too, she joined the worldwide planning debate through her leading role in Herbert Hoover's macroeconomic planning initiatives, in the International Industrial Relations Institute (IRI), and in the Taylor Society, the chief American organization for the promotion of scientific management.[4]

Van Kleeck was not the only Taylorite concerned with scientific management's wider social applications. Morris Cooke and Harlow Person, among others, shared this interest. Nor was she the only woman. Lillian Gilbreth and Ida Tarbell, like Van Kleeck, were members of the Taylor Society, and worked to apply the movement's principles to the home. But perhaps more than any Taylorite, Mary Van Kleeck worked to bring scientific management to bear on social welfare. She saw scientific management's emphasis on research into the factors of production as the key to achieving social work's goal of raised living standards. Scientific management, Van Kleeck believed, its standard of rationality informed by social work's concern for the common weal, could

determine the proper coordination of all aspects of modern economies, from industrial relations within firms to the balancing of
national production and consumption. And she pursued this belief
over a career that traversed the difficult terrain from liberal reform
through Hooverian corporatism to Soviet fellow traveling.[5] Largely
ignored by scholars, Van Kleeck's activities illuminate the appeal
of Taylorism to professions and professionals seeking wider public influence, the meaning and place of scientific management in
the interwar movement toward macroeconomic planning, and the
ironies of one woman's very large role in these matters.[6]

Mary Van Kleeck's commitment to social work antedated her
discovery of scientific management. Her vocation took shape
while she was a student at Smith College from 1900 to 1904.
There, her leading role in the Smith College Association for
Christian Work and exposure to the early industrial work of the
YWCA drew her into a wider world of woman-led reform. Upon
graduation, and with a postgraduate fellowship in hand, she
joined the College Settlement on New York's lower east side and
began graduate work in social economy with Edward T. Devine
and Henry R. Seager at Columbia University. The College Settlement had already served as a training ground for such other
women reformers as Mary Simkhovitch, Frances Kellor, and
Eleanor Roosevelt. And there, Lilian Brandt, Florence Kelley, and
the Women's Trade Union League of New York introduced the
young social worker to a women's network of industrial investigation and reform. From 1905 through 1907, she studied child labor
and overtime in women's work in New York City and soon came
to the attention of the then-new Russell Sage Foundation.[7]

Inaugurated in 1907, the Sage Foundation reflected the scientizing currents then running strongly through philanthropic circles,
and the determination to move beyond charity and relief into the
systematic study of poverty's causes. To this end the foundation
sponsored, among other things, the Pittsburgh Survey, the first
social survey of an American city, dedicated itself to profession-
alizing social work, and would function for the next forty years as
Mary Van Kleeck's institutional base.[8]

Initially, the new foundation sponsored the continuation of Van
Kleeck's early researches, operating now under the auspices of an
independent Committee on Women's Work chaired by Henry

Seager, and in 1910 brought this committee formally into the foundation. Between 1910 and 1917, Van Kleeck's department launched investigations of the poor conditions, night work, and unemployment suffered by New York City's women workers in the artificial flowers, millinery, and bookbinding trades. "Intensive in method, dealing with a concrete, limited subject of inquiry," these studies, she explained, produced "not theories but evidence gathered slowly from those who know the facts through experience—the workers and the employers."[9]

Van Kleeck's investigations emphasized the disorganization and irregularity of business operations. She called, among other things, for worker-management wage boards and employment exchanges to address these problems. In 1910 and again in 1915, she was instrumental in the establishment of state prohibitions against night work for women workers. Reflecting later upon the value of her early projects, she remarked that for "a view of the industrial system which comprehends not only the factory but the homes of the people . . . , the best subject of study is the status of women in industry." By 1914, however, convinced by her work "that distress and poverty among women workers are but phases of" larger "industrial and social conditions," Van Kleeck welcomed the foundation's decision to enlarge her department's scope to include study of men's as well as women's work. This broadened mandate was made formal in 1916 with the creation of a new Division of Industrial Studies under her leadership.[10]

These projects revealed a stubborn faith in the potential of social science to provide both the vision and the means necessary for social transformation. They were, Van Kleeck noted in 1915, "carried on in the faith that a well-informed community will develop, step by step, a new order, the outgrowth of a new philosophy pressing toward the control of the industrial causes of poverty and misery. . . ." Management and labor, in other words, would be brought to a more balanced and just accommodation through a public opinion informed by social research. And because her studies also indicated that poor business management lay behind unemployment, Van Kleeck soon would be among those encouraging the fusion of scientific management and social work in the assault on economic instability.[11]

By 1915 and Taylor's death, scientific management had been moving for some time toward just such a wider application of its principles. Taylor's later writings and pronouncements, together with the popularization of his ideas by Louis Brandeis, Ida Tarbell, and others, strongly suggested the movement's applicability to the cause of national reform and renewal. Under Harlow Person's presidency, the Taylor Society from 1914 through 1919 was increasingly receptive to the consideration of social ideals and to the participation of social scientists and reformers.[12]

Van Kleeck surely was aware of this ferment; while the origins of her association with the Taylor Society remain unclear, her first reference to Taylorism, so the available evidence indicates, came in a syllabus for a course on industrial problems at the New York School of Philanthropy, where she taught from 1914 to 1917. There, in 1915, she introduced students of social work to the proposition that scientific management's "big contribution" to their field lay in its "expert study of working conditions." Such study, she argued early in 1917, had already led some management engineers to recognize the inefficiencies of unemployment and haphazard personnel policies. Here she pointed approvingly to the ideas of Richard Feiss and Ordway Tead, and to the efforts of Robert Valentine to promote an "Industrial Audit," in which the management of human relations within firms would be subject to the scrutiny accorded the management of production. Taylorites, it seemed to Van Kleeck, were beginning to share social work's preoccupation with the "human element"; in order to further these merging tendencies, she urged the adoption of the industrial audit as the first step in training social workers to assume personnel management positions in industry.[13]

As they developed from 1915 to 1924, Van Kleeck's views on the relations between social work and scientific management were complex and contradictory. Convinced that both social workers and scientific managers had much to teach each other, she encouraged their merger and welcomed their contributions to the new field of personnel management. At the same time, she resisted the tendency of Taylorites and others to view the growing emphasis on human relations in industry as an improvement upon and departure from the ideas of Frederick W. Taylor. Occasionally, she seemed to suggest that scientific management needed no lessons in wider social vision from anyone. Because an unreconstructed Taylorism's scientific, and thus disinterested, approach to industrial management could help to rationalize the firm, she reasoned, it could not help but rationalize and make just the firm's relationship with its workers and community. Scientific management, for Van Kleeck, was thus a social science of utopian potential. With its pretensions to transcendent authority, moreover, such a fundamentalist scientism likely held an additional appeal: it could enable insecure professionals, social workers as well as management engineers, to cast themselves as social arbiters with important and independent roles to play in stabilizing the industrial system.

Van Kleeck was acutely conscious of social work's uncertain professional status. With its attention split between the results and the causes of human suffering, between casework and social reform, and lacking an esoteric technique and independent source of income, social work's identity was unclear, its disinterestedness in question. Since it functioned best as a "mediating" contact among various groups, Van Kleeck argued, it should view its professional mission as one of encouraging other groups and professions to think in terms of the community, the social ideal. "Only as social workers are prepared consciously to formulate their experience as a guide for the practice of others . . . can they lay claim to the possession of technique." Recent "experience seems also to show," she noted, "that the more socialized the other professions become, the more they turn to social workers for light." The best evidence for this proposition, Van Kleeck felt, lay in the warming relations between social workers and management engineers.[14]

The first world war's demand for labor management intensified the linkages between these groups, encouraging both the development of the personnel management movement and fresh opportunities to illustrate scientific management's importance to women workers. Together with Morris Cooke, for example, Van Kleeck sought to advance the interests of wartime women workers by establishing labor standards through the Storage Committee and Industrial Service Section of the Ordnance Department. With the trade unionist, Mary Anderson, she expanded upon this work in the Woman in Industry Service of the Labor Department, forerunner of the U.S. Women's Bureau. Despite employer resistance, exploitation, and discrimination, women workers, she found, often succeeded in men's work. "Hundreds of jobs," Van

Kleeck noted proudly, "became sexless." Such success, however, depended mostly upon intelligent and efficient business management. "The war record," she wrote in *The Atlantic Monthly*, ". . . is clear. Management in industry, and not feminism, opened the way to novel work for women." Nonetheless, Van Kleeck suggested, feminism and scientific management shared ultimate goals. "Efficiency," she averred elsewhere, "is not the ultimate aim. . . . The goal is the establishment of just relationships."[15]

> It is the method of industry to attach the individual to his limited, specified place in the whole scheme of production; while the aim of feminism is to make the whole recognize a hitherto unrealized obligation to the individual . . . it busies itself with the issues that the times create.
>
> The economic issues of the time, as they are reflected in women's industrial status, were never more baffling. She must win a more secure place in the shop as a skilled worker. She has as yet only a limited . . . recognition in the labor movement. . . . She is accused of aiming to undermine the home, just when she may be working hardest at uncongenial tasks to support it. So discouraging is the outlook . . . that one is almost inclined to agree with certain anti-feminists about the effects of industrialism on all our social institutions, including the family as a whole and women individually. Not feminism, however, but industrial organization, uncontrolled in the common service, has done the damage.[16]

Scientific management, Van Kleeck was certain, could help undo the damage. And while in the immediate postwar years, she would continue to work on behalf of women workers through her association with the U.S. Women's Bureau, by far the bulk of her energies would be devoted to furthering the merger of social work and Taylorite perspectives. Here, her own ties to scientific management would intensify, as she would be elected to the Nominating Committee and the Board of Directors of the Taylor Society.[17]

"The management engineer and the social worker," she concluded in 1922, "have found cooperation necessary." "The management engineer has discovered . . . that the efficiency and cooperative attitude of a labor force is directly affected by the organization of life in the community." The social worker, "approaching from a different direction has also arrived at the place where recognition of the relations of these two groups . . . become highly desirable for the success of each . . ." Van Kleeck was probably right, although in more ways than she admitted. During the years just before and after the world war, elements within each group were interested in securing greater influence and autonomy, both within and without the corporation: engineers by claiming possession of a scientifically informed social vision, social workers by establishing a new professional authority resting on the research and skills they could bring to bear on the economic sources of social distress. "Industry," she proclaimed, "is being invaded by social workers, who are bringing their experience to bear upon problems of personnel and research as they affect human relations." For a social worker like Van Kleeck, eager to see her profession take up an important role in social reconstruction, the assault was providential.[18]

Closer ties to scientific management, Van Kleeck seemed to think, would help to "scientize," and thus make more effective, social work's claim to a place in the larger postwar debate over capitalist instability and unemployment. Personnel management already had emerged, in part, from this linkage, and Van Kleeck looked forward to further developments along these lines, toward an entirely new profession for industrial sociologists like herself. For a time in 1921 and 1922, she worked with Lucy Carner, Frances Perkins, Molly Dewson, Louise Odencrantz, and George Soule attempting to organize a field of "industrial social work," but nothing came of this effort. Still, as she reminded her friend, Morris Cooke, "the analogy is close between social work and engineering." "We wish," she continued, "that we could find a more inclusive title than social work which has been so strongly associated with case workers." Briefly, she considered the term "social engineering," but regarded it as inaccurate and confusing. Still, "a term of that kind which denotes our interest in constructive social problems and in research would give us the broader basis necessary for . . . professional organization."[19]

While Van Kleeck welcomed the development of mutually informing links between social work and scientific management, ties that would alter each profession, she resisted any suggestion that Taylor's thought had ignored the "human element." "My own experience," she would tell the Taylor Society in 1924, "began with what is called the human element in industry, and I saw it first outside the shop in the community." There, her search for solutions to the long hours and repetitive unemployment characteristic of women's work "led back into the causes of these conditions in the shop itself, and nowhere did I find so many questions in process of being answered as in the Taylor Society."[20]

> Those answers did not relate merely to what is called the human element in industry, conceived as a separate problem in a different compartment of the manager's desk. My interest in the contribution of scientific management . . . was not solely in its emphasis upon personnel relations, but in the technical organization of industry as it affects wage-earners. The constructive imagination which can spend seventeen years studying the art of cutting metals is the imagination which can make industry and all its results in human lives harmonize with our ideals for the community. That kind of constructive imagination, though it may deal with one technical problem, will not fail to envisage the whole significance of industrial management. Nor will it be content merely to increase profits. The philosophy and the procedure which it represents will ultimately build a shop whose influence in the community will be social in the best sense, because the shop and all its human relations are built on sound principles.
>
> Therefore, my interest in the Taylor Society is not directed toward challenging the technical engineer to give attention to problems of human relations. I am not worried about that, because if he is a good engineer he cannot fail to contribute to human relations. I am concerned rather with the other end of the story. I am eager to have those people who see the present disastrous results of industrial organization in the community realize how the art of management in the shop can fundamentally change those social conditions in the community.[21]

By the early 1920s, Van Kleeck's efforts to merge social work and scientific management had led her irretrievably from the world of women's reform to the heart of the management reform movement. While she would maintain some contacts among the women's network of social reformers, she would not be central to their progress through the interwar years. Instead, her commitment to scientific management as social science would lead her into a range of new activities, international associations, and political commitments. Postwar economic turmoil and industrial conflict already had prompted her to reorient her Department of Industrial Studies toward systematic analysis of employee-management plans within several industries. More importantly, in terms of our story, her efforts would take her now into the developing arenas of national and international planning.[22]

These, in the most immediate sense, were the product of the first world war's various national planning experiments. Against the backdrop of postwar dislocations, some of those who had played the largest roles in the wartime mobilization of the economy—management engineers, social scientists, a few businessmen, and labor leaders—struggled to build new national managerial capabilities. The chief figure in this story was the new Commerce Secretary, Herbert Hoover. But around him, from 1921 through the early 1930s, would gather an array of planners, and among these was Mary Van Kleeck.[23]

Van Kleeck saw Hooverian planning, at least at its outset, as an opportunity to further the rationalization of business and its relation to the community, and to do so now on a national scale. Early in 1921, Hoover sponsored the Federated American Engineering Societies' study, *Waste in Industry.* While criticizing the report as vague, Van Kleeck nonetheless found valuable its emphasis on managerial responsibility for social as well as industrial welfare. Still, she was skeptical when in the fall of 1921, amidst a severe depression, Hoover presided over the President's Conference on Unemployment. Van Kleeck doubted Hoover's grasp of labor issues and unemployment. And with both the Labor Department and its Women's Bureau excluded, she feared the Conference would promote the Commerce Department at their expense. Still, she retained some hope. "Perhaps," she wrote to her Sage Foundation associate, Shelby Harrison, "this means that the main objective will be to emphasize the responsibility of employers for avoiding unemployment, and, if so, the results may be worthwhile."[24]

This was precisely Hoover's emphasis in the conference. To institutionalize it, he invited Mary Van Kleeck and others to join a continuing committee to supervise an unprecedented investigation into the nature of business cycles and the utility of scientific management in their prevention. A key vehicle of Hooverian planning, the committee reflected Hoover's desire to construct a better ordered and balanced society through the application of technical expertise to economic problems. It reflected, too, Hoover's antistatism, and his determination to achieve these goals through a corporatist arrangement in which private bodies were encouraged by the Commerce Department to assume larger public responsibilities. [25]

Such planning, while sponsored by the Commerce Department, would be funded by the major foundations and built upon the investigations of social scientists affiliated with them, universities, and public policy research organizations such as the National Bureau of Economic Research. The idea was that the new knowledge developed about the business cycle and the countercyclical benefits of scientific management would be broadcast to the nation's businessmen by a Commerce Department eager to see them stabilize their operations and tailor their investment decisions to the cycle's swings. And to the extent that they did so, the argument ran, then the sum of their individual actions would add up to a national economy of greater stability and less unemployment. [26]

Still skeptical, Van Kleeck was willing to give Hooverian macroeconomic planning a chance. With the economist, Wesley C. Mitchell, and the chairman of General Electric, Owen D. Young, she played a leading role in the Cycle Committee's deliberations, and authored one chapter of the committee's final report, *Business Cycles and Unemployment.* Published amidst wide publicity in 1923, the report seemed at the time to have helped to moderate both the upward swing and subsequent decline in business activity at mid-decade, thus vindicating, apparently, Hoover's approach to the economy. But the story of Hooverian planning would not end well, and turned out to be more a story of tentative efforts soon to be overwhelmed by the economy's deeper structural dilemmas and the coming of the Great Depression. [27]

By the late 1920s, in any case, Van Kleeck had become increasingly impatient with Hoover's approach. Her impatience prompted a reassessment. The evidence of rising unemployment amidst general prosperity had mounted; neither social work's "invasion" of industry nor scientific management, it seemed, were strong enough to compel capitalism's reorganization of work and welfare. Thus the time had come, she now argued, to ask whether the problem of stabilizing employment and raising living standards could any longer be left to business management alone.[28]

Scientific management was as important as ever to addressing these problems, she maintained, but without greater public and worker control of the economy it would never fulfill its promise of rational production and social abundance. "It is not enough," she insisted as early as 1927, "to leave the problem of employment and unemployment to leaders of business." The "scientific method of approach to social and economic problems needs to be utilized by unions." This was a theme she carried even into the Taylor Society, where she urged consideration of the "claim of the public upon the social uses of the science of management." It was a theme, too, that would only intensify, as the coming of the Great Depression accelerated her commitment to socialism.[29]

Insisting that Van Kleeck was "one of the best-fitted women in the country for a Cabinet position," Alice Hamilton spoke for those early in the 1930s who regarded Mary Van Kleeck, in Lillian Gilbreth's words, "as the best research woman I know." Van Kleeck's militant and newfound socialism, however, made a New Deal cabinet appointment unlikely. She was offered a post on the Federal Advisory Council of the U.S. Employment Service, but resigned it abruptly to dramatize her opposition to the NRA's insufficient support for collective bargaining and the labor movement. "I find myself forced to stand outside and criticize," she told her good friend Morris Cooke. "I have to work out in my own mind the right direction for my present activities." Her activities since the late 1920s increasingly had involved her in the worldwide search for a new international economic order, a search that had originated more than a decade before in her first efforts to "internationalize" the merger of social reform and scientific management in the work of the International Industrial Relations Institute (IRI).[30]

The IRI arose early in the 1920s as the result of international efforts by a group of mostly women personnel specialists to address the postwar debate over scientific management's place in industrial relations. While corporate welfare and personnel work had been developing both in Europe and the United States since early in the century, the war's labor demands created openings in many firms for women interested in managing the "human factor." And, in a chateau in Normandy in July, 1922, a small group of such women, representing eleven countries, came together in the First International Welfare Conference.[31]

Louise Odencrantz, the wartime personnel manager for the New York ribbon-making firm, Smith & Kaufmann, and Van Kleeck's former associate at the Sage Foundation, was the American representative to the conference. Mary Fledderus, the personnel manager of the Leerdam Glassworks, just outside Rotterdam, Holland, and soon to become, together with Van Kleeck, the motive force behind the IRI, also attended.[32]

Appointed by the conference to organize a larger and more permanent organization, Fledderus was responsible in June 1925 for convening in Holland the new International Association for the Study and Improvement of Human Relations in Industry. More than fifty delegates, most of them women, representing twenty-one countries, attended the conference. Among them were sympathetic employers, such as Dorothy Cadbury, a managing director of England's Cadbury chocolate empire, and Cees van der Leeuw, a partner in Rotterdam's Van Nelle coffee operation and longtime friend of Fledderus. Sweden's chief Inspector of Factories, Kersten Hesselgren, was elected president, and three American members, Odencrantz, Lillian Gilbreth, and Van Kleeck, were elected to the organization's permanent Council.[33]

"Though the principles of Scientific Management and Efficiency are in themselves to be hailed with enthusiasm," Fledderus wrote in the introduction to the congress's report, "unless they are applied with a corresponding study of their effect upon humanity serving in Industry, they hide within their depths the possibility of a great and subtle cruelty." Here, in another form and place, was Van Kleeck's linkage of industrial social work and scientific management. The new congress envisioned its role as one of collaboration with such established bodies as the International Management Institute (IMI) and the International Labor Organization (ILO). As such it could be a forum for the frank discussion of contending schemes for the "promotion of satisfactory human relations and conditions in industry."[34]

The Association met regularly in summer sessions during 1926 and 1927 in order to prepare for its first triennial conference, one that was to test this self-appointed function. The "Fundamental Relationships Between All Sectors of the Industrial Community" was the theme, then, in June 1928, when more than one hundred delegates from twenty countries met for a week at Girton College, the women's college of Cambridge University. There, Paul Devinat of the ILO, the British scientific management enthusiast, Lyndall Urwick, former Principal Woman Inspector of Factories, Dame Adelaide Anderson, and Paul Kellogg, editor of the *Survey* magazine, were in attendance. Both Holland's and Britain's progressive employers were represented by Cees van der Leeuw and by the Rowntrees and Cadburys.[35]

Their discussions, Van Kleeck noted in her remarks to the congress's closing session, had ranged over the philosophies of individualism and collectivism, differences in national experiences, workers' education, and the contributions of scientific management to improved human relations. "Now if anyone complains that there are not enough 'brass tacks' . . . in our discussions," she admonished, "I think we have to ask, is there anything more tangible or more concrete . . . ," than "bringing together the points of view of labour, of employers, of managers, and of those who are students of industry?"[36]

This seemed to be the view of many, both in the conference and among the attentive public, who in the late 1920s looked upon the IRI as an interesting, if modest, "factory of ideas." The organization was all the more remarkable, Van Kleeck was to note later, because it did not have a formal staff, instead relying upon carefully developed triennial conferences, themselves arising out of previous summer meetings and reports. These materials and conference proceedings, then, would be published, usually in book form, as the favored method of bringing the organization's work to a wider and international public.[37]

In truth, the IRI by the late 1920s relied almost exclusively upon Fledderus and Van Kleeck. As director and associate director, respectively, they ran the organization from its office in The Hague and from Van Kleeck's offices in the Sage Foundation, relying for funds on membership dues, a few guardian angels, and the Sage Foundation. And when early in the 1930s the coming of the Depression, the emergence of fascist parties in Europe, and the Soviet Union's turn toward central planning brought a new urgency to world affairs, they turned the IRI's next triennial conference into an opportunity to investigate the implications of these new developments. The result was the Amsterdam World Social

Economic Congress of 1931, the high water mark of the IRI's influence.[38]

"The situation in Europe is indescribably serious," Van Kleeck warned Morris Cooke in the fall of 1930. And "modest as is the I.R.I., it seems to find itself in the position of being the only organization able to offer a platform at this moment to labor, employers, scientific managers, and economists. . . ." The platform's strength, Van Kleeck felt, would depend upon turning the Amsterdam Congress into an international version of the President's Unemployment Conference of 1921. Then, "Mr. Hoover . . . was trying to lift the subject of unemployment to a higher plane of industrial statesmanship, getting leaders of business to use the results of economic research to enlarge the judgment of businessmen." With unemployment now worsening, she argued, "international economic co-operation . . . toward a planned development of productive capacity and standards of living," was necessary. Van Kleeck envisioned nothing less than the fusion of scientific management and social welfare in an international "Social-Economic Planning."[39]

Returning to a favorite theme, Van Kleeck insisted that social economic planning "traces directly back to the scientific management movement," and asks "whether the mastery of knowledge which is slowly being accepted in the workshops can be transferred to the community as a whole. . . ." Planning, she later wrote, "will soon be another commonplace expression," meaning everything and nothing. "But rarely is the expression 'economic planning' used in combination with the word 'social' as denoting the common welfare — the one word from which it should never be severed." Social-economic planning, she asserted in Amsterdam, "is the name for a definite procedure." It had yet to be fairly tested, "but its underlying principles have been developed in the scientific management movement . . . ," and its central task is to utilize the world's productive capacities "to raise the standards of living."[40]

This was the theme that appealed to the Taylorites, scholars, socialists, and trade unionists who assembled in Amsterdam's Koloniaal Institute in late August of that year. Delegates from the United States included Harlow Person, Edward A. Filene of the Boston department store and 20th Century Fund, and Lewis Lorwin of the Brookings Institution. But drawing the most attention was a delegation of the State Planning Commission of the Soviet Union (Gosplan).

The Soviet delegation's presence alone was news, as they were among the first Soviet officials to travel to the west to discuss the Five Year plans. More than this, they were representatives of the world's first society attempting comprehensive and socialized planning, and thus "their coming did not merely add one nation to the list," Van Kleeck noted, "but brought to the discussion the record of experience with social economic planning under communism, as it is actually in effect." Led by the Gosplan economist, Valery V. Obolensky-Ossinsky, the Soviet delegation even presented their chief discussion of Russia under the plans as "The Nature and Forms of Social Economic Planning." Their presentations were eagerly attended by a congress and international press curious to learn more about the details of central administration, goal setting, the role of scientific management in labor relations, and the allegedly democratic and collaborative ethos underlying the Soviet administration of industry, agriculture, and trade. But of these matters, the Soviets really had little new to say, preferring instead to emphasize, sometimes angrily, the contrast between a Soviet Union enjoying planned and democratic full employment and a prostrate western capitalism.[41]

Following the Amsterdam Congress, Van Kleeck and her allies in the IRI worked to establish a World Commission for the Study of Social Economic Planning, one capable of developing statistics and other materials necessary for the construction of world plans. "But is not this world task too big for us?" she asked rhetorically. It was, of course. The IRI never attained direct and continuous influence in the planning debates of the 1930s. Unable to generate additional funds for their ambitious plans amidst the Depression, Van Kleeck, Fledderus, and a few associates continued their work, coming together in IRI conferences every year until war in Europe effectively brought their enterprise to an end.[42]

While the Amsterdam Congress marked the height of the IRI's career, it marked only the beginning of the final stage of Mary Van Kleeck's efforts to merge social work and scientific management for the planned raising of living standards. During the Great Depression, she advocated a greater role for both in the construction of social economic planning. "The Amsterdam Congress convinced me," she said in a speech early in 1932, "that the place to begin planning is to study the production and distribution of raw materials" as the first step toward a "better social plan for economic life." To this end, she turned the Department of Industrial Studies and the IRI to new studies of natural resource industries, technological change, and living standards, and urged the creation of a National Economic Council to promote such planning.[43]

Increasingly, too, she pointed to the Soviet Union as a source for comparative study in these matters. "If we can be objective and scientific in our attitude, what an opportunity this is for our generation to observe two systems — capitalist and communist — and to compare their results." And by 1933, she had little doubt where such comparison would lead.[44]

> It is impossible to discuss a planned economy without calling attention to the actual example of it in the Soviet Union. There all of the branches of economic life are planned as an integrated whole. It would be worthwhile for us to study its actual technique . . . as examples of the way in which the whole range of managerial problems is studied in their interrelationships. I am frank to say that I believe that the planned economy of the Soviet Union brings us face to face with the real issue . . . [of] whether capitalism as we know it now . . . must claim our permanent allegiance, or whether we are ready with entirely open minds to consider the fundamental questions of economic organization which the present crisis of unemployment presents us.[45]

Van Kleeck, like other curious engineers and observers, had visited the Soviet Union in 1932, studying its efforts toward social economic planning under the Five Year Plans. And upon her return she presented her findings to the Taylor Society.

> The universality of the principles of scientific management emerges as one observes their applicability in the new economic system of the Soviet Union. The outstanding difference is that in the United States limits are set to the application of knowledge because the area of control through ownership is not comprehensive enough to plan and control the relationship of factors which are essentially interrelated. . . . [T]he Soviet

Union has given to scientific management in that country a scope which is new in the history of modern industry. It will take time to perfect its application. . . . But meanwhile . . . this large-scale integration of industries reaches far beyond the widest stretch of the management engineer in America. Here scientific management is tied to a hitchingpost, when it should be free to follow as far as electricity can carry it.[46]

To untie scientific management so that it could assume its rightful social role, Van Kleeck advocated public trusteeship over corporate use of national resources. For a time during the mid 1930s she attained national prominence promoting this vision, especially among social workers, leading them and other professionals as national chairman of the Inter-Professional Association for Social Insurance, an organization designed to forge cross-class alliances between workers and professionals. But it would be her growing identification with the Soviet Union that most marked these latter years of her career.[47]

An advocate of closer U.S.–Soviet trade and diplomatic recognition, she soon became a staunch advocate of the Soviet state, linking the prospects for social economic planning to the fate of the Soviet Union. She defended its persecution of Trotsky, its purge trials, its invasion of Finland, and its short-lived pact with Hitler. She became, in other words, a fellow traveler, apparently never joining the Communist Party, but lending the Soviet Union and American Communists her energies and the support of her intellectual authority. Having dedicated her life to the scientific construction of social welfare, she was tired of capitalism's continuing imbalances. And like many reformers of her generation, she looked upon the Soviet Union as the single, courageous alternative, trying to build the planned society but beset on all sides by enemies, thus requiring her help and defense. For these reasons, she joined or worked with various pro-Soviet organizations during the 1930s and 1940s, leading to her surveillance by the FBI, and to an appearance before Senator Joseph McCarthy's Permanent Subcommittee on Investigations in 1953, at the age of sixty-nine.[48]

Mary Van Kleeck's Taylorism reveals much, but at the same time poses questions beyond the immediate scope of this essay.

Her career emphasizes the point that Taylorism, whatever else it may have been, was a utopian project, one that sought through technocratic direction to produce a rational industrial order and a liberating abundance. Its attractions to reformers thus are not hard to understand. But until now there has been little interest in the question of women reformers' relation to Taylorism. Nor has there been sufficient recognition that one such woman played an unusually large role in the story of scientific management after Taylor.

There has been little recognition, in other words, of Mary Van Kleeck's efforts to merge Taylorism and social work following World War I, to bring to scientific management the social feminist concern for living standards while bringing to the professionalization of social work Taylorism's scientism. But why did so few women join her in this quest? Why was Mary Van Kleeck, virtually alone among the women's reform network of her day, so powerfully attracted to Taylorism and its utopianism? What part did the Russell Sage Foundation play in encouraging or enabling her to set out on this independent path? And on what terms, at what cost, did she leave the worlds of woman-led reform to enter the male-dominated worlds of Taylorism and planning?

Van Kleeck would play a large part in Taylorism's contribution to the interwar debate over national and international planning. Here, especially, few pursued scientific management's utopian implications as far as she did and at such cost. Together with Morris Cooke, Harlow Person, and Henry Dennison, Van Kleeck in the 1920s helped to make the Taylor Society an imaginative forum for the discussion of scientific management's relation to problems of macroeconomic coordination. But why did few if any Taylorites in the 1930s follow Van Kleeck into an uncritical admiration of Stalinist central planning? How, in the absence of personal papers and autobiographical statements, can we account for her increasingly inflexible fellow traveling?

Blinded as well as guided by faith and conviction, Van Kleeck seemed unable to grasp the political implications of her Taylorism. Generous and sincerely committed to advancing human welfare, she nonetheless promoted the antidemocratic tendencies of technocratic direction and centralized control, never appreciating the paradox at the heart of her ambitions. Simultaneously unusual and representative, finally, Mary Van Kleeck still informs us about the fate of scientific management and the history of a generation and its hard-edged confrontation with capitalism, expertise, and utopian hope.

NOTES

1. On Taylorism's origins, see Frederick W. Taylor, *Scientific Management* (New York, 1947); Milton J. Nadworny, *Scientific Management and the Unions, 1900–1932* (Cambridge, MA, 1955); Daniel Nelson, *Managers and Workers: Origins of the New Factory System in the United States, 1880–1920* (Madison, WI, 1975); Nelson, *Frederick W. Taylor and the Rise of Scientific Management* (Madison, 1980). On Taylorism's diffusion, see Daniel Wren, *The Evolution of Management Thought* (New York, 1972); Samuel Haber, *Efficiency and Uplift: Scientific Management in the Progressive Era, 1890–1920* (Chicago, 1964); Judith A. Merkle, *Management and Ideology: The Legacy of the International Scientific Management Movement* (Berkeley, 1980); Raymond E. Callahan, *Education and the Cult of Efficiency* (Chicago, 1962); Hindy Lauer Schachter, *Frederick Taylor and the Public Administration Community: A Reevaluation* (Albany, 1989); Loren Baritz, *Servants of Power* (Middletown, 1960); Sanford M. Jacoby, *Employing Bureaucracy: Managers, Unions, and the Transformation of Work in American Industry, 1900–1945* (New York, 1985). Scientific management's politics or ideological content is treated variously in Reinhard Bendix, *Work and Authority in Industry: Ideologies of Management in the Course of Industrialization* (New York, 1956); Harry Braverman, *Labor and Monopoly Capitalism: The Degradation of Work in the Twentieth Century* (New York, 1974); Les Levidow and Bob Young, eds., *Science, Technology, and the Labour Process: Marxist Studies*, 2 vols., (London, 1981, 1985); David F. Noble, *America By Design: Science, Technology, and the Rise of Corporate Capitalism* (New York, 1977); Stephen Wood, ed., *The Degradation of Work? Skill, Deskilling and the Labour Process* (London, 1982); Paul Thompson, *The Nature of Work: An Introduction to Debates on the Labour Process* (London, 1983); Magali Sarfatti Larson, *The Rise of Professionalism* (Berkeley, 1977); Peter F. Meiksins, "Scientific Management and Class Relations," *Theory and Society* 13 (1984), pp. 177–209; Kerreen M. Reiger, *The Disenchantment of the Home: Modernizing the Australian Family, 1880–1940* (Melbourne, 1985); "All but the Kitchen Sink," *Theory and Society* 16 (1987), pp. 497–526; Ruth Schwartz Cowan, *More Work For Mother: The Ironies of Household Technology From the Open Hearth to the Microwave* (New York, 1983); Susan M. Reverby, *Ordered to Care: The Dilemma of American Nursing, 1850–1945* (Cambridge, MA, 1987); Margery W. Davies, *Woman's Place Is at the Typewriter: Office Work and Office Workers, 1870–1930* (Philadelphia, 1982); Susan Porter Benson, *Counter Cultures: Saleswomen, Managers, and Customers in American Department Stores, 1890–1940* (Urbana, 1986).

2. Georges Friedmann, *Industrial Society* (Glencoe, 1955), chap. 1; Merkle, *Management and Ideology*, chap. 8; Charles S. Maier, "Between Taylorism and Technocracy: European Ideologies and the Vision of Industrial Productivity

in the 1920s," *Journal of Contemporary History* 5, no. 2 (April 1970), pp. 27–61. Maier also treats aspects of what he terms "the politics of productivity" in several essays in his *In Search of Stability: Explorations in Historical Political Economy* (Cambridge, England, 1987).

3. Howard P. Segal, *Technological Utopianism in American Culture* (Chicago, 1985); H. G. Wells, *The Open Conspiracy* (New York, 1928); Merkle, *Management and Ideology*, chap. 4; W. H. G. Armytage, *The Rise of the Technocrats: A Social History* (London, 1965), pp. 200; 219–26; Kendall E. Bailes, *Technology and Society Under Lenin and Stalin: Origins of the Soviet Technical Intelligentsia, 1917–1941* (Princeton, 1978), p. 50; Mark R. Beissinger, *Scientific Management, Socialist Discipline, and Soviet Power* (Cambridge, 1988), pp. 22–23; Ellis W. Hawley, "Herbert Hoover and Economic Stabilization, 1921–1922," in Hawley, ed., *Herbert Hoover as Secretary of Commerce* (Iowa City, 1981), pp. 43–77; Hawley, *The Great War and the Search for a Modern Order* (New York, 1979), pp. 226–29; Guy Alchon, *The Invisible Hand of Planning: Capitalism, Social Science, and the State in the 1920's* (Princeton, 1985).

4. The quoted phrase is from Nancy Cott, "What's in a Name? The Limits of 'Social Feminism'; or, Expanding the Vocabulary of Women's History," *Journal of American History* 76, no. 3 (December 1989), p. 823. Cott's is an analysis of the limited utility of "social feminism" as an explanatory category. Historians usually apply the term to the social reform activities of the first generations of college educated women, circa 1880–1940. It commonly refers to women's projection of prevailing notions of their "domestic responsibilities" onto a larger "public household" in which women, children, and workers require protection from exploitation. Like Van Kleeck, whose early career was devoted to these struggles, these reformers often sought especially to advance women's opportunities by recognizing and defending women's difference from men. Van Kleeck's feminism, then, seems to embody what Cott in another context terms "feminism's characteristic doubleness, its simultaneous affirmation of women's human rights and women's unique needs and differences." See Nancy Cott, *The Grounding of Modern Feminism* (New Haven, 1987), p. 49. On social feminism, see, for example, William O'Neill, *Everyone Was Brave: A History of Feminism in America* (New York, 1971); J. Stanley Lemons, *The Woman Citizen: Social Feminism in the 1920s* (Urbana, 1973); Estelle Freedman, "Separatism as Strategy: Female Institution-Building and American Feminism, 1870–1930," *Feminist Studies* 5, no. 3 (Fall 1979), pp. 512–29; Naomi Black, *Social Feminism* (Ithaca, 1989). Brief surveys of Van Kleeck's life include Eleanor M. Lewis, "Van Kleeck, Mary Abby," in Barbara Sicherman and Carol Hurd Green, eds., *Notable American Women* (Cambridge, 1980), pp. 707–9; Jan L. Hagen, "Van Kleeck, Mary Abby," in Walter Trattner, ed., *Biographical Dictionary of Social Welfare in America* (Westport, 1986), pp. 725–28.

5. On Cooke, see Wren, *The Evolution of Management Thought*, pp. 173–76; Kenneth E. Trombley, *The Life and Times of a Happy Liberal* (New York, 1954); Jean Christie, *Morris Llewellyn Cooke: Progressive Engineer* (New York, 1983); Schachter, *Taylor and the Public Administration Community*, chap. 6. On Person, see Wren, *The Evolution of Management Thought*, pp. 181–82; Person

"The Manager, The Workman, and the Social Scientist," *Bulletin of the Taylor Society* 3, no. 1 (February 1917), pp. 1–7. A listing of women officers of the Taylor Society appears in Person to J. H. Williams, Van Kleeck, et al., September 8, 1927, Box 17, Folder 344, Mary Van Kleeck Papers, Sophia Smith Collection, Smith College (hereafter cited as MVK Papers). For Gilbreth, see Edna Yost, *Frank and Lillian Gilbreth: Partners For Life* (New Brunswick, 1949); Guy Alchon, "Lillian Gilbreth and the Science of Management, 1900–1920," *Essays in Economic and Business History*, vol. 7 (1989), pp. 25–39; Lillian Gilbreth, *The Homemaker and Her Job* (New York, 1927). Tarbell is mentioned in Julie A. Matthaei, *An Economic History of Women in America* (New York, 1982), chap. 8; Susan Strasser, *Never Done: A History of American Housework* (New York, 1982), pp. 172–73; Ida Tarbell, "The Cost of Living and Household Management," *Annals of the American Academy of Political and Social Science* (hereafter cited as *Annals*) 48 (1913), pp. 127–30; Tarbell, *The Business of Being a Woman* (New York, 1912).

6. No full study of Van Kleeck's life or career exists. Aspects of her work are treated in Clarke Chambers, *Seedtime for Reform: American Social Service and Social Action, 1918–1933* (Minneapolis, 1963); Chambers, *Paul U. Kellogg and The Survey: Voices for Social Welfare and Social Justice* (Minneapolis, 1971); Maurine Weiner Greenwald, *Women, War, and Work: The Impact of World War I on Women Workers in the United States* (Westport, 1980); Cletus Daniel, *The ACLU and the Wagner Act: An Inquiry Into the Depression-Era Crisis of American Liberalism* (Ithaca, 1980); Jacob Fisher, *The Response of Social Work to the Great Depression* (Boston, 1980); Harvey Klehr, *The Heyday of American Communism: The Depression Decade* (New York, 1984); Alchon, *The Invisible Hand of Planning*; and two unpublished papers by Ruth Oldenziel, Department of History, Yale University: "Mary Van Kleeck, A Career of Idealism," (1983); "The International Institute for Industrial Relations, 1922–1946," (1987).

7. For the origins of Van Kleeck's social commitment, her college Memorabilia book and the *Annual Report, 1903–1904*, Smith College Association for Christian Work (hereafter cited as SCACW), both in the author's possession, are revealing, especially of Smith students' involvement in the YWCA's summer conferences. See, too, the *SCACW Minutes*, April 1902–April 1905, pp. 9, 13; and the *SCACW Reports*, 1902–1903, and 1903–1904, pp. 82–83, 104, College Archives, Smith College. For the industrial work of the YWCA, see *The YWCA and Industry* (New York, 1928), Box 16, Folder 4, National Board of the YWCA Records, Sophia Smith Collection, Smith College (hereafter cited as YWCA Records); Mary Frederickson, "Citizens for Democracy: The Industrial Programs of the YWCA," in Mary Frederickson and Joyce L. Kornbluh, eds., *Sisterhood and Solidarity: Workers' Education for Women, 1914–1984* (Philadelphia, 1984), pp. 75–106. On the women's networks to arise from the social settlements and urban reform, see Kathryn Kish Sklar, "Hull House in the 1890s: A Community of Women Reformers," *Signs* 10, no. 4 (Summer 1985), pp. 658–77; Nancy Schrom Dye, *As Equals and As Sisters: Feminism, the Labor Movement, and the Women's Trade Union League of New York* (Columbia, 1980); Susan Ware, *Beyond Suffrage: Women in the New Deal* (Cambridge, 1981). On New York City,

unemployment, and social investigations early in the century, see Roy Lubove, *The Progressives and the Slums: Tenement House Reform in New York City, 1890–1917* (Pittsburgh, 1962); Peter Seixas, "Unemployment as a 'Problem of Industry' in Early-Twentieth Century New York," *Social Research* 54, no. 2 (Summer 1987), pp. 403–30. Van Kleeck, "Memorandum No. 1," November 2, 1956, and "Memorandum No. 2," November 14, 1956, both addressed to the Smith College Library, in Box 1, Folder 18, MVK Papers. Van Kleeck, "Working Hours of Women in Factories," *Charities and the Commons* (October 16, 1906), pp. 13–21; "Child Labor in New York City Tenements," *Charities and the Commons* (January 18, 1908), pp. 1405–20.

8. "Russell Sage Foundation: Confidential Bulletin No. 1," 1907, Box 18, Folder 19, Mary Van Kleeck Papers, Reuther Library, Wayne State University (hereafter cited as MVK/R Papers); John M. Glenn, Lilian M. Brandt, and F. Emerson Andrews, *Russell Sage Foundation, 1907–1946*, 2 vols., (New York, 1947); David Hammack, "Russell Sage Foundation," in Harold Keele and Joseph Kriger, eds., *Foundations* (Westport, 1984), pp. 373–80.

9. See, for example, Van Kleeck, "The Artificial Flower Trade in New York City," November 30, 1909, Box 13, Folder 3; Van Kleeck to John M. Glenn, Russell Sage Foundation, March 31, 1910, Box 13, Folder 4; Van Kleeck, "A Program for a Committee on Women's Work," April 25, 1910, Box 13, Folder 6, all in MVK/R. See, too, Van Kleeck, "Memorandum Regarding Investigations for the Winter of 1910–1911"; and the several letters from Van Kleeck to John Glenn, all in Box 15, Folder 132, Russell Sage Foundation Papers, Rockefeller Archive Center (hereafter cited as RSF Papers). Several of these studies were published under Van Kleeck's name: *Artificial Flower Makers* (New York, 1913); *Women in the Bookbinding Trade* (New York, 1913); *A Seasonal Industry* (New York, 1917). See also Louise Odencrantz, *Italian Women in Industry* (New York, 1919). The quotation is from Van Kleeck, "Industrial Investigations of the Russell Sage Foundation," September 17, 1915, p. 4, Box 13, Folder 28, MVK/R Papers.

10. On the idea that irregular business operations and employment could be stabilized, see Henry R. Seager, *Social Insurance: A Program of Social Reform* (New York, 1910); and Herman Feldman, *The Regularization of Employment* (New York, 1925). On the role of Van Kleeck's *Women in the Bookbinding Trade* in the prohibition of women's night work, see Glenn, et al., *Russell Sage Foundation*, pp. 154–56; brief prepared by Louis D. Brandeis and Josephine Goldmark on behalf of the People of the State of New York v. Charles Schweinler Press, Cases and Briefs, NY Court of Appeal, 214 N.Y. 395, 108 N.E. 643 (1915). The quotations are from Van Kleeck to Mary Beard, November 18, 1935, Box 1, Folder 3; Van Kleeck, "Memorandum Regarding Investigation of Industrial Conditions By Russell Sage Foundation," October 26, 1915, Box 100, Folder 1564, both in MVK Papers. On the creation of the Department of Industrial Studies, see Glenn et al., *Russell Sage Foundation*, p. 161.

11. Van Kleeck, "Industrial Investigations of the Russell Sage Foundation," p. 4; *Women in the Bookbinding Trade*, pp. 235–36; *Artificial Flower Makers*, p. 56; Alchon, *The Invisible Hand of Planning*, chap. 1.

12. Person, "The Manager, the Workman, and the Social Scientist"; Haber, *Efficiency and Uplift*, chap. 3; Nelson, *Frederick W. Taylor*, chap. 7; Noble, *America By Design*, chap. 10; Schachter, *Taylor and the Public Administration Community*, chap. 5.

13. "New York School of Philanthropy, Course 3a," October 1914–January 1915; Van Kleeck, "Memorandum Regarding Preparation of Students for Industrial Service," January 26, 1917, both in Box 90, Folder 1412, MVK Papers. On scientific management and the "human element," see, for example, Lillian Gilbreth's remarks in Harlow S. Person, ed., *Scientific Management: Addresses and Discussions at the Conference on Scientific Management* (Dartmouth, 1912), p. 356; Lillian Gilbreth, *The Psychology of Management* (New York, 1914); Richard A. Feiss, "Personal Relationship as a Basis of Scientific Management," *Bulletin of the Taylor Society* 1, no. 6, (November 1915), p. 5; Robert G. Valentine, "The Progressive Relation Between Efficiency and Consent," *Bulletin of the Taylor Society* 2, no. 1 (January 1916), pp. 7–11; Louise Odencrantz, "Personnel Work In Factories," May 18, 1923, Box 25, Folder 4, YWCA Records; Jacoby, *Employing Bureaucracy*, pp. 102–5.

14. "New York School of Philanthropy — Memorandum Regarding Report on Curriculum," November 27, 1916, Box 90, Folder 1412, MVK Papers; Van Kleeck and Graham Romeyn Taylor, "The Professional Organization of Social Work," *Annals* 101 (May 1922), pp. 163–64; Van Kleeck to John M. Glenn, February 5, 1921, Box 19, Folder 7, MVK/R Papers. On social work and professionalization, see Walter I. Trattner, *From Poor Law to Welfare State: A History of Social Welfare in America*, 3d ed., (New York, 1984), chap. 11.

15. See, for example, Van Kleeck to Morris Cooke and reply, July 23, 24, 1917, Box 11, Folder 182; Van Kleeck, "Storage Bulletin No. 9," October 24, November 24, 1917, Box 72, Folder 1125, both in MVK Papers; Van Kleeck, "Memorandum Regarding the Work Done During the War," Box 1, Entry 1, Folder: Labor Department (Secretary of Labor), RG 86, Papers of the U.S. Women's Bureau, National Archives; Van Kleeck, "Women in the Munitions Industry," *Life and Labor* 8 (June 1918), pp. 113–22; A. L. Alford, "An Industrial Achievement of the War," *Industrial Management* 55 (February 1918), pp. 97–100; Charles W. Wood, *The Great Change* (New York, 1918), chap. 3; Mary Winslow, *Woman at Work: The Autobiography of Mary Anderson as Told to Mary Winslow* (Minneapolis, 1951), chaps. 9–12; Greenwald, *Women, War, and Work*, chap. 2; Alchon, *The Invisible Hand of Planning*, chap. 2; Jacoby, *Employing Bureaucracy*, chap. 5; Noble, *America By Design*, pp. 298–99; Glenn et al., *Russell Sage Foundation*, pp. 256–58. The quotations are from Van Kleeck, "Women and Machines," *Atlantic Monthly* 127 (February 1921), pp. 250–52; Van Kleeck, "Industrial Studies of the Russell Sage Foundation," September 16, 1943, p. 53, Box 99, Folder 1549, MVK Papers.

16. Van Kleeck, "Women and Machines," pp. 255–56.

17. On Van Kleeck and the Women's Bureau, see Winslow, *Woman at Work*; reports and correspondence in Box 71, MVK Papers, and Box 1 of the Mary Anderson Papers, Schlesinger Library, Radcliffe College. For Van Kleeck's positions in the Taylor Society, see *Bulletin of the Taylor Society* 5, no. 1 (February 1920), p. 9; H. S. Person to J. H. Williams, Mary Van Kleeck, et al., September 8, 1927.

18. Van Kleeck and Taylor, "The Professional Organization of Social Work," p. 164; Edwin T. Layton, Jr., *The Revolt of the Engineers* (Cleveland, 1971); Jacoby, *Employing Bureaucracy*, pp. 126–32.

19. Van Kleeck to Cooke, June 9 and 11, 1921, Box 16, Morris L. Cooke Papers, Franklin D. Roosevelt Library (hereafter cited as Cooke Papers); Van Kleeck, "Notes for Speech on Industrial Basis of Social Work," March 14, 1922, Box 24, Folder 487; "Minutes, Committee of Industrial Social Work," December 22, 1921, January 13, 1922, Box 99, Folder 1450, both in MVK Papers.

20. Van Kleeck to Person, July 4, 1922, Box 117, Folder 344; "Remarks of Mary Van Kleeck at Annual Business Meeting of the Taylor Society, December 4, 1924," Box 24, Folder 488, both in MVK Papers.

21. "Remarks of Mary Van Kleeck," December 4, 1924.

22. Van Kleeck would not be among the women's network surveyed in Susan Ware's *Beyond Suffrage*. For an example of the contacts Van Kleeck would maintain, see her congratulatory letter to Frances Perkins upon the latter's appointment as Secretary of Labor, Van Kleeck to Perkins, March 7, 1933, Box 17, Folder 343, MVK Papers. On changes within the Sage Foundation, see Glenn et al., *Russell Sage Foundation*, chap. 27; and Van Kleeck, "Industrial Studies of the Russell Sage Foundation," pp. 56–73. On Van Kleeck's postwar plans for her department, see "Memorandum," to John M. Glenn, unsigned, October 25, 1919, Box 23, Folder 456, MVK Papers.

23. Hawley, *The Great War and the Search for a Modern Order*; "Herbert Hoover, the Commerce Secretariat, the Vision of an 'Associate State,' 1921–1928," *Journal of American History* 51, no. 1 (June 1974), pp. 116–40; Alchon, *The Invisible Hand of Planning*.

24. Committee on the Elimination of Waste in Industry of the FAES, *Waste in Industry* (New York, 1921); Layton, *Revolt of the Engineers*, pp. 201–5; Van Kleeck, "Memorandum," June 4, 1921, Cooke Papers; Van Kleeck to Shelby Harrison, September 10, 1921, Box 2, Folder 24, MVK/R Papers.

25. Hawley, "Herbert Hoover and Economic Stabilization"; Carolyn Grin, "The Unemployment Conference of 1921," *Mid-America* 54 (April 1973), pp. 83–107.

26. Evan Metcalf, "Secretary Hoover and the Emergence of Macroeconomic Management," *Business History Review* 49 (Spring 1975), pp. 60–80; Alchon, *The Invisible Hand of Planning*.

27. Van Kleeck to Mary Beard, November 18, 1935; Committee on Business Cycles and Unemployment of the President's Conference on Unemployment, *Business Cycles and Unemployment* (New York, 1923); Willard E. Hotchkiss, "Business Cycles and Unemployment," *Bulletin of the Taylor Society* 9 (April 1924), pp. 86–89; Alchon, *The Invisible Hand of Planning*, chaps. 5–8.

28. Van Kleeck, press release, June 9–10, 1926, Box 2, Folder 5, MVK/R Papers; Van Kleeck, "Barometers of Unemployment," March 1, 1927, Box 26, Folder 508, MVK Papers; Van Kleeck, "What Will You Do Next?" *American Federationist* 34, no. 9 (September 1927), pp. 1090–94; Van Kleeck, "Unemployment in Passaic," *American Federationist* 35, no. 5 (May 1928), pp. 597–602; Alchon, *The Invisible Hand of Planning*, chap. 8.

29. Van Kleeck, "What Will You Do Next?" pp. 1092, 1094; Van Kleeck, "Tentative Draft of Letter of Invitation to Taylor Society Dinner," March 11, 1927, p. 3, in Van Kleeck to Morris Cooke, March 11, 1927, Cooke Papers; Alchon, *The Invisible Hand of Planning*, chap. 8.

30. Hamilton is quoted in Perriton Maxwell to Van Kleeck, January 5, 1933, Box 1, Folder 3, MVK Papers; Lillian Gilbreth to L. W. Wallace, February 3, 1926, Container 124, File 0816-160, Frank and Lillian Gilbreth Papers, Purdue University (hereafter cited as Gilbreth Papers); "Mary Van Kleeck Scores NRA Policy," *New York Times*, August 7, 1933, p. 5, col. 7; "NRA Is Criticized as Failing Labor," *New York Times*, May 26, 1934, p. 14, col. 1; Van Kleeck to Cooke, August 13, 1933, Cooke Papers.

31. Jacoby, *Employing Bureaucracy*, chaps. 2, 5; and Mary Drake McFeely, *Lady Inspectors* (New York, 1988), offer some background to this story.

32. There is little surviving record of the conference, save for a few pieces in the Odencrantz Papers, including a copy of the program, the papers she presented ("Personnel Work in America"), and a report of her impressions. See especially Folder 1, Louise Odencrantz Papers, Schlesinger Library (hereafter cited as Odencrantz Papers).

33. "Report of the Interim Committee Appointed at the First International Conference on Industrial Welfare," Folder 8, Odencrantz Papers; and "Officers and Members of Council," in *Report of the Proceedings of the International Industrial Welfare (Personnel) Congress* (Zurich, 1925), p. 486. Organized initially as an Association, the IRI would reorganize and rename itself the International Industrial Relations Institute in March, 1932, but even from its earliest days was known by the letters *IRI*.

34. The quotation is from the "Introduction to the Report of the Proceedings of the International Industrial Welfare (Personnel) Congress, Flushing, 1925," Folder 8, Odencrantz Papers. It is attributed to Fledderus by Van Kleeck, "Comments on Work of Mary L. Fledderus," February 17, 1945, Box 1, Folder 19, MVK Papers.

35. See "Ten Years IRI," a short history of the organization written, apparently, by Fledderus and Van Kleeck, in 1935, and found in Box 15, Folder 142, of the Paul U. Kellogg Papers, Social Welfare History Archives, University of Minnesota; "IRI Summer School: Preliminary Suggestions," Container 131, File 0830-9, Gilbreth Papers; Mary Fledderus, ed., *Report of Summer School: The Elimination of Unnecessary Fatigue in Industry*, Raveno, Italy, June 1927 (The Hague, 1930); "List of Persons Present," IRI Cambridge Congress, Box 84, Folder 1318, MVK Papers.

36. Van Kleeck, "Summary of the Conference," Box 84, Folder 1319, MVK Papers.

37. The quoted phrase appears in Van Kleeck's remarks in the "Report of the IRI Summer Meeting, Schloss-Elmau, June–July, 1929," p. 7, Box 83, Folder 1311; on the IRI's methodology, see Van Kleeck, "Comments on Work of Mary L. Fledderus: Addendum," February 17, 1945, Box 1, Folder 19, both in MVK Papers. See, too, the "Informal Notes of a meeting," October 27, 1928, Folder 8, Odencrantz Papers. The IRI, from its inception, was able to function as a truly international organization due to the linguistic abilities of

Mary Fledderus, who was capable of simultaneous translations in Dutch, French, English, and German. These skills carried over into the IRI's major publications during the 1920s and 1930s, with English, French, and German versions appearing within each single volume.

38. The IRI material in the two main Van Kleeck collections, and the IRI papers at the International Institute for Social History in Amsterdam, are revealing of most of these points.

39. Van Kleeck to Cooke, October 6, 1930, Cooke Papers; Van Kleeck, "Memorandum," April 17, 1930, Box 23, Folder 467, MVK Papers; "Call For the Congress," February, 1931, IRI Papers, 1925–1939, Folder: IRI Social-Economic Congress, Amsterdam, 1931, International Institute for Social History, Amsterdam (hereafter cited as IRI Papers/1).

40. Van Kleeck, "Social Economic Planning," February 20, 1932, Box 4, Folder 2, MVK/R Papers; "Ten Years IRI," p. 3; "Statement at Final Session By Mary Van Kleeck," August 23–28, 1931, IRI Papers/1.

41. Van Kleeck, "Analysis and Review of the Congress," p. 3; V. V. Obolensky-Ossinsky, "The Nature and Forms of Social Economic Planning," reprinted in Fledderus, ed., *World Social Economic Planning* (The Hague and New York, 1932), pp. 291–340. Press coverage included such articles as "Geneva and Soviet in Clash at Parley: Russians at Amsterdam Congress Assail Labor Organization Delegate as Pro-Capitalist," *New York Times*, August 29, 1931, p. 4, col. 4; and a live radio address by Van Kleeck, broadcast from Amsterdam to the United States. See "Radio Address of M. Van Kleeck, Delivered August 26, 1931," in MS 1091, Folder 3.1/63, Otto and Marie Neurath Isotype Collection, Department of Typography and Graphic Design, University of Reading. See also George Soule's review of the congress and its published proceedings, "A World Symposium," *The Saturday Review of Literature* 9, no. 16 (November 5, 1932), pp. 228–29.

42. On the IRI's immediate plans following the Amsterdam Congress, see "Minutes of the Meeting of the Interim Committee," Paris, September 20, 1931, File 353, Folder: International Industrial Relations Institute, 1931–1952, F. M. Wibaut Papers, International Institute for Social History, Amsterdam; Van Kleeck, "Report on Present Outlook," January 19, 1932, Box 9, Folder 7, MVK/R Papers. The quotation is from Van Kleeck, "Social Economic Planning," p. 15.

43. Van Kleeck, "Social Economic Planning," p. 15; "Social Planning and Social Work," draft article, January 12, 1932, Box 26, Folder 512, MVK Papers; "Statement of Miss Mary Van Kleeck," *Establishment of a National Economic Council: Hearings Before a Subcommittee of the Committee on Manufactures, United States Senate*, 72d Cong., 1st Sess., part 2, December 1, 2, 3, 4, 11, and 19, 1931, (Washington, GPO, 1931), pp. 491–524. On the Department of Industrial Studies' and IRI's work during the 1930s, see Glenn et al., *Russell Sage Foundation*, chap. 37; Van Kleeck, *Miners and Management* (New York, 1934); "Planning for the Coal Industry," *Bulletin of the Taylor Society* (November 1934), pp. 4–13; Van Kleeck and Fledderus, *On Economic Planning* (New York, 1935); "Memorandum on Optimum Productivity in the Workshop as an Area for Social and Technical Research," March 21, 1938,

Cooke Papers; Fledderus and Van Kleeck, *Technology and Livelihood: An Inquiry into the Changing Technological Basis for Production as Affecting Employment and Living Standards* (New York, 1944); Fledderus and Van Kleeck, *The Technological Basis for National Development* (New York, 1948).

44. Van Kleeck, "Social Economic Planning," p. 14.

45. Van Kleeck, "A Planned Economy As a National Objective for Social Work," *The Compass* (May 1933), p. 23.

46. Van Kleeck, "Observations on Management in the Soviet Union," presented before a meeting of the Taylor Society, New York, December 8, 1932, Box 4, Folder 3, MVK/R Papers. See also Van Kleeck, "Notes on Six Weeks in the Soviet Union, July 25 to September 4, 1932," Box 29, Folder 541, MVK Papers.

47. Van Kleeck, "Social Economic Planning," p. 20; Van Kleeck, *Creative America: Its Resources for Social Security* (New York, 1936). On the IPA, see Fisher, *The Response of Social Work to the Great Depression*; the relevant material in Box 80, Folders 1267 and 1268, MVK Papers; Box 11-12, MVK/R Papers.

48. Van Kleeck's relations with the Soviet Union during the 1930s are extensively documented in correspondence, speeches, and articles in both major collections of her papers. See, for example, Van Kleeck to Senator Robert F. Wagner, December 24, 1931, Box 188, Folder 125, Robert F. Wagner Papers, Georgetown University Library; Van Kleeck, "Scientific Management in the Second Five Year Plan," *Soviet Russia Today* (June 1933), p. 4; "Soviet Planning," *Soviet Russia Today* (November 1937), p. 17. Some of her activities on behalf of the Soviet Union are further documented in Eugene Lyons, *The Red Decade* (New York, 1941); Harvey Klehr, *The Heyday of American Communism: The Depression Decade* (New York, 1984). On the nature and history of fellow traveling, see David Caute, *The Fellow Travelers: Intellectual Friends of Communism*, rev. ed. (New Haven, 1988); Paul Hollander, *Political Pilgrims: Travels of Western Intellectuals to the Soviet Union, China, and Cuba, 1928–1978* (New York, 1981). Some of Van Kleeck's State Department and FBI files have been released to the author and to the Sophia Smith Collection, Smith College. Leonard Boudin represented Van Kleeck before an executive session of McCarthy's Permanent Subcommittee on Investigations in 1953, "where she astounded McCarthy and Roy Cohn with the statement that she had never been a member of the Communist Party." Boudin to author, February 27, 1989.

KATHY BURGESS

6 Organized Production and Unorganized Labor: Management Strategy and Labor Activism at the Link-Belt Company, 1900–1940

The Link-Belt Company occupies an important place in the history of scientific management. After 1907, as one of Frederick W. Taylor's famous showcase firms, it epitomized the "mental revolution" in cooperative and efficient production. The company's top executives, James Mapes Dodge and Charles Piez, ranked among Taylor's most ardent supporters, and Link-Belt employees often expressed their satisfaction with Taylor's system. However, there was another side to the Link-Belt experience. An examination of the firm's industrial relations from 1900 to 1940 underscores the limited impact of scientific management in an important area of industrial management: contrary to their statements, Link-Belt executives never relied on scientific management to promote industrial peace. The company's labor management strategy had combined trade association and corporate welfare activities with Taylorism from the beginning, and after World War I, scientific management became even less important in defining the relations between employer and employees.

Similarly, a reluctance to join in organized labor's attack on scientific management did not signify that Link-Belt workers were indifferent to trade union promises of higher wages and better working conditions. On three occasions labor activists threatened to organize the company's Chicago plant. With each

The author thanks Daniel Nelson, Walter Licht, and James A. Sauls for their valuable comments on the manuscript, and PT Components, Inc. for providing access to the Link-Belt records.

challenge, Link-Belt executives used every available means to oppose unionization and collective bargaining. Far from a celebration of Taylor's methods and the "mental revolution," the Link-Belt experience exposes the limits of scientific management in satisfying workers' aspirations.

The Link-Belt Company grew out of a small Chicago enterprise that began manufacturing a new detachable-link chain for agricultural equipment in 1875. Link-Belt chain quickly transcended its original use in farm equipment and became an important component in elevating and conveying machinery. Over the next five decades, the company expanded its facilities and diversified its product line, initially to meet customer demand and later to maintain its position in a competitive market. By 1930, Link-Belt was a well-established engineering firm specializing in materials handling equipment, with corporate headquarters in Chicago and primary manufacturing facilities in Chicago, Philadelphia, and Indianapolis. Although some work at the three manufacturing sites overlapped, each plant specialized in particular activities, serving complementary purposes in the company's overall manufacturing business. The Indianapolis plant made a wide variety of chain products sold to basic industries and used in Chicago and Philadelphia as components of other Link-Belt goods. The Chicago facilities did contract engineering and produced cranes, steam shovels, electric hoists, and other heavy earth moving equipment. Link-Belt's Philadelphia shops specialized in designing and installing the customized transmission and conveying systems that fueled the growing mass-production industries.[1]

At first, Link-Belt's expansion and diversification had little effect on the company's social structure or management practices. Before 1906, several levels of authority existed in the Chicago shops. Each department foreman set wages and controlled hiring, firing, and shop discipline in his own area. The foremen coordinated the efforts of a highly skilled, technically knowledgeable, and versatile work force, but the workers themselves determined production methods. Company executives and engineers, including Charles Piez, Link-Belt president and head of the Chicago operation, maintained offices right in the shops, where they did estimating, engineering, designing, drafting, and experimental work in conjunction with foremen and craftsmen. Everyone from the greenest hand to the company president intermingled on the shop floor.[2]

While foremen and individual workers ironed out most labor grievances at the point of conflict, sometimes workers resorted to other means. Occasionally, they appealed to the plant superintendent or higher company officials to resolve disputes. In other cases, they looked to unions for support. Link–Belt carpenters, millwrights, machinists, and molders successfully organized the Chicago plant at the turn of the century. As part of a citywide drive to gain union recognition, the nine-hour day, and better working conditions, machinists and molders waged at least four strikes at Link–Belt between 1900 and 1906. In conjunction with other Chicago metal trades employers, Link–Belt signed agreements with the International Association of Machinists (IAM) between 1900 and 1903, and during these years the union's business agent and shop stewards had considerable voice in settling grievances, setting wage rates, and defining production norms.[3]

Responsibilities for meeting production schedules fell on foremen's shoulders. In fulfilling these duties, they exerted far less control than in dictating the terms of employment. In addition to a work pace determined by the craftsmen's notion of a fair day's work, foremen had to cope with periodic shortages of material, machinery breakdowns, production bottlenecks that disrupted work flow between departments, and the continual need to set aside partially completed work to produce rush orders. Often the obstacles delayed shipments until well after the delivery dates promised to customers.[4]

The nature of Link–Belt products limited the use of rigid production techniques and schedule. Except for the company's wide variety of standard chain products, business was done by special order. Marketing heavy machinery and conveying systems designed to meet the specific needs of each client called for customized chain, special devices, and new forms of conveyors. Producing an order for a production-line conveyor system used to refine Cuban sugar might be followed by another for a coal storage system capable of handling two hundred tons per hour and involving feeders, crushers, bucket carriers, storage bins, a cable car system, and a locomotive crane.[5] The shops required a wide variety of skills and enough flexibility to accommodate such dramatic switches in production.

The foundation for scientific management at Link-Belt was laid in Philadelphia. To eliminate some bottlenecks and systematize the shops, James Mapes Dodge, who headed Philadelphia's operation, hired Louis Wright, a former apprentice under Frederick W. Taylor, as plant superintendent in 1889. Dodge credited Wright with giving Link-Belt its "first jolt in [the] direction" of scientific management, stating that "as soon as he became our superintendent he put in all the new wrinkles he brought with him from the Midvale Steel Co." Wright's efforts included the introduction of a bulletin board, shop notices spelling out job instructions and rules, and new routing procedures, involving "circulating bills-of-material" that documented worker accountability for specific tasks.[6]

Louis Wright left Link-Belt after two years, but systematization continued throughout the decade. Company executives departmentalized production and implemented new accounting methods, work rules, and bureaucratic labor control mechanisms, including a "Time Recorder." Between 1890 and 1903, the supervisory staff doubled and the nonproduction managerial staff nearly tripled. Higher management chipped away at the foremen's empire by delegating some supervisory tasks to "assistant foremen," and by restricting the foremen's ability to hire, fire, and set wages at will.[7] By the turn of the century, Link-Belt management had paved the way for a smooth transition to scientific management.

Link-Belt was among the first companies to install Taylor's system. Taylor's most orthodox student, Carl Barth, oversaw the installations. Barth's work coincided with retooling the plants to utilize high-speed steel cutting tools, converting from partial to full electrification, and installing individual motor drives on all machinery. In 1904, Barth began his preliminary work in Philadelphia by standardizing and upgrading machinery, tools, and other equipment, redesigning the shop floor layout, and experimenting to determine the proper speeds and feeds for machining different types of metal with high-speed steel. Gradually, skilled workers were promoted and trained as functional foremen. Some former foremen and skilled workers joined draftsmen and engineers in setting up the planning room and designing instruction cards and other recordkeeping forms.[8]

More than a year passed before Dwight Merrick, a former Link-Belt draftsman promoted to assist Barth, began time studies. Merrick proceeded cautiously after Philadelphia's machine shop workers objected to the stopwatch. Barth and Link-Belt Superintendent Willis Adams took two of the younger machinists aside to explain how they could earn 35 percent over their day rate by "working under instructions and direct supervision." The young machinists agreed to try it and their wages immediately averaged 40 percent more than those of veteran coworkers. The two machinists worked under functional foremen, but their work involved no time study, no slide rule calculations, no detailed instruction cards, or any discernable new work methods. Other Link-Belt machinists stood on the sidelines for some time, comparing their relatively thinner pay envelopes to those of the two young men. Eventually, a worker with fifteen years' seniority succumbed, deciding he wanted a chance to earn the higher wage. Thereafter, others approached Adams asking "to be put on that kind of work." As resistance eroded, Barth and Adams introduced new elements of the system "little by little," including "time study and task work with bonus, for which, later on, Mr. Taylor's differential rate was substituted."[9]

To maintain the employees' confidence throughout this process, Link-Belt managers assured workers that once time studies were taken and fair piece rates established, there would be no tampering with the rates. It was management's duty to eliminate disruptions and provide workers with the best equipment and materials. No matter how much money a worker might make, rate changes were not allowed unless new machinery or technology rendered old production methods obsolete. In Dodge's words: "We would not dare to cut the rate. Scientific management would evaporate like snow in sunshine if we did not keep our word with our men."[10]

With reorganization and time study work well under way in Philadelphia, Barth departed for Chicago to introduce the system in June 1906. Conditions there differed substantially from those in Philadelphia. First, there is no evidence that Louis Wright's work was duplicated in Chicago. Second, while Philadelphia's labor relations were generally friendly, in Chicago they were strained. Barth entered the Chicago shops in the aftermath of a six-year unionization drive involving citywide labor unrest and considerable violence at the Link-Belt plant. For example, during the IAM strike of 1900, fights between strikers and nonunion employees led to some serious injuries. "[M]en were knocked out in the shop, windows . . . and machinery were broken, . . . and mobs [went] through the Chicago shops three times" during subsequent machinists and molders strikes. Furthermore, the molders' shop steward ordered what Charles Piez considered "a steady and insidious reduction in output," cutting production on some operations by 30 percent. A management study estimated that Link-Belt's Chicago machine shop workers had reduced their output by 35 percent. Such challenges led to stormy labor relations at the firm. Consequently, following a citywide strike beginning in May 1904 and lasting into 1905, Link-Belt refused to renew its contract with the IAM. The company also rejected the molders' contract demands after a general strike in 1906. Thereafter, Link-Belt management vowed to operate as an open shop in Chicago.[11]

Chicago's branch of the National Metal Trades Association (NMTA), an organization spawned and nurtured by the strikes, aided Link-Belt in this endeavor. Initially, when member firms realized they could not keep unions out of their plants, the NMTA served as bargaining agent for all its members, bringing metal manufacturers and unions together under citywide contracts between 1900 and 1903. When contract negotiations broke down in 1904, the NMTA developed new tactics aimed at breaking the unions. Two weeks after the IAM called its members out on strike, NMTA recruiters began scouring midwestern and northeastern cities for replacement workers. In the midst of a depression, recruiters found "an unusual number of unemployed mechanics" who willingly travelled to Chicago.[12] The NMTA's national secretary opened a temporary office in Chicago to coordinate recruitment, interview incoming workers, match up their qualifications with the needs of member firms, and dispatch them under guard to their new employers.[13]

Link-Belt and other NMTA members intended to teach the strikers "that they cannot leave their positions and still have them." Recruiters had instructions to engage only permanent replacements, not temporary strikebreakers, and member firms pledged to protect the nonunion machinists throughout the strike and offer them preferential employment afterwards. Travel advances, deducted from the strikebreakers' wages in the first two weeks of employment, were refunded to those who "rendered faithful service" for sixty to ninety days. Apparently, many received their refunds. Five months after the strike broke out, the NMTA declared a "crushing defeat" of the IAM, reporting that 75 percent of the NMTA "certified mechanics" remained on the job along with about 20 percent of the strikers who defected from the union and returned to work. In a move to further cripple the IAM, the NMTA worked with the Chicago Employers' Association to prosecute sixty machinists on criminal charges.[14]

Heralding its new focus, the NMTA changed the name of its monthly publication from the *Bulletin* to *The Open Shop*. To further its objectives after defeating the machinists, the Association converted its emergency organization into a permanent labor bureau to screen prospective employees for member firms. Association members refused to hire workers without cards on file with the NMTA. Besides recording the employment histories, qualifications, and union activities of workers who consented to the process, clerks kept similar records on many unsuspecting Chicago metal workers through a network of secret informants in the plants. The NMTA's extensive card index served as a powerful blacklist in the following years, and Link-Belt's Charles Piez felt it was "perfectly proper" to use it for that purpose.[15]

James Dodge offered ambiguously worded denials when asked if Link-Belt had "discharge[d] the entire force in Chicago" before introducing scientific management. He denied that any "whole-sale exodus of men" had taken place, and he refused to connect individual dismissals with the success of scientific management. Undoubtedly, few, if any, IAM activists were reinstated. Link-Belt officials demanded undivided loyalty from their workers after the strike. Anyone expressing discontent or having union connections was fired on some other pretext. Describing the situation at Link-Belt a decade after the strike, Chicago's IAM business agent complained: "I do not believe you can find a union man with a fine-tooth comb."[16]

Reshaping Link-Belt's labor force did not completely satisfy the company's needs. Like other firms, it soon detected "wide-spread disloyalty" among foremen and superintendents. The NMTA's "special agents" reported that supervisors had shown "a strange antipathy toward the newcomers," by using everything from subtle discouragement to discharge without cause to rid their departments of strikebreakers. Most of the wayward supervisors held withdrawal cards from the union. Early in the 1904 strike, the

NMTA convinced its members that such attitudes compromised their efforts, and the employers began hosting dinner meetings with their production supervisors and NMTA officials to discuss "the question of a superintendent or foreman's true position" in the firm. In December, the Chicago Metal Trades Association Superintendents' and Foremen's Club was officially organized. Among those elected to office at this meeting were Link-Belt Assistant Superintendent L. I. Yeomans and Foreman J. D. Wiggins.[17] No doubt others participated as well.

Consequently, Barth arrived in Chicago to deal with a restructured Link-Belt production force consisting of longtime employees who sided with management during the strikes, newcomers who replaced striking machinists, and a supervisory staff purged of incorrigible union sympathizers and instilled with a new sense of responsibility toward the company. The economic downturn beginning in October 1907 further reinforced the new order. In November, Link-Belt laid off its entire night shift and many workers on the day shift; the remaining employees worked short hours. The depressed market extended well into 1909. Under such circumstances, Barth met little resistance. While he had required over four years to develop and install scientific management in Philadelphia, he took only eighteen months to transplant it to Chicago. By relying on prior experience and data from Philadelphia, Barth and his assistants dispensed with much time-consuming experimentation and preliminary work.[18] Barth quickly installed what he considered to be an operational system, and then he left it to the superintendent and newly trained functional foremen to keep things running.

After the installations, Link-Belt became a prominent stop on the tours Frederick W. Taylor arranged for potential clients who wished to see a working model of scientific management. Dodge and Piez welcomed both admirers and critics to tour the Link-Belt plants. Even skeptical visitors were impressed by the orderly, efficient plants they saw and the promotional pitch they heard. With the introduction of scientific management, Link-Belt officials explained, worker productivity had more than doubled and wages ran 25 to 35 percent above the straight day rate, prices of Link-Belt products had decreased by 10 to 20 percent, and yet the corporation's profit margin had increased 15 to 20 percent. After stressing that all this was accomplished without a hint of labor trouble—sometimes even crediting the system with solving Chicago's labor problems—they invited members of the audience to get the workers' firsthand reactions. Most visitors left the premises convinced of scientific management's unqualified success in the Link-Belt shops.[19]

The promotional rhetoric fell short of fully disclosing the complex series of changes influencing the statistics. State-of-the-art machinery, high-speed steel cutting tools, and more extensive and effective use of electricity in the shops also help to explain increased output. Link-Belt officials who described the plants frequently used wage data from 1904 to emphasize the workers' higher earnings in the 1910s. However, they failed to acknowledge that 1904 was a depression year, disregarded inflation, and overlooked the portion of workers' higher earnings attributable to their increased skill or length of service. Nor can scientific management alone explain growing corporate profits. For example, the Indianapolis plant was profitable although it operated under traditional management methods until 1916.[20] Many interrelated factors account for increased profits between 1904 and 1915, including product development and more sophisticated marketing techniques. Finally, Link-Belt officials told half-truths in describing the labor situation, obfuscating the strikebreaking and blacklisting that suppressed labor activity in Chicago, and disregarding factors other than scientific management that encouraged worker cooperation.

Despite outward appearances, the uneven application and administration of the "system" at these showcase plants cannot be emphasized too strongly. Some work was readily adapted to the system, other applications took years to implement, and in other cases, scientific management proved entirely impractical. Link-Belt continued using several payment methods, including straight day work, piece work, and bonus rates in the shops, long after it installed scientific management. Fully 50 percent of the work done in Chicago was paid on a straight day work basis. Regardless of the payment methods, workers' rates were not uniform and earnings did not depend solely on output, since management made individual adjustments based on seniority and the foreman's assessment of ability.[21]

Since the planning department routed work to minimize material handling and to avoid foreseeable delays, the system affected all production workers to some degree. However, Link-Belt's most highly skilled workers, such as the pattern makers, tool makers, electricians, maintenance workers, and structural steel workers, maintained their autonomy under scientific management. For less skilled workers, the system's effect varied from day to day, depending on the feasibility of conducting time studies of work moving through the shops at any given time. Scientific management's impact also changed from one shift to the next. During the day, labor crews moved raw materials and work in progress from one machinist to the next while tool boys ran errands, gathered tools, stood on line to collect and return time cards, and even fetched water for the machinists. Machinist Michael Donnelly, who eventually refused to work under the system at Link-Belt, complained of losing his bonus "quite frequently" because this advantageous support network did not exist for him on the night shift, and time studies made no compensating allowances.[22]

Although management methods and the physical arrangement within the plants changed, Link-Belt's special-order, custom-designed products remained the same, requiring small batch production, flexibility, and highly skilled labor. Dodge described Link-Belt workers as "ambidextrous," capable of moving easily from one machine and operation to another. He insisted that "specialists" would be detrimental in shops like his, where most production jobs involved a complicated series of operations rather than a few repetitive tasks. Although workers might repeat the same work process several times, the typical machine shop job required one and a quarter hours to complete. On average, workers changed jobs seven times a day. This work pace was faster under scientific management, but it did not involve deskilling. In most cases, well-paid versatile machinists concentrated their efforts where skill was essential, while low-paid common laborers took over menial tasks and routing of material. Link-Belt machinists apparently paid more attention to their wages than to "any particular system of management in the shop." Of the few Link-Belt workers' voices appearing in the scientific management sources, Michael Donnelly alone complained, while the others reported satisfaction with the system based on their high earnings.[23]

Upon Barth's departure, local managers began simplifying, adapting, and improving the system to meet each plant's specific needs. In December 1907, Link–Belt eliminated the speed-bosses; in early 1908 it altered some forms to reduce some paper work; and by 1913 it had abandoned functional foremen in favor of conventional general foremen and subforemen.[24]

After being lured into working under the differential piece rate, machinists turned it to their advantage. In many cases, the workers knew more than Dwight Merrick and the other time study experts and protested to the rate setter, the foreman, and even higher management if they considered a rate too low. By establishing informal limits on production among themselves, workers influenced the process of determining methods, defining operation times, and setting rates. Moreover, Chicago's management encouraged employee initiative in improving methods by awarding three monthly prizes for the best suggestions. To their credit, Link–Belt managers took the workers' complaints and suggestions seriously and kept their promise to uphold established piece rates.[25]

From their first experience with Taylor's methods, Link–Belt managers recognized the system's deficiencies in maintaining the worker's cooperation. At a conference on scientific management, Dodge argued:

> Certainly, where human elements are introduced into a problem, scientific methods alone will hardly achieve a complete solution. It must be a combination of scientific analysis and methods plus consideration for the interest and well-being of the workers, and tact in meeting their inherent resistance to change. . . . Truly *Scientific* Management takes account of both sides of the problem, and the method of approach should lie along both these lines [emphasis Dodge's].[26]

As early as the 1890s, Link–Belt introduced an impressive and growing array of employee benefits, incentives, and welfare measures, designed to personalize the relationship between management and labor. These activities lacked the elaboration and sophistication of programs developed by companies such as Joseph & Feiss. Link–Belt had no welfare department or special staff. Some Link–Belt welfare efforts developed piecemeal to address specific needs, while others grew out of close contact and genuinely friendly relations between management and workers during the late nineteenth century. Dodge and Piez believed in maintaining personal contacts and in giving workers a "square deal," but they disapproved of "soup-house philanthropy." Consequently, most Link-Belt initiatives required matching employee contributions in effort, talent, or funding. From the Beneficial Society's support for ill or disabled workers to company events providing family entertainment, managers and workers collaborated in organizing and operating the company's welfare programs. One observer aptly termed such Link-Belt activities the "philanthropy of self-help."[27]

In January 1915, James Dodge wrote to his friend Frederick W. Taylor: "I believe that it would be perfectly possible to harmonize Scientific Management with Trade Unionism if an earnest effort were made by both parties." In a subsequent letter, Dodge informed Taylor that at Link-Belt's annual meeting the executives discussed introducing worker-elected shop committees to permit employee participation in "the determination of base rates and piece rates so as to . . . disarm organized labor in their claim that we are all arbitrary and heartless in our determination of these figures. . . ." Taylor minced no words in his reply: "I think you are making a great mistake in doing this. I do not believe there is the silightest [sic] dissatisfaction among your men and having these Shop Committees would only have the effect of stimulating you[r] men in the direction of trades unionism."[28]

Dodge's views in this exchange expose his ambivalence toward labor unions. While "gradually coming to the opinion that . . . intelligent labor leaders might overcome their opposition . . .[to] scientifically-managed shops," Dodge stopped short of sanctioning unions at Link-Belt. His practical alternative was to enlist workers into a Link-Belt association. However, other Link-Belt executives were less enthusiastic. Taylor's firm opposition to the shop committees gained a sympathetic response from Charles Piez, who feared that any form of organization might revive the IAM in Chicago. He wrote to Dodge: "I want to move very cautiously before taking a step that may haunt us later on. . . . There is . . . no great haste about the appointment of these committees, so that we will have ample time for further reflection." Link-Belt never established shop committees, and management dropped the debate after Dodge's death in December 1915.[29]

Link-Belt managers clung to familiar methods to discourage union inroads. They expanded their traditional social and welfare measures and continued to play active roles in the NMTA.[30] These additional methods complemented scientific management at Link-Belt in a three-pronged strategy designed to enhance management authority: scientific management controlled the labor process and individualized bargaining between labor and management; corporate welfare encouraged workers to identify with management; and trade association activities shaped the labor market. In trying to block later unionization efforts all three elements of the company's management strategy came into play.

Industrial mobilization during WWI posed the first challenge to Link-Belt's smooth operation under scientific management. The trouble rose from a booming market as American industries began to supply the European combatants. In 1916, Link-Belt filled the largest number of orders in its forty-one year history. The boom revealed "every weak spot and laid bare every defect in organization, in facilities, in method" at Link-Belt, and "carried with it ugly portents," according to Charles Piez. In particular, the company faced increasing difficulty in recruiting and retaining employees. Workers of all skill levels demanded and received more money. In May 1916, Link-Belt offered its entire manufacturing workforce a 10 percent bonus, regardless of output or the type of work performed. Thereafter, the company advanced "certain wage rates . . . almost weekly." During January 1917, "in order to secure labor at all," the Chicago plant had to raise the hourly rate of common laborers from 23 to 27.5 cents in addition to the 10 percent bonus. This amounted to average earnings of 30 cents per hour, nearly 50 percent above the prevailing rate of January 1916. In April 1917, union demands for the eight-hour day at neighboring establishments forced the company to reduce its work week from 54 to 50 hours and cut back to a 45-hour week a year later. Since production demands necessitated long working hours, the shorter work week translated into extra overtime pay for Link-Belt workers.[31]

In this tight labor market, the company could ill afford to depend on "scientific" methods to set wages or determine production methods. As Link-Belt and all other metal manufacturers strained to keep pace with rising wages in the defense industries, its incentive wage came to closely resemble the community wage norm for a given occupation. Wartime wage inflation effectively negated the economic incentives of working under scientific management at Link-Belt.

Despite wage and hour concessions, a shortage of skilled workers and labor turnover plagued Link-Belt. Superintendents and foremen gladly hired anyone who walked through the door, even applicants lacking NMTA labor bureau credentials. Labor turnover reduced efficiency and managerial control over production in three important ways. First, the firm's skilled workforce was "continually besieged by other employers with flattering offers." Second, new recruits were seldom trained well enough to begin producing Link-Belt's special-order products immediately. Furthermore, they became "a source of expense rather than profit," by simply quitting their jobs if management proved too demanding.[32] Third, the process of on-the-job training enhanced the power of skilled workers in defining and controlling work methods.

These problems notwithstanding, Link-Belt managed to double production and earn substantial profits by expanding facilities, running night shifts, and hiring large numbers of inexperienced workers. The aspects of scientific management directly affecting labor played a surprisingly minor role in this accomplishment. Although central planning and accounting, efficient routing, and the use of time study data remained in force, supervisory controls and systematic efforts to reduce costs by increasing worker efficiency fell into disuse. In the wartime market, inefficiency had no effect on company profits. The pressing demand for Link-Belt products allowed the company to pass rising costs along to customers by qualifying all contract proposals with the warning: "prices are subject to change with market conditions."[33]

Once conditions returned to normal, management renewed the quest "for economy, method and efficiency." However, scientific management came to represent a set of guiding principles, rather than a system of specific methods. New initiatives often reflected Taylor's philosophy, but not his methods. For example, in coming years, Link-Belt's efficiency experts would characterize time studies taken with a "slow and clumsy" stopwatch as "half-baked." New rate-setting methods involved motion-time analysis and "synthetically constructed" elementary times based on "practically universal" body movements. Moreover, new work methods and economic incentives often focused on white-collar workers. After the war, superintendents and foremen also implemented new efficiency measures on the shop floor, but they considered their efforts as outgrowths, rather than components, of Taylorism.[34]

Although company officials again argued that wages must be tied to production, Link-Belt's wartime experience had dramatically transformed Taylor's most controversial practices. Both managers and workers knew that the bonuses and pay increases every few months from 1916 to 1920 bore no relationship to individual productivity. With time study thus exposed as just one of many factors in establishing piece rates, Link-Belt employees of the postwar period joined in the universal demand for wage adjustments based on the cost of living. No opposition developed over time study or piece rates per se, but growing pressure for across-the-board raises kept Link-Belt wages in line with the pay scales at neighboring plants.[35]

As scientific management's overt significance receded at Link-Belt, trade association activities and corporate paternalism took on greater importance. Charles Piez was particularly concerned about the postwar upsurge in labor conflict. On leave from Link-Belt as Director of the U.S. Shipping Board's Emergency Fleet Corporation, he and Seattle, Washington's mayor had broken the five-day Seattle general strike of January 1919. Piez believed that Seattle's workers had relinquished control to radical, foreign leaders who aimed to "wrest control of industry from its owners. . . ." During the steel strike several months later, he appealed to steel users "to keep 'hands off' the strike situation and to accept inevitable business losses . . . rather than embarrass the steel companies by bringing pressure on them to surrender to the strike leaders." He called for "a fight to the finish," since he believed the ultimate control of industry was at stake.[36]

Piez's fears and impressions filtered down to Link-Belt even before he returned to the company in May 1919. Link-Belt officials carefully monitored national labor unrest and looked for signs of contagion in their own shops. In assessing prospects for the New Year of 1919, Link-Belt's acting president, Staunton Peck, sensed undercurrents of "anarchy, Bolshevism, socialism, populism, and other isms." He had evidence to suggest that an unnamed union (probably the IAM) had planted organizers in the Chicago shops. Carefully avoiding the attention of foremen, the organizers approached fellow workers, "pouring into them radical ideas about the wage scale and shop conditions."[37]

Company documents do not explain how the union infiltration was discovered. Quite possibly, Link-Belt lathe operator James

Cousland provided the information. Cousland, who started working at Link-Belt in 1916, commenced spying on his coworkers shortly thereafter. From 1918 to 1936, Cousland sent weekly or monthly reports to the NMTA. An Association secretary copied the information and sent it to the Chicago plant superintendent. Cousland insisted that he only reported on "piece work trouble," workers' complaints about safety hazards, and production problems, not on "labor activities."[38] However, his denials are unconvincing in view of Link-Belt management's own account, which identified agitation and dissatisfaction over "the wage scale and shop conditions" as the inspiration for "labor activities." There is no record of how the shops were purged of radical elements, although it is likely that workers who publicly expressed grievances were fired.

Dispelling distrust took more concerted effort. Upon resuming control at Link-Belt, Piez realized that the plants had grown to the point where he and other top executives could no longer personally sway worker opinion. He favored regaining loyalty in the shops by preparing the superintendents, foremen, and subforemen "to meet this insidious doctrine that is being spread to the detriment of industry." He believed the first-line managers could "create sound public opinion" in the shops. But, before assuming this role, the supervisors had to cease supporting the "aggressive, vociferous, minority" of workers who advocated unionization. Piez persuaded Link-Belt's directors to expand a stock option plan to give production managers a personal stake in the company's growth, and to supplement the efforts of the NMTA Supervisors' and Foremen's Club to eradicate union sympathy among production supervisors. To "build and maintain a high esprit de corps," foremen gathered in the plant superintendent's office for special weekly meetings to address "pure labor questions."[39]

Link-Belt officials knew that labor espionage and supervisory training programs provided only partial solutions to their problem. Piez opposed some popular programs of the 1920s, such as profit sharing and company unions, which he characterized as "a great deal of bosh." Consequently, Link-Belt expanded its welfare programs, self-help initiatives, and company-sponsored social affairs to reinvigorate employee loyalty. During the early 1920s, each plant organized an Employment Office and appointed a manager with a threefold agenda: to administer nonwork related activities, to raise management's consciousness of the "human aspect of production problems," and to preserve employee morale. The Employment Office recruited labor, selected potential candidates for job vacancies, settled grievances, and processed dismissals and resignations. The employment managers compiled detailed histories of each active and former employee to identify workers suitable for promotion, pay raises, disciplinary action, or reinstatement. The records were also used for statistical analyses of labor turnover and accident rates. The office investigated worker complaints and offered solutions, recommended amenities such as men's locker rooms and women's rest rooms, and managed the operation of dispensaries and cafeterias. Finally, the employment managers oversaw the company's Beneficial Societies, Building and Loan Associations, Credit Unions, charitable activities, athletic teams, and worker education and training programs, and administered a growing number of other benefits, such as newly inaugurated paid vacations for shop workers. To enhance employee morale, individual plants hosted outings and elaborate social events featuring the talents of Link–Belt employees. In 1925, the entire corporation celebrated "half a century of successful operation" and Charles Piez's retirement as president.[40]

Other than the recession of 1921–1922, when workers suffered wage cuts and layoffs, Link–Belt enjoyed a decade of growth, prosperity, steady employment, and minimal worker dissatisfaction. The surviving records reveal no hints of strikes, union organizing efforts, or overt labor problems, and little management paranoia.[41]

If these factors did not entirely subvert union sympathy during the 1920s, the failing economy and insecure labor market of 1930–1933 certainly had a chilling effect. Management employed a step-by-step strategy developed during earlier economic slumps to minimize disruption of the workforce. Initially, as special orders dropped off, nonessential overtime was eliminated and workers produced stock items or did repairs and odd jobs around the shops. As stopgap jobs ran out, foremen closed early on weekdays and suspended Saturday schedules and night shifts. When work fell off further, management instituted work sharing by limiting some workers to a three- or four-day work week. It later reduced benefits and periodically cut hourly wages, piece rates, and salaries, but the company laid off employees only as a last resort.

Many Link-Belt employees worked without layoffs throughout the Depression, and those forced out of work or placed on part-time schedules for extended periods often returned to their full-time jobs when work picked up again. Consequently, Link-Belt employees considered themselves fortunate and felt satisfied with their work, or at least refrained from complaining about wages or working conditions. During this difficult period the company enhanced its reputation as a good employer.[42]

As Link-Belt's business began a fitful recovery, management faced new challenges from the federal government. Link-Belt officials generally disapproved of government interference in industry. In public statements, advertising literature, and internal communications, they vigorously opposed New Deal legislation. However, as Assistant General Manager E. L. Berry phrased it, "in order to sort of cooperate with the spirit of the N. I. R. A.," the Chicago plant management organized the Link-Belt Employees Board. Existing records do not reveal whether fear of local labor activity or pressure from corporate headquarters prompted the decision.[43]

On arriving at work one Monday morning in 1933, Chicago workers found a notice posted on the bulletin board suggesting that they establish an Employees Board and calling for nominations and an election of representatives. Although Link-Belt workers recognized this as a company initiative, they willingly gave it a try. As established, the Board provided a monthly forum for E. L. Berry and seven employee representatives to discuss health and safety; education, recreation, and benefit programs; wages, hours, and working conditions; "continuity of employment," industrial conditions, and "economy and waste prevention." Dividing the plant into seven electoral areas ostensibly insured "fair representation to each department," but in fact, it diluted the potential power of the blue collar employees. Three divisions contained predominantly white-collar and professional personnel, one division combined white-collar, professional, and highly skilled craft workers, and three divisions represented the majority of Link-Belt's blue-collar employees. The seven elected "voting members" served advisory roles, while authority rested with management's "non-voting representative."[44]

Louis Salmons, a maintenance electrician and former AFL member with nine years' service at Link-Belt, was elected as a worker representative. At the board's first session, Salmons proposed holding an open meeting of "the whole rank and file . . . [to] let everybody have a voice instead of leaving it up to the representatives to use their own judgment on all matters." The other representatives—an engineer, a clerk, two foremen, and two oldtimers—unanimously voted Salmons down. For three years Salmons served on the board, persistently trying to represent his constituents by bringing up wage and hour grievances, poor working conditions, and work-related health problems. Assistant General Manager Berry acted promptly on suggestions for repairing or improving facilities, but dismissed wage demands, declaring that the company was losing money.[45]

Dissatisfaction with the Employees Board and knowledge that workers had other options led Salmons to the Steel Workers Organizing Committee [SWOC] in September 1936. He described the Employees Board and working conditions at Link-Belt and asked for the SWOC's assistance in organizing the plant. Assured that the organization would back him "100 per cent," he requested fifty application cards to start organizing Local 1604 of the Amalgamated Association of Iron, Steel and Tin Workers.[46]

Sensing that there would be retribution, Salmons proceeded cautiously. The application cards required an organizer's signature, so Salmons signed each one, guarding against someone else bearing the consequences of his actions. He asked seven coworkers to assist him in organizing, and they began passing out cards to fellow workers whom they considered trustworthy. Salmons' position allowed him to move freely through the plant doing routine inspection, maintenance, and troubleshooting when machinery broke down. Salmons started discussing the Amalgamated Association as he worked and, when the opportunity rose, he slipped Local 1604 application cards among literature he distributed for the Employees Board. "I was elected to represent the men . . . not [to] represent the company," Salmons recalled. "I took the stand that I would represent them. And when I couldn't represent them properly through the employees board, I took other steps to represent them."[47]

After a week of discreet recruiting netted eleven members, the organizers met to discuss strategy. Salmons told his friends that management would soon learn of the organizing and fire him. He warned the other organizers: "I will have to work on the outside.

Then it will be up to you fellows to keep this thing going on the inside." Salmons was right. A batch of application cards disappeared from one organizer's toolbox, and some employees turned the cards over to E. L. Berry. The morning following the strategy session, Berry discharged Salmons. Salmons shrugged it off, bluffing: "It is all right, we have 370 men signed up." The rumor spread through the plant, generating interest in the "big drive" and making the inside organizers' efforts a bit easier.[48]

Within six months, Local 1604's membership caught up with the rumor. Salmons went on the SWOC payroll and began rallying forces on the outside—at the plant gates, at the streetcar stop, and at the neighborhood tavern where Link-Belt workers frequently stopped after work. The tavern owner rented a back room to the union for meetings, posted the local's recruiting sign, and kept a stack of application cards handy. The insiders' ranks gradually grew to include organizers in every department, and evidence suggests that the Amalgamated won broad support, fairly evenly distributed among the skilled, semiskilled, and unskilled blue-collar ranks. While some workers with ten or more years' seniority played important roles in organizing the union, employees hired during the depression years—who identified least with management and whose jobs were most vulnerable—seemingly joined in larger numbers. Meanwhile, the Regional National Labor Relations Board [NLRB] Director negotiated Salmons's reinstatement. Berry's conditions for putting Salmons back to work in December 1936 were "no more running around the plant" and "no more organizing." Berry isolated Salmons by placing him at bench work where he repaired only small items brought directly to him, but the feisty electrician challenged Berry's second condition, responding: "there will be no more organizing in the plant, but there will be lots on the outside." After attracting about 400 members, the union elected Salmons as President in April 1937.[49]

The company kept tabs on the union's activities for months as James Cousland attended organizing meetings and spied on workers throughout the plant. Cousland briefly served as a union member, but his usefulness to the company diminished after the LaFollette Committee exposed him as an NMTA operative. Since the unionists could not directly link Cousland's spying to any damage, they reported his activities to the membership but took no further action against him.[50]

Link-Belt management and a substantial number of loyal employees found another way to fight back. After the *Jones & Laughlin* decision held employer-dominated organizations illegal, the Employees Board disbanded and several former representatives formed a new organization, the Independent Union of Craftsmen [IUC]. During the three-day IUC recruitment drive, foremen conveniently disappeared or turned their heads while employees worked their way through the shops requesting, cajoling, bribing, or coercing fellow workers to obtain signatures on IUC petitions. Many workers willingly signed, particularly white-collar employees, skilled blue-collar workers with long terms of service, and those in line for promotion, while others felt they had no choice. In one flagrant move, a foremen "signed up" several illiterate workers without seeking their consent. Such tactics obtained signatures from 760 of approximately 1,000 Link-Belt employees in three days. A committee of self-appointed delegates presented the petitions to Berry on April 20, 1937, and the following day he signed an agreement officially recognizing the IUC as the employees' bargaining agent.[51]

Imposing the IUC on the workforce and intimidating workers through discriminatory dismissals and layoffs stalled the Amalgamated's efforts for nearly five years. As in 1904 and 1919, when unionization threatened Link-Belt, management purged the labor activists. Nine workers lost jobs at Link-Belt because of their actual or suspected union activity during the organizing drive, and other workers believed that they were targeted for layoffs during the economic slump of 1937 because of their union affiliation.[52]

Unlike past experiences, the fired unionists had means of fighting back after 1937. With Louis Salmons's determination and the SWOC's support and guidance, the aggrieved workers took their cases to the NLRB. The NLRB disestablished the IUC, and ordered the company to end its spying activities and reinstate the labor activists with back pay. Although Link-Belt won a favorable ruling in Federal Appeals Court, the union activists triumphed in January 1941, when the United States Supreme Court reversed the lower court's decision.[53]

Thus for Link-Belt executives, scientific management provided a vital mechanism for organizing and managing production, but it offered no answer to another pressing problem, the turmoil associated with union organizing campaigns and collective bargaining. Incentive wage plans and good working conditions, coupled with the company's traditional benefit programs and later efforts in systematic personnel management, helped attract and retain a capable labor force, but they could not satisfy additional demands inspired by members of the metal trades unions. Although the company refused to deal with unions after 1906, replaced strikers, resorted to labor espionage, and discharged men identified as union partisans, the problem did not go away. Consequently, Taylor's promise of industrial harmony under scientific management proved elusive. It took four decades of considerable conflict before Link-Belt executives reluctantly returned to the bargaining table.

### NOTES

1. The Link-Belt Company, *The Story of Link-Belt, 1875–1925*, (Chicago, 1925), pp. 19–32; *Link-Belt News*, May–June 1939, pp. 1–3.
2. U.S. House of Representatives, *Hearings before the Special Committee of the House of Representatives to Investigate the Taylor and Other Systems of Shop Management under the Authority of H. Res. 90*, vol. 3, (Washington, DC, 1912) (hereafter cited as *Taylor Hearings*), p. 1699; U.S. Congress, Senate, *Evidence Taken by the Interstate Commerce Commission in the Matter of Proposed Freight Rates by Carriers*, 61st Cong., 3d sess., 1911 (hereafter cited as *Eastern Freight Hearings*), pp. 2692–93, 2738–39, 2741–43.
3. *Taylor Hearings*, pp. 1684–85, 1689–93; U.S. Congress, Senate, *Report of the Commission on Industrial Relations*, vol. 1, 64th Cong., 1st sess., 1916 (hereafter cited as *U.S. CIR*), p. 872; *Eastern Freight Hearings*, pp. 2743, 2747; *U.S. CIR*, vol. 4, pp. 3176–77; *The Bulletin of the National Metal Trades Association* 3, no. 10 (1904 [hereafter cited as *NMTA Bulletin*]), pp. 450–51; David Montgomery, *The Fall of the House of Labor: The Workplace, the State, and American Labor Activism, 1865–1925* (Cambridge, England, 1987), pp. 231, 270.
4. *U.S. CIR*, vol. 1, p. 872; *Eastern Freight Hearings*, pp. 2698–99.
5. *Eastern Freight Hearings*, p. 2690; George P. Torrence, *James Mapes Dodge (1852–1915): Mechanical Engineer, Inventor, Pioneer in Industry* (New York, 1950), p. 9.
6. *The Story of Link-Belt*, p. 26; Charles Piez, "Personal Reminiscences of James Mapes Dodge," reprinted from *American Machinist*, January 20, 1916 and February 3, 1916, p. 11; Daniel Nelson, *Frederick W. Taylor and the Rise of Scientific Management* (Madison, WI, 1980), p. 143; *Eastern Freight Hearings*, pp. 2691, 2732–37; Link-Belt Notice Book, notices from April 1890 through March 1891.
7. Link-Belt Notice Book, notices from April 1890 through December 1903; *Eastern Freight Hearings*, pp. 2733, 2742.

8. *Eastern Freight Hearings*, pp. 2740–42; *U.S. CIR*, vol. 1, pp. 862–63; *Taylor Hearings*, pp. 516–17, 1545–46; Piez, "Personal Reminiscences," pp. 16–17; L. P. Alford, "Scientific Management in Use," *American Machinist* 36, no. 14 (April 4, 1912), p. 548. Nelson, *Frederick W. Taylor*, p. 144.

9. *Taylor Hearings*, pp. 516–17, 1546–47, 1638–39.

10. *U.S. CIR*, vol. 1, p. 871.

11. Alford, "Scientific Management in Use," p. 548; *U.S. CIR*, vol. 4, p. 3177; *Chicago Tribune*, March 1, 1900, p. 12; March 9, 1900, p. 1; March 10, 1900, p. 9; March 14, 1900, p. 9; *U.S. CIR*, vol. 1, p. 868; Montgomery, *Fall of the House of Labor*, p. 270. Montgomery provides general background on this strike wave, see pp. 259–75.

12. *NMTA Bulletin* 3 (1904), pp. 518–19.

13. Ibid.

14. *NMTA Bulletin* 3 (1904), pp. 372, 519–20; *The Open Shop* 4 (1905), p. 233.

15. *U.S. CIR*, vol. 4, pp. 3185–86, 3416–17.

16. *Eastern Freight Hearings*, pp. 2743–44; *U.S. CIR*, vol. 4, pp. 3177–79, 3414. Link-Belt refused to reinstate labor leaders after the 1900 strike; see Montgomery, *Fall of the House of Labor*, p. 205. Montgomery suggests that by introducing high-speed steel and scientific management, Link-Belt weaned formerly aggressive workers from both their skills and their unions; see pp. 231–32. Taylor, Dodge, and Piez also claimed that scientific management eliminated the workers' desire to unionize. However, I find no evidence of strong union sympathy in Philadelphia before or after 1904. Although the success of scientific management in Chicago possibly hinged on eliminating the union, that occurred prior to Barth's installation. Link-Belt's reshaped labor force of 1906 was not the same as the union-prone group of 1900–1904. Moreover, while Link-Belt's priority in replacing the strikers and in introducing scientific management was to gain greater control, it was not an assault on skill per se. Link-Belt's production required craft skills. Striking machinists were not replaced by deskilled machine tenders, but by nonunion skilled workers or by less skilled workers whom the company trained to assume skilled positions.

17. *The Open Shop* 4 (1905), pp. 76, 222–24.

18. Link-Belt *Weekly Letter* 548 (October 15, 1920), p. 946 (hereafter cited as *Weekly Letter*); *Eastern Freight Hearings*, pp. 2700, 2742; Alford, "Scientific Management in Use," p. 548.

19. *Eastern Freight Hearings*, pp. 2694–98, 2701; *U.S. CIR*, vol. 4, pp. 3193–94; Alford, "Scientific Management in Use," pp. 548–50; "Methods of Management that Made Money," *Industrial Engineering and the Engineering Digest* (January 1911), pp. 21–27; Lieut. Frank W. Sterling, "The Successful Operation of a System of Scientific Management," in Clarence Bertrand Thompson, ed., *Scientific Management: A Collection of the More Significant Articles Describing the Taylor System of Management* (Cambridge, MA, 1914), pp. 296–365; John R. Commons, *Industrial Government* (New York, 1921), pp. 26–34.

20. *Weekly Letter* 859 (March 2, 1936), p. 242; *Eastern Freight Hearings*, p. 2700.

21. C. W. Adams, "The Differential Piece Rate," *American Machinist* 34 (January 5, 1911) pp. 18–19; *Eastern Freight Hearings*, p. 2740; *U.S. CIR*, vol. 4, pp. 3180, 3182.

22. *Taylor Hearings*, pp. 1637, 1684, 1694–96; "Methods of Management that Made Money," p. 25; *U.S. CIR*, vol. 1, p. 866.
23. *U.S. CIR*, vol. 1, p. 867; *Taylor Hearings*, p. 450; "Scientific Management from the Workman's Standpoint," in Thompson, *Scientific Management*, p. 836.
24. Alford, "Scientific Management in Use," p. 549; J. Christian Barth to Elizabeth G. Hayward, May 25, 1950, Taylor Collection 151; Link-Belt Notice Book, December 12, 1907; "Methods of Management that Made Money," p. 26; Gilbreth Collection, NGTSP 100/0738, see Prof. Mixter's comments, August 27, 1913; Sterling, "The Successful Operation of a System of Scientific Management," p. 296; Commons, *Industrial Government*, p. 28.
25. Alford, "Scientific Management in Use," p. 549; *U.S. CIR*, vol. 4, p. 3182; Charles Piez to James Mapes Dodge, March 1, 1915, Taylor Collection 58B.
26. James Mapes Dodge, "The Spirit in Which Scientific Management Should Be Approached," *Addresses and Discussions at the Conference on Scientific Management at the Amos Tuck School, Dartmouth College* (Norwood, MA, 1912), pp. 142–43.
27. David J. Goldberg, "Richard A. Feiss, Mary Barnett Gilson, and Scientific Management at Joseph & Feiss, 1909–1925," in this volume, chap. 2; Louis Bell, "The Philanthrophy of Self-Help," *Cassier's Magazine* 24 (May–October 1903), pp. 439–46; *U.S. CIR*, vol. 1, p. 865; Link-Belt Notice Book, notices from 1890 to 1915.
28. James Mapes Dodge to Frederick W. Taylor, January 18, 1915 and February 18, 1915; Taylor to Dodge, February 25, 1915, all in Taylor Collection 58B.
29. James Mapes Dodge to Frederick W. Taylor, December 14, 1914 and March 9, 1915; Charles Piez to James Mapes Dodge, March 1, 1915, all in Taylor Collection 58B. Other researchers have claimed that Link-Belt formed a company union, based on the letters that circulated among Taylor, Dodge, and Piez in 1915. See Frank Barkley Copley, *Frederick W. Taylor: Father of Scientific Management*, vol. 2 (New York, 1923), pp. 428–29; Nelson, *Frederick W. Taylor*, p. 145. I find nothing in these letters or in other company records to indicate that Link-Belt executives moved beyond discussing the merits and drawbacks of shop committees. In response to an NMTA questionnaire in 1919, Piez wrote: "The Link-Belt Company has never organized any shop committees. . . ." See *Weekly Letter* 521 (September 1, 1919), p. 701.
30. *Synopsis of Proceedings of the Annual Convention of the National Metal Trades Association* (hereafter cited as *NMTA Proceedings*), 1910, and 1916–1922; U.S. Senate, Committee on Education and Labor, *Industrial Espionage*, Report no. 46, part 3, 75th Cong., 3d sess., 1937 (hereafter cited as *LaFollette Committee Hearings*), pp. 984, 988, 991, 997, 1053, 1055, 1087, 1088; Metal Manufacturers' Association of Philadelphia Collection, Temple University Urban Archives, URP 44, Box 4, Folders 22, 23, 30.
31. *Weekly Letter* 455 (September 15, 1916), p. 262; 464 (January 2, 1917), pp. 332–33; 465 (January 15, 1917), p. 337; *Link-Belt News* (April 1937), p. 5.
32. *Weekly Letter* 461 (December 8, 1916), p. 313; 466 (January 22, 1917), pp. 342–43. Montgomery notes the high cost of labor turnover at other firms during this period; see *Fall of the House of Labor*, pp. 239–40.

33. *Weekly Letter* 464 (January 2, 1917), pp. 332–34; 490 (January 2, 1918), pp. 519–20; 507 (January 1, 1919), pp. 581–82; 522 (September 15, 1919), p. 711; 461 (December 8, 1916), p. 313.

34. E. L. Berry and H. C. Robson, "Motion Study in the Job Shop," in Allen H. Mogensen, *Common Sense Applied to Motion and Time Study* (New York, 1932), pp. 120–27; *Weekly Letter* 507 (January 1, 1919), pp. 581–82; 508 (January 15, 1919), pp. 587–88; 511 (March 15, 1919), pp. 604–5; 515 (June 2, 1919), p. 642; 516 (June 23, 1919), p. 649; 517 (July 1, 1919), p. 659; 524 (October 15, 1919), pp. 732–33; 529 (January 1, 1920), pp. 776–78; 551 (December 1, 1920), pp. 988–89.

35. Commons, *Industrial Government*, pp. 27–28; *Weekly Letter* 506 (December 2, 1918), p. 580; 522 (September 15, 1919), p. 713. Link-Belt employee card files document changes in wages.

36. *Weekly Letter* 545 (September 1, 1920), p. 921; 524 (October 15, 1919), p. 725; 515 (June 2, 1919), p. 635; 522 (September 15, 1919), p. 711; 523 (October 1, 1919), p. 718; *NMTA Proceedings* (1919), pp. 84–85; *Philadelphia Evening Bulletin* Files, Temple University Urban Archives, clippings from January 30, 1919 and October 6, 1919.

37. *Weekly Letter* 507 (January 1, 1919), p. 581; 524 (October 15, 1919), p. 727.

38. *LaFollette Committee Hearings*, pp. 1053, 1055, 1087–88; *Link-Belt Company v. National Labor Relations Board; Independent Union of Craftsmen v. National Labor Relations Board and Link-Belt Company*, 110 F. 2d 506 (C.C.A. 7th) (hereafter cited as *Link-Belt v. H.L.R.B.*), pp. 112–21, 128–29, 583–86, 1156–61.

39. *Weekly Letter* 524 (October 15, 1919), pp. 726–27; Commons, *Industrial Government*, pp. 29–30.

40. *Weekly Letter* 524 (October 15, 1919), pp. 725–26; 521 (September 1, 1919), pp. 702–2; 664 (December 23, 1925), pp. 313–14; 845 (February 1, 1935), pp. 27–28; 627 (June 2, 1924), pp. 181–82; 639 (January 2, 1925), p. 1; Link-Belt Notice Book, notices from 1919 to 1930; Anonymous handwritten journal; Philip Scranton and Walter Licht, *Work Sights: Industrial Philadelphia, 1890–1950* (Philadelphia, 1986), p. 248; Link-Belt Bulletins, January (n.d.), 1925 and March 9, 1925; Link-Belt Company Fiftieth Anniversary Dinner Program Book, pp. 3, 25–26; Charles Piez to "My Friends and Associates of the Link-Belt Company," February 20, 1925.

41. *Weekly Letter* 573 (January 3, 1922), p. 189; Link-Belt Notice Book, notices from 1920 to 1930; Link-Belt Bulletins, 1920–1930; *The Story of Link-Belt*; Link-Belt Company Chronology, May 23, 1956; Anonymous handwritten journal, 1888–1937; Link-Belt employee card files; Alfred Kauffmann, "Knowing Men Is Keystone of Management," *Iron Age* 124 (1929), pp. 81–82; Philadelphia Labor Market Studies, Folders 5, 9–13, 15–16.

42. *U.S. CIR*, vol. 1, pp. 864–65, 867; *Weekly Letter* 573 (January 3, 1922), p. 189; Link-Belt Notice Book, notices for September 18, 1893, October 4, 1893, January 1, 1931, July 20, 1931, February 25, 1932, and March 31, 1932; Anonymous handwritten journal; Link-Belt Union Book, list of wage adjustments for 1931–1943; Philadelphia Labor Market Studies; *Link-Belt v. N.L.R.B.*, see workers' testimony throughout.

43. *Link-Belt v. N.L.R.B.*, pp. 1127, 1296; Link-Belt Bulletin, July 10, 1933.

Guidelines for establishing similar representation plans spread throughout the corporation, although local management had final say over implementing such a program. In 1933, the Indianapolis plant established an Employees Board with bylaws nearly identical to those written in Chicago. Philadelphia management rejected the idea of installing an Employees Board.

44. *Link-Belt v. N.L.R.B.*, pp. 146–52, 204–5, 280–82, 815–24, 1127, 1202–3, 1296–1305.
45. *Link-Belt v. N.L.R.B.*, pp. 150–52, 178, 182–88, 1301–4.
46. *Weekly Letter* 854 (November 1, 1935), p. 158; *Link-Belt v. N.L.R.B.*, pp. 150–52, 190, 813–15.
47. *Link-Belt v. N.L.R.B.*, pp. 152–53, 155, 170–71, 196, 280–90, 813–15, 1230. Louis Salmons and the "union pioneers" of the electrical industries shared many characteristics. See Ronald Schatz, "Union Pioneers: The Founders of Local Unions at General Electric and Westinghouse, 1933–1937," *Journal of American History* 66, no. 3 (December 1979), pp. 586–602.
48. *Link-Belt v. N.L.R.B.*, pp. 153–54, 188–89, 282, 353, 714, 1230, 1232–33.
49. *Link-Belt v. N.L.R.B.*, pp. 153–54, 161, 163, 171, 190–91, 196, 211–13, 1229–31, 1234. Information on occupations and length of service of Amalgamated members is found throughout the testimony of NLRB witnesses.
50. *Link-Belt v. N.L.R.B.*, pp. 120–46, 178–82, 191.
51. *Link-Belt v. N.L.R.B.* Accounts of this organizing drive and information on occupations, length of service, and subsequent promotion of IUC members are found throughout the testimony of NLRB, Respondent, and Intervener witnesses.
52. *Link-Belt v. N.L.R.B.*, pp. 142–227, 228–40, 370–420, 569–81, 697–709, 1027–39, 1062–97, 1105–1111, 1125–1207, 1214–22, 1228–34, 1265–67.
53. *Link-Belt v. N.L.R.B.*, pp. 1519–56; *Labor Cases*, vol. 3 (New York, 1941), pp. 51, 116–51.

STEVEN KREIS

7 The Diffusion of Scientific Management:
The Bedaux Company in America and
Britain, 1926–1945

$B$y the time of Frederick Winslow Taylor's death, the
gospel of industrial efficiency preached by American scientific
managers was commonplace on both sides of the Atlantic. In the
following years of world war, reconstruction, and adjustment,
scientific management attracted a new generation of advocates
and practitioners, many of whom would have perplexed and
shocked Taylor and his immediate circle. Of the entrepreneurs of
scientific management who succeeded Frank Gilbreth, Harrington
Emerson, Richard Feiss, and other pioneers, none was more
successful than Charles Eugene Bedaux (1886–1944). Unlike Taylor and his colleagues, Bedaux was and still is a mysterious figure.
Secretive to a fault, he avoided professional contacts, refused to
write for popular or technical journals, and spurned publicity. Yet
he was a master salesman whose operations were global in scope
and impact. Only in recent years, with the discovery of the papers
of the British Bedaux Company, is it possible to gauge the impact
of Bedaux and his extraordinary career.[1]

Bedaux's success was based on simple insights that he and his
engineers applied, apparently with little variation, in a variety of
industrial settings. The Bedaux system brought the intellectual
principles of scientific management down to earth from their lofty
pedestal and put those principles into action. Table 7.1 indicates
the growth of the international Bedaux consultancies between
1918 and 1931. According to a 1934 Bedaux publication, the
Bedaux system had been used in twenty-one countries with
nearly 100 applications in Britain and over 230 in the United States

TABLE 7.1

Breakdown of International Bedaux Offices, 1918–1931

| Year | Number of Engineers | Plants Using Bedaux | Plants under Application | Total Plants |
|------|---------------------|---------------------|-------------------------|--------------|
| 1918 | 2 | 1 | 2 | 3 |
| 1925 | 19 | 70 | 15 | 85 |
| 1926 | 41 | 110 | 35 | 145 |
| 1928 | 94 | 161 | 72 | 233 |
| 1929 | 114 | 278 | 68 | 346 |
| 1930 | 176 | 399 | 81 | 480 |
| 1931 | 205 | 509 | 123 | 632 |

Source: *Bedaux Measures Labor*, p. 9.

and Canada.[2] Bedaux's American clients included American Rolling Mill, General Electric, Standard Oil of New Jersey, Dow Chemical, Eastman Kodak, and Swift. Pierre Laloux estimated that by 1937, 500 American firms, 225 British, 144 French, 49 Italian and 39 Dutch firms had bought Bedaux's industrial services.[3] Clearly, the Bedaux system commanded an international reputation during the 1930s that remained unchallenged by any other post-Taylorite system then available. Furthermore, by 1945 the British Bedaux Company had perfected a system of work measurement and labor management by which other similar systems were often judged.[4]

British managers became a particularly receptive audience to the Bedaux system during the late 1920s.[5] Despite the highly publicized criticism of Taylor and Gilbreth in British engineering and technical journals, many British employers were nonetheless attracted to scientific management because of its promise of increased labor productivity without great investments in plant or machinery. Two diverse groups provide a rough measure of this potential. First were the personal efficiency experts such as Herbert Norris Casson, Edward Purinton, and T. S. Knowlson, who offered diluted yet passionate forms of scientific management in the guise of short, readable pamphlets and how-to manuals. These manuals carried such titles as *How to be Healthy in Business* (1911), *How to Become Efficient: An Introductory Study of First Principles* (1914), and *Increasing Your Mental Efficiency* (1915). Regardless of how sophomoric or jejune these manuals may seem, the experts in efficiency helped sell the principles of scientific management to British managers.

Second, throughout the 1920s and 1930s, British industrial psychologists urged works managers and employers to experiment with workshop reorganization. New methods of reorganization took the form of job grading and analysis, time and motion study, vocational guidance and selection, and wage incentive schemes, the most popular and widely adopted being the premium bonus system.[6] These methods were freely borrowed from the generation of British mechanical engineers who were influenced by Taylorian "science." Led by Charles S. Myers, founder of the influential National Institute of Industrial Psychology, the industrial psychologists professed to be critics of Taylor and Gilbreth and the engineers' approach to work.[7] Yet by the 1920s, the psychologists' work came to signify nearly the same thing. Their language and techniques differed but their aims were quite close. The fact that the scientific manager aimed at "maximum" production and the industrial psychologist at "optimum" production ought not to obscure the significance of either of these two movements. The more the industrial psychologist tried to distance himself from Taylorism, the closer he came to embracing similar ideals. As paid consultants in industry, industrial psychologists helped to highlight the entrepreneurial quality of the scientific management movement as a whole.[8]

In such an atmosphere, Bedaux's system of labor management and work measurement became the most widely utilized system of scientific management in Britain.[9] By 1945, more than 500 British firms had used the Bedaux System, including such industry giants as Joseph Lucas, Pilkingtons, Joseph Lyons, Ferranti, and Imperial Chemical Industries. Extensive applications were made in the chemical and allied trades, food processing, motor vehicle components (although not motor vehicles), textiles, and mechanical engineering. The appearance and success of the system, despite frequent managerial indifference and labor hostility, has led more than one historian to remark that the history of scientific management in interwar Britain is largely the history of Bedaux.[10]

## Early Training

The Bedaux system was grounded in Taylor's scientific principles of work and management and in Harrington Emerson's twelve principles of "ethical" efficiency. This combination situates Bedaux well within the ranks of the American Taylorites. But what Bedaux added to the movement was his ability, unmatched by his contemporaries, to market and sell scientific management. As one of Bedaux's former British employers once remarked, Charles Bedaux was "the world's first true entrepreneur in scientific management."[11] Bedaux's first biographer, Janet Flanner, put it this way in 1945:

> His genius was his promoter's faculty for making men want to believe what he said. He had a demagogic gift for convincing hardheaded businessmen that they were public benefactors, as he essentially believed he was himself. When some millionaire Scrooge in Chicago would frankly say that he was interested only in profits, Bedaux would tell him that he, the poor millionaire, was really interested in bettering man's conditions, in bettering himself, his community, his little Illinois world. The triple miracle of making the Scrooge believe this, buy the Bedaux system, and actually start bettering something besides his bank account was an accomplishment Bedaux pulled off so often that he dazed and even silenced his most critical employees.[12]

While personal efficiency experts and industrial psychologists struggled to impress and win over the sometimes obstinate employer with simple advice and scientific research, Bedaux was much more direct in his approach. Only practical and immediate results in terms of increased profits would impress the average executive. Bedaux promised and in most cases delivered lower unit costs, increased output, and greater efficiency.

Charles Eugene Bedaux was born at Charenton-le-Pont, Department of the Seine, on October 10, 1886.[13] For the first sixteen years of his life Bedaux led a rather precarious existence on the streets of Paris, doing odd jobs and usually avoiding school. The details of his formal education are unclear and there is no record of his having received a regular degree. The young Bedaux found work in a bookstore and in a quarry, where his biographer, Jim Christy, says he first began to analyze motions and various work procedures.[14] Early in 1906, the twenty-year-old Charles Bedaux left France and emigrated to the United States where he found work as a dishwasher, sandhog with the crews building the Hudson River tunnels, and insurance salesman. He also worked a short stint at the New Jersey Worsted Mills in Hoboken. It seems unlikely that such a meager training would have prepared Bedaux for a successful career as an industrial engineer, but between 1909 and 1916 Bedaux conceived and perfected his own system of scientific management.

In 1909, Bedaux found employment in the clerical department of the Mallinckrodt Chemical Company of St. Louis. He noted that inefficient production was due to a lack of common sense on the part of management. An efficiency engineer was secured to do time studies. Bedaux studied the work of the efficiency expert and concluded that the expert had accomplished very little. Bedaux brought his findings to the attention of management and was himself promoted to efficiency expert.[15] The following year, Bedaux was introduced to Wilfred Sellers, who was then President of the Sellers Kitchen Cabinet Company of Ellwood, Indiana. The Sellers organization was proud to have devised a new approach to the "traditional kitchen" and stressed greater efficiency by the better arrangement of tabletops and appliances.[16] Sellers and Bedaux became close friends, and Sellers told a number of his friends in the Grand Rapids area about Bedaux. It was at this time that Bedaux began to conceive his system while engaged as an individual consultant for several furniture companies.[17]

After a brief trip to Paris in 1912, Bedaux returned to the United States as consultant for the McKesson & Robbins Company of New York. It was at McKesson & Robbins the following years that Bedaux was introduced to A. M. Morrini, an Italian industrial engineer who came to the United States to investigate scientific management. Morrini left for France with three Emerson engineers and Bedaux was secured as an interpreter for the group.[18] After his contract with Morrini ended, Bedaux worked with L. B. Duez, advising furniture factories in Paris, and automobile and airplane factories at Agenteuil. It was also at this time, according to Christy, that Bedaux read Taylor, Emerson, and other scientific management writers.[19] Bedaux supposedly developed his own system at a direct reaction to Taylor's work. He rejected Taylor's approach to "Schmidt" and proposed that a more equitable method of measuring labor could be developed.[20] The result was the Bedaux work unit, or *B*, which will be discussed in the next section.

By 1914, Bedaux was confident that he could compete successfully with the leading consultants. With the outbreak of war he served briefly in the Foreign Legion, then returned to the United States where he worked as Morrini's assistant at the Wolverine Brass Company of Grand Rapids. Bedaux broke his contract with Morrini and with financial backing from a sales executive, Frederick Brearly, formed the Charles E. Bedaux Company of Cleveland.

A training manual that he published shortly thereafter, *The Bedaux Efficiency Course for Industrial Application*, reflects his debts to Taylor and Emerson.[21] For Bedaux, efficiency was the science that teaches the best way to produce the maximum result with minimum effort; it is logic, common sense, and the concentration of effort. "Efficiency applied to industry, scientific management," Bedaux wrote, "is not an occult science but it is, on the contrary, an elementary, organized, classified knowledge within the reach of all."[22] Bedaux realized that efficiency was something new and vital. "Is efficiency a new science?" he asked. "When was it born and why was it born? Why do we see the word written and spoken everywhere, while a decade ago, although in the dictionary, it was practically unknown to humanity? What is efficiency?"[23] In a series of object lessons, admonitions, and case studies, Bedaux diagnosed modern industry and offered his solution to the world.[24]

## The Bedaux System

The Bedaux system was a labor management control system founded on the premise that all human labor could be measured in terms of definite units of effort and fatigue. Bedaux claimed to have solved the problem that plagued the Taylorites, namely the precise, scientific relationship between effort and fatigue. Bedaux identified a unit of work, which he called the *B* and defined as "a fraction of a minute of work plus a fraction of a minute of rest, always aggregating unity, but varying in proportions according to the nature of the strain."[25] Of course, the discovery that an hour of work contained sixty units of effort combined with rest should hardly surprise us, but with this revelation Bedaux believed he had stumbled upon a fundamental law in the science of work. This law he proudly called the "principle of human power measurement."

Bedaux used time and motion study, which he called "work study," to produce an elaborate chart of effort and relaxation values.[26] All tasks were assigned a specific $B$ rating, and from this rating the Bedaux engineer could determine the proper rate of remuneration according to the skill, experience, and responsibility required of a specific job. The average worker, working under average conditions, with a sufficient supply of raw materials and with machinery in good repair should have been able to reach an output of 60$Bs$ per hour (Normal Performance Level). However, the Bedaux engineers regarded a standard of 80$Bs$ (Standard Performance Level) as being entirely possible, especially where labor, process, and management were 100 percent efficient. According to J. A. Edwards, Bedaux engineer at the short-lived application at J. R. Freeman & Son,

> The attainment of an 80 unit hour is rendered possible not by an increase in the operator's speed of working, but by the removal of certain unnecessary elements in the operation, by better arrangement of working materials, by adequate servicing, and by the analysis and elimination of the cause of lost time.[27]

Bedaux himself reasoned that "less than 80$Bs$ a hour" indicated the "incomplete use of labor and incomplete realization of maximum earning power."[28] The bonus for each premium $B$ was one-sixtieth of the base rate of wages, and Bedaux recommended that 75 percent of the bonus be paid to the worker and the remaining 25 percent to supervisors and indirect workers whose labor facilitated production in excess of the 60$B$ standard.[29]

The determination of wages under Bedaux's system was a complicated affair, which often confused workers as much as it did works managers. The Bedaux organization was aware of this tendency, and in the late 1920s and early 1930s produced short handbooks designed to explain the calculation of wages.[30] Its distinctive jargon aside, the Bedaux method closely resembled L. H. Gantt's "task and bonus" system. It was based on preliminary improvements in plant organization and working conditions (though not the comprehensive reorganization that Taylor favored), the use of time studies to establish standards, and a guaranteed base rate regardless of output.[31] Individual performance was measured through the aggregate number of Bs produced. At the end of each shift, the worker's total number of Bs were tallied, and posted the following day. The Daily Posting Sheet showed the hours worked and the B or "point hour" attained. Daily premium wages were also posted so the worker could check his performance and determine his wages. Wages were paid in two envelopes, one containing base wages, the other containing the premium earned. In this way, "an atmosphere of prosperity is . . . produced that twice the amount given in the same envelope in the form of a raise would not create."[32] In addition, each department head received a consolidated Weekly Analysis Sheet showing the performance of all operators and the average point hour attained for specific departments (see table 7.2). The "Reference B Hour" refers to the B rating before the Bedaux system was installed. In nearly every case, the Reference B hours were surprisingly low.

Such were the fundamentals of the Bedaux system. Bedaux engineers would enter the factory and over a period of three or four weeks conduct countless work studies in order to measure current efficiency and show how and where inefficiencies could be rectified by the more rational organization of machines and labor. Every evening the engineer had to prepare a detailed report outlining the progress of his work, which he submitted to management the following day. He also sent copies of his reports, with recommendations, to London where they were carefully reviewed by Bedaux's Technical Department.[33] The reports pointed out to management the amount of savings that could be expected over any projected period of time. This was part and parcel of Bedaux's sales pitch: the only way the engineers could overcome employer obstinacy and hesitancy was to confront them with immediate profits. If the Bedaux Archives reveal anything, it is that works managers and employers were literally bombarded by statistical evidence that their factories could be run much more efficiently.

Bedaux engineers reorganized machines, adjusted feeds and speeds, constructed new conveyor systems, and in many cases urged employers to invest in new and sometimes costly machinery. For instance, during a ten-month application at Cooper's & Co., a Glasgow manufacturer of biscuits, Bedaux fees were

TABLE 7.2

Sample Bedaux Weekly Analysis Sheet (1929)

| Operation | Reference B Hour | Daily B Hours | | | | | | Average |
|---|---|---|---|---|---|---|---|---|
| | | T | F | S | M | T | W | |
| packing | 32.9 | 50 | 43 | 58 | 54 | 60 | 66 | 55.2 |
| soldering | 18.7 | 29 | 46 | 54 | 43 | 42 | 46 | 43.3 |
| nailing | 32.0 | 39 | 49 | 53 | 39 | 38 | 54 | 44.3 |
| wire/attach seal | 24.2 | 40 | 40 | 51 | 35 | 36 | 42 | 40.1 |
| nail cases | 15.9 | 19 | 13 | 29 | 13 | 13 | — | 17.4 |
| truck cases | 27.4 | 32 | 30 | 38 | 27 | 28 | 32 | 31.2 |
| weighing | 17.5 | 39 | 35 | 39 | 33 | 38 | 36 | 36.6 |
| cutting hoop | 18.8 | 43 | 43 | 49 | 43 | 43 | 40 | 43.5 |
| strapping | 33.0 | 38 | 40 | 51 | 45 | 57 | 60 | 48.5 |
| nail strapping | 29.9 | 50 | 40 | 53 | 43 | 49 | 60 | 49.1 |
| reverse cases | 11.5 | 32 | 30 | 37 | 31 | 28 | 28 | 31.0 |
| truck to lorries | 17.4 | 31 | 29 | 35 | 31 | 27 | 27 | 24.8 |
| AVERAGE: | 23.2 | 37 | 37 | 46 | 36 | 38 | 45 | 39.8 |

Source: Bedaux Archives, British-American Tobacco Co., Ltd., March 7, 1929, Film 3G.

reckoned to be in excess of £3,000. Upon the recommendation of the Bedaux engineer, a further £12,000 was invested in new machinery. Wage costs also increased by £5,000 per year. The net effect of the application was that, at the end of the period, the firm was losing about £2,000 per year.[34]

The Bedaux organization nevertheless proclaimed that any firm could expect annual savings of up to 35 percent, and in some cases would save even more. Unit costs would decrease by 20 percent and wages would increase by 15 or 20 percent. Management would gain valuable experience and be prepared to reorganize other departments as the need arose.[35] Laborers would come to expect the increased earnings promised by the Bedaux engineers and gladly better their performance. "The main point to be mastered," as Bedaux himself once wrote, "should be the placing of labor in a frame of mind such that everyone grows to believe the efficiency man wishes nothing but good to the worker."[36]

The whole process of Bedaux applications was, at least when compared with other systems, extremely rapid. From 1926, the year that Bedaux opened his London office, until 1948, more than 46 percent of a total of 606 British applications were completed in twelve months or less.[37]

## Bedaux in Britain, 1926–1945

The response to the introduction of the Bedaux system in Britain by labor and management was both varied and outspoken. While the British Bedaux company continued to attract a lengthy list of clients throughout the 1930s and 1940s, both managers and workers frequently expressed their hostility toward the system. Numerous works managers and foremen saw the Bedaux system as a direct assault upon their authority. They often reacted to the introduction of the system with sabotage, exposing the carefully conducted work studies of the Bedaux engineers as incorrect and unscientific. Workers reacted more sharply and deliberately. Work stoppages and strikes against the introduction of the system were numerous during the 1930s. Between 1929 and 1939, thirty-six work stoppages and strikes against the Bedaux system were reported to the Chief Conciliation Office of the Ministry of Labour. Strikes were most frequent in the chemical and allied trades, engineering, and the textile industry. In twenty-eight strikes for which reliable information is available, the average duration was twenty days. Twelve strikes lasted between thirty and sixty days, and strikes at Boulton & Paul (1931) and Richard Johnson & Nephew (1934) persisted for more than four months.[38] While the majority of these strikes were precipitated by Bedaux time studies, agitation by Communists also added to the overall hostility exhibited by the British worker toward Bedaux. The Trades Union Congress (TUC) and General Federation of Trade Unions (GFTU) issued independent reports on Bedaux and resolved that their members fight the system to a standstill.[39] Where Bedaux could not be defeated, the TUC recommended that their members work to modify the system. Yet despite such suspicions and fears, Bedaux continued to attract even more clients as the years passed.

By 1948, the Bedaux system was well known in British industrial management circles and had been installed in more than six hundred firms with varying degrees of success. As table 7.3 indicates, by the 1930s an average of twenty-five new clients were being added every year. Nearly half of the applications before 1939 were in food processing, chemical and allied trades, and textiles, but after the outbreak of World War II, metal manufacture, mechanical engineering, and textiles made up about 60 percent of Bedaux's business in Britain (see table 7.4). These figures call for further comment. First, it was rare that an entire plant was totally reorganized by Bedaux engineers. Second, there are a few instances in which applications were not conducted by Bedaux engineers. Instead, works managers learned of the system through their contact with other managers and applied what they thought was the Bedaux system. In such cases the system usually ran aground because the firm's engineers were not trained in Bedaux methods. In the hands of "foolish or avaricious employers," such a development helped Bedaux earn an even poorer reputation among British workers.[40]

British workers argued that the Bedaux system was antisocial and contrary to the principles of trade unionism. Percy Glading, a prominent leader of the London engineering workers, bitterly complained that the Bedaux system "has succeeded in increasing production in various industries where other well-known systems of payment by results, bonus systems, straight piecework systems, and similar swindles have been less successful."[41] Horace Moulden wrote of Bedaux that "this system . . . promises to become a great factor in the path of trade unionism."[42] "That hellish system," and "absolutely ridiculous" were phrases used by British workers in the 1930s to describe the system. Even the name "Bedaux" came to symbolize an attempt on the part of management to increase the speed of production and cut established rates. For this reason, the British Bedaux office soon cautioned its engineers not to use the name of Bedaux while on assignment. When William Smyth, a Bedaux engineer, was assigned to Joseph Lucas in 1938, he was requested "not to mention the name Bedaux at any time at . . . [the] Works. This is a matter of policy we have determined from a point of view of labour relations and is most important."[43] By the late 1930s, Bedaux terminology was also altered to quiet opposition. The Bedaux Office became the Bonus and Control Office, Premium Hours became Bonus Hours and the B Hour was simply referred to as Performance. Finally, the great symbol of the system, the B, was replaced by less obnoxious terms such as the Allowed Minute (AM) or Point (P).[44]

TABLE 7.3

Number of British Firms Using the Bedaux System
by Year, 1926–1948

| | | | | | | | |
|------|----|------|----|------|----|------|----|
| 1926 | 3 | 1932 | 29 | 1938 | 22 | 1944 | 20 |
| 1927 | 4 | 1933 | 15 | 1939 | 24 | 1945 | 31 |
| 1928 | 5 | 1934 | 27 | 1940 | 23 | 1946 | 33 |
| 1929 | 9 | 1935 | 16 | 1941 | 18 | 1947 | 44 |
| 1930 | 13 | 1936 | 11 | 1942 | 26 | 1948 | 31 |
| 1931 | 30 | 1937 | 22 | 1943 | 21 | | |

Source: Bedaux Archives, Organization Charts, Films OC 1–6.

TABLE 7.4

Distribution of the Bedaux System in Britain by
Industrial Sector, 1926–1949

| | Number of Firms Using Bedaux | |
|------|------|------|
| **Trade Group** | **1926–1939** | **1939–1949** |
| Food, Drink and Tobacco | 22 | 13 |
| Chemical and Allied Trades | 26 | 28 |
| Coal and Petroleum | 3 | 2 |
| Metal Manufacture | 18 | 42 |
| Mechanical Engineering | 10 | 57 |
| Electrical Engineering | 9 | 6 |
| Motor Vehicle Components | 8 | 1 |
| Textiles | 36 | 115 |
| Services/Distribution | 11 | 58 |
| Other | 35 | 66 |
| TOTAL | 178 | 388 |

Source: Bedaux Archives, Organization Charts, Films OC 1–6.

Nevertheless, by the 1940s, Bedaux's work study techniques had become the standard by which other systems were measured. The British Bedaux office trained numerous work study engineers, many of whom either went on to open their own management consultancies or who created work study departments within specific firms. For instance, former Bedaux engineer Leslie Orr left the British office in 1932 and joined British scientific management devotee Lyndall Urwick to form Urwick, Orr & Partners.[45] Two years later, R. Bryson and W. H. Craven left Bedaux and together established the P. E. Group, and in 1943 E. E. Butten left Bedaux and set up Personnel Administration Ltd. Americans Frank Mead and Colwell Carney left the British office in 1938 and returned to the United States. After World War II they were both back in Britain and together established Mead, Carney & Partners, a management consultancy specializing in work measurement techniques.[46] Bedaux engineers often remained at individual factories where they created their own work study departments, such as at Imperial Chemical Industries. By the late 1930s, similar developments were under way at Pilkingtons, Kodak, and Joseph Lucas. According to William Smyth, "in the field of work measurement, and particularly, of time study, present day practice probably owes more to Bedaux than to Taylor."[47]

## Conclusion

The career of Charles E. Bedaux underlines the possibility of "a brilliant campaign of salesmanship" in an industrial world sensitized to the possibilities of rationalized production.[48] Bedaux had no original ideas or special insights into industrial management; he offered no more than had a score of competitors in the 1920s and 1930s. By the standards of Taylor, his immediate followers, and his intellectual heirs in the Taylor Society, Bedaux was little more than a quack or charlatan. Yet by the 1930s he had become a leading practitioner of scientific management on both sides of the Atlantic. Indeed, Bedaux's international reputation probably surpassed that of Taylor, Gilbreth, and their most orthodox disciples. Bedaux succeeded because his clients had already been educated to the potential of scientific management and because his approach was simple, logical, direct, and, from the executive's perspective, highly appealing. Unlike Taylor, Gilbreth, and others, he did not demand new investment, radical changes in management systems, or a long transitional period; a "mental revolution," if it occurred at all, was an incidental feature of a Bedaux reorganization. Bedaux nevertheless promised increased output and lower unit costs, largely at the expense of the workers' mental and physical health. His efforts boldly emphasized the narrow line between the highminded theorists, who offered workers a better life via planning, system, and order, and less exalted efficiency engineers who offered marginally higher wages for substantially greater effort.

Was the British experience typical? Until more is known about the activities of Bedaux's American, French, Italian, German, and other European and global agents, it is impossible to be certain. British employers on average devoted more attention to labor costs and the possibilities of reducing those costs. The meager record that survives suggests that American managers of the interwar years were receptive to simple, nondogmatic appeals and were cognizant of the possibilities of the Bedaux system. Certainly there is no evidence that Bedaux suffered in the competition for their attention. The handful of references that have come to light suggest that Bedaux's approach was similar everywhere and that American managers and workers who were employed by firms that hired Bedaux had many of the same complaints as their British compatriots. In America as well as in Britain, the Bedaux Company insured that the controversies that had marked the early years of the scientific management movement did not disappear altogether.

NOTES

1. For biographical details of Charles Bedaux, see Janet Flanner, "Annals of Collaboration: Equivalism," *The New Yorker* (September 22, October 6 and 13, 1945), pp. 28–41, 32–43, 32–47; Jim Christy, *The Price of Power: A Biography of Charles Eugene Bedaux* (Toronto, 1984); Steven Kreis, "The Diffusion of an Idea: A History of Scientific Management in Britain, 1890–1945," (Ph.D. diss., University of Missouri—Columbia, 1990), chaps. 5 and 6.

2. For a list of Bedaux's American clients see the unpublished International Bedaux Company's *Representative List of All Bedaux Companies* (New York, 1934). Bedaux's work in the United States has received little attention, but see Jeremy Egolf, "The Limits of Shop Floor Struggle: Workers vs. the Bedaux System at Willipa Harbor Lumber Mills, 1933–35," *Labor History* 26 (Spring 1985), pp. 195–229. David Montgomery refers to Bedaux as a "scientific manager" and "French Taylorite" in his *The Fall of the House of Labor: The Workplace, the State, and American Labor Activism, 1865–1925* (Cambridge, England, 1987), pp. 87, 440. See also John Purcell, *The Worker Speaks His Mind* (Cambridge, 1953), chap. 11; L. C. Morrow, "Application of Bedaux Management Methods in the Robbins & Meyers Plants," *American Machinist* 57 (August 17, 1922), pp. 249–55, 294–98.

3.  Pierre Laloux, *Le Système Bedaux Calcul Des Salaires* (Paris, 1951), p. 11. Similar figures can be found in Spencer Miller, Jr., "Labor's Attitude Toward Time and Motion Study," *Mechanical Engineering* 60 (April 1938), pp. 289–94, 338; and Harlow S. Person, "The Bedaux System," *New Republic* 93 (November 24, 1937), p. 17.

4.  See, for example, Sylvia Shimmin, *Payment By Results: A Psychological Investigation* (London, 1959); and the scattered references to Bedaux in two reports issued by the Dartnell Corporation, *Job Evaluation Methods and Procedures*, Report no. 531 (Chicago, 1945); and *Experience of 117 Companies with Wage Incentive Plans*, Report no. 561 (Chicago, 1948). See also the British Productivity Council reports, *Cutting Costs for Productivity* (London, 1958); and *Work Study in the West* (London, 1958). Bedaux work study is also reviewed in the National Industrial Conference Board's report, *Systems of Wage Payment* (New York, 1930); and the International Labour Office handbook, *Payment By Results* (Geneva, 1951).

5.  The literature on British economic performance in the interwar years is immense, although the role of scientific management in British industry has been neglected. See, for instance, Derek Aldcroft, "The Performance of British Machine-Tools in the Interwar Years," *Business History Review* 40 (Autumn 1966), pp. 281–96; Sidney Pollard, *The Development of the British Economy, 1914–1950* (London, 1962); Peter L. Payne, "Industrial Entepreneurship and Management in Great Britain," in Peter Mathias and M. M. Postan, eds., *The Cambridge Economic History of Europe*, vol. 7, part 1 (Cambridge, England, 1978), pp. 180–230; Jonathan Zeitlin, "The Emergence of Shop Steward Organization and Job Control in the British Car Industry: A Review Essay," *History Workshop* 10 (Autumn 1980), pp. 119–37; William Lazonick, "Industrial Organization and Technological Change: The Decline of the British Cotton Industry," *Business History Review* 57 (Summer 1983), pp. 195–236. Two other works of interest are A. L. Levine, *Industrial Retardation in Britain 1880–1914* (New York, 1967); and Martin J. Weiner, *English Culture and the Decline of the Industrial Spirit, 1850–1980* (Cambridge, England, 1981).

6.  The premium bonus system (PBS) was a payment by results scheme whereby workers were paid a bonus for producing above a standard output. The PBS substituted a time allowance for a piece work price. Initially, output was determined by foremen but by 1900 rate fixers had assumed the responsibility for determining rates. The literature on the PBS in Britain is extensive but see, David F. Schloss, *Methods of Industrial Remuneration* (New York, 1892); G. D. H. Cole, *The Payment of Wages: A Study in Payment By Results Under the Wage System* (London, 1918); J. A. Hobson, *Incentives in the New Industrial Order* (New York, 1925); William Graham, *The Wages of Labour* (London, 1921). For an excellent survey of the PBS in the engineering industry see James B. Jeffreys, *The Story of the Engineers 1800–1945* (London, 1946).

7.  Charles S. Myers, *Mind and Work: The Psychological Factors in Industry and Commerce* (London, 1920), p. 23.

8.  The institutional implications of British industrial psychology and scientific management are explored at length in D. C. Doyle, "Aspects of the Institu-

tionalisation of British Psychology: The National Institute of Industrial Psychology 1921–1939" (Ph.D. diss., University of Manchester, 1979). On American industrial psychology, see the useful but dated work by Loren Baritz, *The Servants of Power: A History of the Use of Social Science in American Industry* (Middletown, CT, 1960).

9. The Bedaux system was not the only scheme of scientific management to have emerged in the interwar period. Numerous systems of wage incentives and workshop reorganization flourished in Britain after the 1890s: some developed out of the British engineering workshop (eg. the Weir, Rowan, Mavor and Priestman-Atkinson systems), while others had been imported from the United States. This influx of systems and their subtle modifications was as much a product of the British engineering workshop experience as it was a transatlantic dialogue between engineers and works managers.

10. Craig Littler, *The Development of the Labour Process in Capitalist Societies: A Comparative Study of the Transformation of Work in Britain, Japan and the U.S.A.* (London, 1982), p. 108; P. Livingstone, "Stop the Stopwatch," *New Society* (July 10, 1969), p. 49.

11. Mildred Brownlow to the author, January 17, 1987. Brownlow worked in the Technical Information Department and Library at Bedaux's London office from 1926 to 1972. I am indebted to this extraordinary woman for supplying me with numerous details of some of the finer points of the system and the company.

12. Flanner, "Annals of Collaboration," (September 22, 1945), p. 30.

13. The biographical details that follow are taken from Christy, *The Price of Power*. See also the unpublished and informal history of the Bedaux companies, "History of the Bedaux Companies and Albert Ramond and Associates, Inc., 1910–1955." This document was kindly sent to me by Elizabeth A. McDonough of Albert Ramond and Associates (Chicago). Albert Ramond was a close friend of Bedaux's and was selected by Bedaux to direct several American offices. By 1938, however, thanks to some personal intrigues between Bedaux's son and Ramond's wife, Ramond led a palace revolt against Bedaux and subsequently took total control of all the American Bedaux companies.

14. Christy, *The Price of Power*, pp. 12–13. Records of the youthful Taylor reveal a similar preoccupation. See in particular, Sudhir Kakar, *Frederick Winslow Taylor: A Study in Personality and Innovation* (Cambridge, MA, 1970).

15. Christy, *The Price of Power*, pp. 23–25.

16. See the lengthy section on mechanization and the twentieth-century household in Siegfried Gideon's seminal essay, *Mechanization takes Command: A Contribution to Anonymous History* (New York, 1948), pp. 512–606.

17. The account of Bedaux's friendship with Sellers is related in "History of the Bedaux Companies," p. 1. Christy does not mention this episode in his biography.

18. Charles Lytle, *Wage Incentive Methods: Their Selection, Installation and Operation* (New York, 1942), p. 224n. See also Christy, *The Price of Power*, pp. 27–28.

19. Christy, *The Price of Power*, p. 28.

20. See Charles D. Wrege and Amedeo G. Perroni, "Taylor's Pig Tale: A Historical Analysis of Frederick W. Taylor's Pig-Iron Experiments," *Academy of Management Journal* 17 (March 1974), pp. 6–27. See also Reginald Marriott, *Incentive Payment Systems: A Review of Research and Opinion* (London, 1957), p. 338.

21. *The Bedaux Efficiency Course* was initially published by the Bedaux Industrial Institute in 1917, and a revised edition with the cover title "Industrial Management" appeared in 1921. The manual was used extensively in Britain and the United States throughout the 1920s, and was then replaced by the following manuals: *Code of Standard Practice* (1928), *Code of Application Principles* (1930), *Training Course for Field Engineers* (1930), and *Standard Bedaux, Weekly Analysis Sheet: Notes on Use* (1933).

22. Bedaux, *The Bedaux Efficiency Course*, p. 12. This is the only direct reference Bedaux made to scientific management. Elsewhere he discusses a "scientific form of management" (p. 70) and the "science of efficiency" (p. 108).

23. Bedaux, *The Bedaux Efficiency Course*, p. 2.

24. The discussion that follows is based on a detailed analysis of the Bedaux Archives. The archives are located at the Business Office of INBUCON Management Consultants Ltd., near Haywards Heath, West Sussex, Great Britain. The files consist of several thousand reports documenting Bedaux's work with British clients from 1926 to the present. Although extremely repetitive, this extensive collection provides a complete picture of the daily operation of the Bedaux system from the standpoint of the Bedaux engineers. Craig Littler was the only other scholar to have used these records, although he failed to cite their location in his published works. I am indebted to D. M. Wilford and Sandra Silke of the London Office and Sheila Fernee at Haywards Heath for granting me permission to use this important collection. None of my research would have been at all possible had it not been for Howard Gospel of the Business History Unit of Economics, for helping me to discover the location of the Bedaux Archives.

25. Charles E. Bedaux, *Bedaux Measures Labour* (London, 1928), p. 3. See also L. C. Morrow, "The Bedaux Principle of Human Power Measurement," *American Machinist* 56 (February 16, 1922), pp. 241–45.

26. All efforts to locate this chart have been fruitless. I have contacted former Bedaux engineers, management consultants, and management historians in both Britain and the United States regarding this chart and none have any recollection of its existence. We can only surmise that this curious chart was the product of Bedaux's own observations rather than "scientific objectivity." British trade unionists and other critics of Bedaux were always quick to point to this singular failure of the system as a whole. It is perhaps possible that this chart was a clever bit of salesmanship on the part of Bedaux. Regardless, the discovery of this chart would reveal a great deal about Bedaux's claim to have produced a science of work.

27. Bedaux Archives, J. R. Freeman & Son, September 22, 1934, Film 19D.

28. Bedaux, *Bedaux Measures Labour*, p. 5.

29. By the late 1930s, the 75 percent bonus for direct workers was changed to 100 percent owing to increased trade union demands made upon manage-

ment. In the United States, this important modification took place some-what later, in the 1950s. See Purcell, *The Worker Speaks His Mind*, p. 237.

30. See, for instance, Hoffman Manufacturing, *The Bedaux Method of Wage Payment* (1928); Hayes Cocoa, *The Bedaux Method* (1931); Venesta, *The Bedaux System* (1932).

31. See F. A. Halsey, "The Premium Plan of Paying for Labor," *Transactions: American Society of Mechanical Engineers* 22 (1891). See also William B. Cornell, ed., *Organization and Management in Industry and Business* (New York, 1928), pp. 274–88; and NICB, *Systems of Wage Payment*, pp. 55–64.

32. Bedaux, *The Bedaux Efficiency Course*, p. 292.

33. These daily reports were extremely detailed and were about ten pages in length. The London office became so swamped by this mass of statistical and technical data that by the late 1930s it urged engineers to submit one or two reports per week. By the early 1940s, the reports were filed once or twice per month.

34. Report of J. B. Galbraith, Glasgow Chief Conciliation Officer, Ministry of Labour, October 3, 1935, Public Record Office, Ministry of Labour, Industrial Relations Department, LAB 2 2061/1, Ref. IR(G) 105/1/1934. See also Bedaux Archives, Cooper & Co, Film 19C.

35. Integral to the smooth operation of the Bedaux system was the selection of several workers to serve as time study trainees. This was necessary so that Bedaux's work could be continued after the assignment was terminated. One key to the system was maintenance, and the time study practitioners served just such a purpose. They also acted as liaison between the Bedaux engineer, fellow workers, and management.

36. Bedaux, *The Bedaux Efficiency Course*, pp. 186, 188.

37. Bedaux Archives, Organization Charts, Films OC 1–6. Applications that lasted more than five years represented almost 24 percent of the total number of firms where the Bedaux system was installed.

38. The dispute at Richard Johnson & Nephew between 1932 and 1934 is well documented. On the dispute, see "Bedaux Dispute at Richard Johson & Nephew, 1932–1934," a file located at the Working Class Movement Library in Old Trafford, Manchester. See also Mick Jenkins, "Time and Motion Strike—Manchester 1934–7: The Wiredrawers' Strike Against the Bedaux System at Richard Johnson's," *Our History* 60 (Autumn 1974), pp. 3–34; Littler, *Development of the Labour Process*, pp. 128–40. Unfortunately, there are no records of the Bedaux applications at Richard Johnson in the Bedaux Archives because the film on which they are located (Film 16) is now missing.

39. See Trades Union Congress, *The TUC Examines the Bedaux System of Payment By Results* (London, 1933); General Federation of Trade Unions, *Report on the Bedaux and Kindred Systems* (London, 1932).

40. See GFTU, *Report on the Bedaux and Kindred Systems*, p. 2.

41. Percy Glading, *How Bedaux Works*, Labour White Paper, no. 45 (London, 1934), p. 4.

42. Horace Moulden, "Interim Report on the 'Bedaux System of Labour Measurement,'" March 2, 1931, Public Record Office, Ministry of Labour,

Industrial Relations Department, LAB 2, File 2060/5, Ref. IR(Bi) 73/1. Moulden was Secretary of the Leicester Amalgamated Hosiery Workers' Union and key figure in the lengthy strike by Wolsey workers against Bedaux in 1931. See also Littler, *Development of the Labour Process*, pp. 118–28.

43. Norman Pleming to William Smyth, April 6, 1938. This letter was kindly sent to me by Willie Smyth.

44. Bedaux Archives, Linoleum Manufacturing Co., June 19, 1948, Film 26D.

45. See the short prospectus prepared by Urwick, "Profit on Principle: A British Service for British Business in the Application of the Principles of Direction and Control," (London, 1934). Urwick mentions Taylor, Emerson, Gilbreth, Gantt, and Fayol, but Bedaux's name is curiously absent.

46. Mead and Carney were originally sent by Bedaux to Britain to open the London office in 1926. Both men had trained under Bedaux at several firms in the Rochester, New York area. Their earliest assignments in Britain were at the Wealdstone plant of Kodak and at Goodrich Rubber.

47. William A. Smyth, "Bedaux—The Man and His Work," *Work Study* (October 1966), p. 7.

48. Edwin T. Layton, Jr., "The Diffusion of Scientific Management and Mass Production From the U.S. in the Twentieth Century," *Proceedings of the XIVth International Congress in the History of Science* 4 (Tokyo, 1974), p. 383.

JOHN C. RUMM

# 8 Scientific Management and Industrial Engineering at Du Pont

Frederick W. Taylor's death did not signal the passing of scientific management. On the contrary, in the years after 1915, the techniques of scientific management were applied as part of a broad effort to rationalize production and enhance managerial control over the workplace. A new figure in American industry — the industrial engineer — played a key role in this continuing effort to apply scientific management. Industrial engineers utilized techniques derived from scientific management to reduce information about production to a set of standard data that managers could use for more effective labor control. They sought to develop for management "scientific facts [that could] be used to reach a reasonable solution" to the question of "what should be considered a 'fair day's work.'"[1] In doing so, they hoped to effect what Taylor termed "the substitution of exact scientific investigation and knowledge for the old individual judgment or opinion, either of the workman or the boss, in all matters relating to the work done in the establishment."[2]

This essay reviews the application of scientific management at a leading American firm, E. I. du Pont de Nemours & Company,

This essay is a revised version of a paper presented at the annual meeting of the Society for the History of Technology in Wilmington, Delaware, in October 1988. The author wishes to acknowledge the comments of Edwin T. Layton, Jr., Steve Kreis, and Daniel Nelson on that paper; Marjorie McNinch, of the Hagley Museum and Library, for her assistance in locating Du Pont Company records; and Lyn Stallings and Brian Greenberg for their continuing support.

during the first half of the twentieth century. Until the late 1920s
and early 1930s, efforts to apply techniques of scientific management within the company were limited, largely because managers
did not give their full support. As they struggled to reduce labor
costs in the wake of the Great Depression, however, company
managers increasingly turned to Du Pont's industrial engineering
force for assistance in implementing techniques intended not only
to increase efficiency, but also to enhance managerial control over
the work force. By the 1950s, industrial engineers had succeeded
in Taylorizing the workplace at Du Pont.

## Early Efforts to Apply Scientific Management
## at Du Pont

Du Pont has long been regarded as a paragon of modern
managerial and organizational techniques. The executives who
reorganized the company at the turn of the century, including
Pierre and Coleman du Pont, Arthur J. Moxham, J. Amory
Haskell, and Hamilton M. Barksdale, introduced improved administrative methods, new accounting techniques, and systematic internal communication procedures. The result, as Alfred D.
Chandler, Jr. stated, was that by World War I "few American
industrial enterprises had as modern a management as Du Pont."[3]
Yet these reforms affected the administration of the enterprise as a
whole; they had relatively little impact upon factory management.
For the most part, labor at Du Pont's fifty-odd plants was still
managed under the paternalistic practices developed during the
first century of the firm's existence.[4]

Only in Du Pont's High Explosives Operating Department
(HEOD) was much consideration given to reforming factory
management. Senior managers emphasized the need to reduce
labor costs, improve methods, and find the most effective way of
performing tasks.[5] The department held regular superintendents'
meetings to discuss improvements and set up special commissions
to develop and adopt new machinery and processes. In the spring
of 1911, these efforts received new impetus with the formation of
an "Efficiency Division."[6] The decision to organize it reflected
the vogue for "efficiency" that followed the publication of Frederick W. Taylor's *The Principles of Scientific Management*. Hamilton
M. Barksdale, until recently director of HEOD and now the

company's general manager, read Taylor's book and decided that an effort should be made to apply scientific management at Du Pont.[7] As Harry G. Haskell, Barksdale's successor at HEOD, reminded superintendents, "to feel satisfied of the men as working *hard* is not sufficient in our days; [you] must know that the men are all working *well*, and that is the gist of the efficiency idea." The Efficiency Division, he stated, would try to determine "by scientific trial" whether employees were indeed working well.[8]

Rather than utilize the services of Taylor or another consultant, the HEOD turned to two of its own staff in the Efficiency Division. Edward Montgomery Harrington, the director, was an MIT graduate (1886) with some twenty years' experience in the explosives industry; his assistant, W. Maxwell Moore, had worked for nearly a decade at Repauno, the HEOD's largest plant.[9] From 1911 to 1914, the two men visited all of the HEOD's dozen plants, conducting time and motion studies of workers. They determined standard times and methods for tasks, set standard speeds for machinery, and made suggestions for rearranging the flow of work, improving tools, and installing labor-saving equipment.[10]

The Efficiency Division's efforts were hampered, however, by several problems. Not the least was a lack of clear support for, or understanding of, its work. Its findings remained strictly advisory; plants were not required to adopt its recommendations. Harrington sought to expand the work of the division to include studies of fatigue, the scientific selection of workers, and employment departments, but these studies were referred to other divisions or were not approved.[11] Some HEOD officials and plant superintendents were skeptical of its efforts or showed little understanding of scientific management. Neither of the company's other manufacturing departments—Black Powder and Smokeless Powder—established efficiency divisions, and officials in these departments took only passing interest in the work of the HEOD's. Apart from Hamilton Barksdale and his assistant, Irénée du Pont, both of whom received the division's reports and attended HEOD meetings at which its work was discussed, other top company executives apparently paid little attention to its activities.[12]

Another problem related to the hazardous nature of explosives manufacturing: the threat of an explosion prohibited the use of incentives that might encourage workers to speed up their production. This imperative conflicted with a key tenet of Taylorism and other efficiency systems—that workers should earn a bonus for completing a task in or before a standard length of time. As Harrington stated, it was difficult "to make employees see where they are to gain by changing methods of operation which may give increased production [but] with no monetary gain to themselves." The division never resolved the conflict.[13]

The Efficiency Division also faced challenges over its approach. Harrington warned against expecting quick results, arguing that only prolonged studies of work would lead to increased efficiency.[14] Senior officials and superintendents, however, sought immediate gains in efficiency and measurable reductions in labor costs. As one superintendent bluntly stated, "the Efficiency Division would have to show a saving in dollars and cents or there would be no reason for [its] existence."[15] In 1913, Harrington estimated that the division had produced savings amounting to $6,500 during 1912; he also admitted, however, that it had found "comparatively little for which [it had] recommended remedies."[16] The division's failure to produce more significant results disappointed senior officials, who expected a greater return on their investment. Hamilton Barksdale, for example, warned that if the quest for efficiency was "left to a desultory sort of consideration . . . [it] will not get anywhere." He urged Harrington to make a "clear cut, well defined method of getting at" efficiency, proposing that the division undertake trials of functional foremanship.[17]

In September 1913, Harrington began these tests in a dynamite mixing house at the Repauno Plant. Only a day after "an old hand" was placed in the building as a functional foreman, however, an explosion levelled the house, killing him and three other workers, and injuring six others. Harrington shifted his experiments to another building housing a different process. In December, however, an explosion destroyed another dynamite mixing house, killing and injuring several more workers, causing "a wild scramble among employees," and throwing residents in neighboring communities into a state of panic. As rumors spread that the accidents were the result of "the foremen . . . rushing the men," Harrington and Repauno officials suspended further experiments. Damages to plant property from the two explosions, together with payments made to dependents, exceeded $34,000, or nearly six times the estimated savings for 1912.[18]

Following the disasters at Repauno, the Efficiency Division's operations were scaled back considerably; early in 1915, the HEOD suspended its work entirely.[19] This action temporarily ended further systematic efforts to apply scientific management at Du Pont. The division's experiences, moreover, suggested that future attempts to install scientific management would likely fare poorly unless managers at all levels gave their full support—something this initial effort never received.

During World War I, "efficiency" or "time-study" departments were organized by some of the company's larger smokeless powder plants. At the Haskell Plant in New Jersey, for example, an efficiency section made time and motion studies, set standards for a "fair day's work," and installed labor-saving materials handling equipment. Such efforts, however, should be placed in proper perspective. The resulting improvements were minor; as one plant manager observed, "the labor situation did not warrant the expenditure of the money" required for full-scale efforts to improve efficiency. Interest in efficiency emerged only at a late point in the war effort; not before the spring of 1918. Moreover, attention centered upon a small segment of the work force—laborers and construction gangs—rather than on the much larger group of production workers.[20]

Similar limited efforts were made to apply techniques of scientific management during the 1920s at plants operated by Du Pont or by its subsidiaries. "Planning" departments in some plants conducted time and motion studies to analyze jobs and develop standard work crews.[21] Other plants used scientific management techniques to resolve specific labor problems. In 1921, for example, the Du Pont Viscoloid Company (a wholly owned subsidiary that manufactured "pyralin" plastic articles) formed a "Time Study Section" to study the jobs of production workers at its Arlington Plant in New Jersey.[22] The Viscoloid Company's efficiency engineers installed a "task and bonus system," similar to that devised by Henry Gantt, under which workers began earning a bonus on each piece produced when their output attained a certain level (typically 45 percent) of the standard established for their task. By 1927, the system covered nearly all production workers, most of whom earned bonuses.[23] Another subsidiary, the Du Pont Rayon Company, in 1926–1927 adopted a similar plan to reduce turnover among female workers in its Richmond and Buffalo plants. These employees worked at highly repetitive manual tasks; their work was tedious and fatiguing, and annual turnover often exceeded 100 percent. To keep workers from leaving, the levels at which they began earning bonuses were set very low—as little as eight percent of standard. Turnover fell sharply after the system was installed; at Richmond, for example, it dropped to 5 percent by 1930. The earnings of many workers rose markedly as they reached or even exceeded the theoretical maximum 100 percent standard.[24]

These instances should not obscure the fact that interest in applying scientific management techniques at Du Pont during the 1920s was not widespread within the company as a whole. Two particular factors served to reduce interest. One was a preference for other company measures designed to increase efficiency, chiefly the "Merit Pay Plan." Open to all hourly workers employed more than one year, the plan paid a monthly bonus of 5 to 20 percent over their regular pay, based on length of service and attention to factors such as care, quality, and attendance. Officials who promoted Merit Pay argued that it was preferable to other incentives since it not only promised to increase efficiency, but also, thanks to its service provision, to stabilize employment. However, high annual rates of turnover (170 percent in 1923) and an annual cost of $770,000 to administer the plan, convinced senior managers in 1925 to end Merit Pay as a companywide program. Some departments, however, continued their own merit pay plans through the 1940s.[25]

Another factor that lessened interest in scientific management among executives was Du Pont's prosperity during the 1920s. Apart from the years immediately after World War I, the company's business expanded as production shifted from explosives to chemicals and synthetics. Sales rose from $74 million in 1923 to $203 in 1929, fueled by new products such as tetraethyl lead, rayon, and cellophane. This prosperity, along with the need to strengthen Du Pont's position within the chemical industry, led executives to emphasize research and development, diversification, and market expansion more than efficiency.[26]

## The Great Depression and the Rise of Industrial Engineering

The company's rosy earnings picture changed dramatically with the onset of the Great Depression. Du Pont's sales dropped to

$186 million in 1930, and to $118 million by 1932. Hardest hit were the departments and subsidiaries that made acids, fertilizers, paint, coated fabrics, and other chemical products used in the automotive, mining, steel, construction, and agricultural industries. Struggling to maintain profits despite decreased production and falling sales, managers faced two alternatives: raising prices or cutting manufacturing costs. They chose the latter option. Labor, as a major cost item, did not escape the pressure for economy; the need to cut costs heightened interest in measures aimed at improving labor efficiency.[27]

These developments coincided with the emergence of industrial engineering as a separate function at Du Pont. In 1928, an "Industrial Engineering Division" (IED) was formed within Du Pont's Engineering Department to wage what one official termed a "continuous struggle to reduce operating costs."[28] The company's hard fortunes during the depression years of the 1930s gave added impetus to cost-reduction efforts; indeed, Du Pont's Executive Committee advised departmental managers to give full attention to "perfecting the efficiency of their operations, by intensive study of manufacturing processes, elimination of waste, discard of superfluous practices, development of labor-saving devices, substitution of mechanical for manual operations, and other means of reducing costs."[29] The IED quickly moved to the vanguard in coordinating cost-reduction and efficiency work within the company.

The rapid growth of the IED offers a good measure of the interest Du Pont management took in its work. From a staff of twenty-eight engineers in 1928, its ranks swelled to over 200 by 1940, and to some 500 six years later. The IED's engineers specialized in every aspect of production, including chemical processes, materials handling, packaging, waste recovery, water filtration, power conservation, instrumentation, maintenance, lubrication, equipment development, and plant design.[30] Its ranks also included engineers, trained in such techniques of scientific management as time and motion study, wage incentives, and job analysis, whose efforts were directed at making "continuing studies . . . which should result in . . . more effective use of manpower."[31]

The techniques applied by industrial engineers who were concerned with labor efficiency dovetailed with managers' perceived need for "fair standards of productivity to be expected of employees."[32] As one company executive observed, among the responsibilities facing management was that of "making certain that our working force produces a fair day's work for a fair day's pay under good operating conditions."[33] Increasingly, however, managers asserted that the diversified and varied nature of Du Pont's production made it much harder to be sure that workers were performing efficiently. One manager, whose plant turned out over 3,000 separate products, stated that while he once felt confident "that he knew what a day's work was and that his operators were effectively busy," he now believed that "it is impossible for him and his supervisors to know the content of a day's work in a multiproduct unit."[34] Company managers also believed that foremen and lower-level supervisors could not be relied upon to evaluate workers' performance. "The foreman doesn't know what a normal work pace is," one official stated, since "he is expected to be judge and prosecutor at the same time; and he omits part of a job because he doesn't analyze it sufficiently."[35] Another official stated the problem somewhat more pointedly: "The bodies are moving, but how effectively we don't know."[36] This need to determine "how effectively the bodies were moving" led Du Pont managers to devote increased attention to scientific management from the 1930s onward.

## Work Measurement, Incentive Wages, and Labor Standards

Initially, Du Pont's industrial engineers focused upon improving the efficiency of chemical workers in production operations demanding a high degree of manual labor. They assumed that "the science of time and motion study" would "increase [chemical workers'] productive efficiency considerably."[37] Labor costs constituted a lower percentage of overall costs in chemical production than in the manufacture of rubber, automobiles, steel, and other products; however, in the production of many chemicals they remained high. In the "batch" operations, which typified the manufacture of small quantities of paints, dyes, resins, explosives, coated fabrics, and other specialized products, production remained highly labor intensive. Workers hauled and conveyed raw materials and semifinished products during processing; cleaned, repaired, adjusted, and set up equipment; and sorted and inspected finished products. Finishing operations in the production of rayon, plastic, or cellophane articles also demanded considerable manual labor. Continuous-flow automatic (or nearly so) equipment was used for the high-volume processing of acids, ammonia, methanol, and other fluid chemical products. The force of workers needed to operate such equipment was small, but manual labor was still needed to handle ingredients, charge boilers with fuel, maintain equipment, and remove wastes and byproducts.[38]

The application of scientific management techniques at a Du Pont plant began with a preliminary survey of its operations to "indicate the number of men in [each] building and what each one is doing and how they can best be handled to improve their work or become better fitted for it." Based on the survey, industrial engineers consolidated processes, rearranged the layout of work areas, installed materials handling equipment, and trimmed work crews.[39] Engineers then made motion and time studies of workers in specific operations. To analyze motions, they utilized stroboscopic, micromotion, and memo-motion (time-lapse) photography, and the chronocyclegraph, in which flashlight bulbs were fastened to a worker's wrists and long-exposure photographs were taken to create "light patterns" tracing the movements followed in performing a task. While Du Pont engineers relied on the traditional stopwatch to make time studies, they also consulted published tables of predetermined standard time values for basic motion elements. Using such tables, they simply "synthesized" the time values of individual elements to obtain the net time for a task.[40]

The net time, along with any allowances for fatigue or difficult working conditions, established the "standard time" for an operation; a standard or "normal" production level was also defined. Together, they comprised the "job standard," in which, barring unusual conditions, workers were expected to achieve normal levels of production. Engineers also defined a "100 percent effective point," a theoretical maximum limit that only the best workers could achieve. Workers were rated in terms of their efficiency: if the job standard for an operation was 500 pounds in four hours and a worker produced 250 pounds, he or she was rated 50 percent efficient.[41]

The job standards and ratings served as the basis for incentive wages designed to stimulate employees to become "more efficient and better operators." Encouraged by news of the satisfactory results obtained in plants that had installed incentive plans during the 1920s, officials in other Du Pont departments and subsidiaries increasingly became interested in placing their production employees under an incentive wage plan. By 1938, at least thirty plants had installed such plans, covering 9,400, or 27 percent, of the company's 34,000 hourly employees. Coverage ranged from three percent of the work force at some plants, to as much as 90 percent at others.[42]

Du Pont's wage incentive plans took various forms. At least three plants installed the Bedaux Company's system. While generally good results were reported with the Bedaux System, it contained some undesirable features that limited its wider use within the company. Du Pont managers objected to the Bedaux consultants' "insistence on their plan being worked in, even if some of it does not fit," while the sizable expenditure required to install the system — over $200,000 in some cases — dissuaded other plants from applying it.[43] A few plants used a similar though cheaper plan, the "KIM System," named for the three engineers (King, Irvin, and MacLachan) who developed it.[44] Another alternative — and the one most widely pursued at Du Pont — was for industrial engineers to study existing systems, both within and outside the company, and then to borrow liberally from them to create an "in-house" version tailored to the conditions of a particular plant. Ammonia Department officials, for example, sent an industrial engineer to the Dye Works to "skim off as much of the cream as we can" about the Bedaux System, rather than hire Bedaux consultants to install it at its plants.[45]

Though they differed in detail, all of the incentive plans shared a common principle: employees earned "extra wages for extra effort" based upon their ability to meet or exceed the standard established for their job.[46] Typically, an employee began earning a bonus when he or she attained a 75 percent efficiency rating. Loren I. King, the IED's "Wage Incentive Consultant," described how such a plan covered workers who soldered wires at one plant:

> We . . . set a rate for each bunch of wires to be soldered say 15 minutes and set the normal at 20 minutes giving the operators 5 minutes in which to make a bonus. Penalty values are set up just as are bonuses set up. If an employee fails to do his job in the normal time or fails his duty altogether he is penalized.[47]

The amount of the bonus decreased as the worker's output rose above the standard. The advantage, as one observer noted, was that "the required increase in production is greater than the attainable increase in pay, so that the company shares in the gains of a man's increased output and the labor cost per piece declines as the pay goes up."[48]

Initially, most incentive wage applications covered only production workers whose duties required considerable hand work. At some plants, however, engineers devised plans for operators of continuous-flow equipment, whose duties were more "mental," such as taking readings from instruments or adjusting dials that regulated temperature, pressure, and other variables. The plans set standards for accuracy in monitoring instruments and controlling process variables, for conserving power, water, and materials, and for attaining predetermined levels of quality and yield. Such a plan was installed at the Belle Plant in West Virginia, which manufactured ammonia and antifreeze. As the industrial engineer who developed the incentive plan recalled,

> Usually if [an] operator was watching a chart, for example a temperature chart, [a] pressure chart, and so forth, the basic approach would be how accurately, how closely did he control the temperature, which was critical to the operation of course, or the pressure. And some of the operators were far more adept at this than others and it showed up in the performance of the operation.

Operators who met or exceeded the standards received bonuses; those who did not were penalized.[49]

The efforts of industrial engineers to study jobs and to place workers under incentive plans produced mixed reactions among Du Pont employees. Some workers opposed such efforts. A carpenter at the Dye Works, for example, recalled he "told the management plain" that the "B-Doe" would "make a man run on one of these rip saws, buzz saws, Lord knows, maybe he'd cut his damned hand off." Management considered his protests, but "they still installed it and run it for quite a while."[50] Similarly, the former manager of the Belle Plant stated that "the men were suspicious" during time studies, refusing to answer questions about their work.[51] The caption of a cartoon published in one plant's employee magazine, showing a stopwatch and a clipboard, was pointed: identifying time study engineers as "the enemy of all piece workers," it asserted that "they never lie boys."[52]

Workers also complained about job standards and incentive wages. Works Councils (Du Pont's employee representation plan) at several plants asserted that workers "[did] not understand" the incentives and could not "calculate at least approximately their current earnings."[53] Some employees of the Dye Works were "kicking" over the Bedaux System, a foreman reported, because "they are not getting their rate of which they are right," and because the plant penalized them for mistakes by "cutting their rates or taking their Bonus away."[54] The "Employes Mutual Association" (an independent union) at the Ilion Plant of Du Pont's Remington Arms subsidiary wrote Lammot du Pont about "excessively tight" job standards, which forced operators "to work at a speed that not only is detrimental to the safety rules of the plant but also to the health and good will of the employees." Remington officials sent industrial engineers to Ilion to review the standards and resolve the situation.[55]

On the other hand, while employees may not have been wholly pleased by their job standards or incentive plan, many apparently welcomed the opportunity to earn extra money. The Dye Works carpenter who initially opposed the Bedaux System, for example, nevertheless praised management for being "always liberal enough to set a price that'd give you the time to do it" (i.e., to make a bonus). As he recalled, many employees also learned how to turn the system to their own advantage: "[The Company would] put a price on [a job] and maybe two or three fellows would have to work on [it] and . . . naturally they'd talk among themselves and find out what was the best way to do it in which you could make more money." Evidence suggests that many Dye Works employees learned "the best way to do" their jobs to earn more money: by the 1950s, workers covered by the Bedaux System were receiving, on average, $688 per year over their regular base pay.[56] At some locations, employees whose work was not covered under an incentive plan protested such "discrimination," demanding that they be given an opportunity to add to their earnings. The Grasselli Chemicals Department, for example, citing "continued requests for extension of the [Wage Incentive] System to now uncovered operations," reported that it was "being extended as fast as accurate studies and evaluations can be made." Similarly, in response to numerous requests, in 1939 the Dye Works began placing maintenance, craft, shipping, clerical, and laboratory employees under the Bedaux System; by 1955, the plan covered 99 percent of the work force.[57]

If workers were divided over wage incentive plans, so too were company managers. Some managers asserted that incentives were necessary to insure that workers give their full effort to keeping output levels high. Other departments reported that industrial engineers' efforts had produced huge savings and gains in productivity. The Grasselli Chemicals Department, for example, stated that its expenditure of $141,500 on time studies and incentive wages had resulted in savings of nearly $850,000. The Organic Chemicals Department claimed that the Bedaux System had caused productivity to increase nearly 31 percent while labor costs fell from $3.47 to $2.81 per pound.[58]

These sanguine opinions, however, were not held unanimously within the company. By the late 1930s, many departments were cutting back or eliminating their incentive plans due to employee dissatisfaction, soaring labor costs, failure to achieve prior levels of quality and output, and the work of administering the plans. The former manager of the Belle Plant, for example, recalled that its plan "became . . . burdensome to the local financial people, the control people, the payroll [people]." When the decision was made to abandon it, he said, "a lot of [them] sighed a sigh of relief." At the Dye Works, management realized that the full-scale extension of the Bedaux System had backfired: clerks objected to the extra paperwork needed to compute payrolls, supervisors found inflated reports of work done, and labor costs rose so high that German and Japanese dye manufacturers undercut the prices of its products. The local union, however, rejected proposals to write the system out of its contract until management granted an increase in base rates to "buy out" the plan.[59]

By the 1940s, despite the belief that "fundamentally, there is nothing wrong with [this] system of payment," the trend at Du Pont was running "toward lessening the number of employees paid on wage incentives."[60] Some plants changed to "Good Performance" plans, under which groups of workers shared monthly bonuses based on output and quality. Others gradually phased out incentives altogether. At the rayon plants, for example, operators who reached maximum levels of efficiency "were changed to a straight hourly rate with practically no loss of earning." By the early 1950s, only a few plants still retained incentive wage plans.[61]

While company managers abandoned incentives, they regarded time study and job standards as essential tools for controlling labor. "Labor measurement based on time study," stated one supervisor, "is a pre-requisite when planning for the effective use of labor."[62] Only "the organized analysis of work," another official asserted, would give management "the necessary elements of control."[63] By the 1940s, most Du Pont plants formed "Methods and Standards Sections," staffed by industrial engineers, to develop information and controls to assist managers in planning production. Using techniques derived from scientific management, these industrial engineers "place[d] the management of [labor] on a truly business basis."[64]

Methods engineers conducted a continuous program of job analysis in the plant, studying the work of production workers and also of "indirect labor" such as maintenance, construction, laboratory, warehouse, shipping, and clerical employees. They made time and motion studies of jobs to determine standard time values for each operation and to see that proper methods were being followed. Engineers also set labor standards for each job, establishing "the content of a fair day's work, or what should normally be expected from each individual for his day's pay."[65]

This ongoing job analysis program was only one of the duties performed by the Methods and Standards sections. Another was the preparation of written work plans. Supervisors and foremen sent all work orders to the section, where analysts converted them into detailed plans before jobs were begun. An industrial engineer described the process:

> The analyst studies the job first. He determines the best methods, tools, materials, safety requirements, and standards for manpower (by using standard time data). He writes store tickets for needed material. He prepares work sketches or photographs to assist foremen . . . and workers in visualizing the work. [The] result . . . is a completely analyzed job written in clear, concise form.[66]

This work plan established the "standard practice" for the job—defined as "a carefully thought out, officially approved method of performing a function."[67] Such a work plan, asserted one methods engineer, would "cause each operation to be performed in a stipulated manner at a designated time for an acceptable cost," enabling management to plan production more effectively.[68] Moreover, if this work plan was "'religiously' adhered to," a Methods and Standards manual promised, it would reduce "the good operation to a habit or routine [and release] the full faculties of management to be directed along other paths of progress."[69]

Du Pont managers relied on labor standards and work plans developed by Methods and Standards Sections to estimate work loads and to schedule crews. "Job methods planning," one analyst stated, gave managers "a measurement tool . . . to calculate the labor required for any job."[70] It also provided them with a tool for evaluating workers' performance. Supervisors could compare the job standard and work plan with the actual time of the job and the methods followed to measure how well workers performed the task. Labor standards, a methods engineer stated, formed "a common unit of measurement, understood by management and labor," which provided "a reliable means of objectively measuring . . . performance."[71] Standards were also used to rate jobs to determine payment differentials and to establish job promotion ladders based on the relative difficulty of different tasks.[72] Because each standard represented a specific output of an individual product, managers also utilized standards as administrative tools for production control. Based on forecasts of anticipated sales and orders, they estimated the volume of production, scheduled equipment utilization, predicted the labor costs of different products, and monitored inventories. At the end of the period, they compared actual production with the estimates to determine the causes of delays and overruns. Standards were also used for allocating labor and overhead costs among various products. "The use of [labor] measurement data," stated one engineer, "takes the elements of guesswork out of many of the problems . . . which management is called upon to evaluate."[73]

In addition to developing labor standards and preparing work plans, Du Pont's Methods and Standards sections engineers oversaw one other element of the company's efficiency efforts: its "Work Simplification" program. Developed by Allan Mogenson, an editor of *Factory Magazine* who was retained by the IED as a parttime consultant during the 1930s, work simplification was a training program designed to "[tap] the available brains in the plant for their constructive ideas."[74] Methods engineers delivered classroom lectures to groups of foreman and workers on basic principles of motion economy, instructing them how "to develop time and labor savings methods and to put that thinking into operation." The trainees then went back to their work sites, where, under an instructor's supervision, they identified jobs needing study and improvement. The trainee broke the job down into its constituent elements; prepared a written description for each element; plotted the job on process flow or work distribution charts; questioned how individual elements might be eliminated, simplified, or combined; and then implemented the improved method.[75] IED representatives stated that work simplification produced significant cost reductions, reduced the need for more sophisticated forms of job analysis, and fostered a "cooperative approach" to improving work methods. Moreover, they asserted, it would be "easier to sell" workers on the need to change their methods, since decisions about such changes would be based on "facts, not opinions" and made by workers themselves.[76]

From the 1920s to the 1950s, industrial engineers at Du Pont developed and implemented a variety of techniques, derived from scientific management, to provide managers with data for reducing production costs and controlling labor. "Those responsible for production," wrote a senior supervisor of one Methods and Standards Section, now "had available [to them] information, validated by established facts, on which to base their decisions."[77] In short, Du Pont engineers effectively "Taylorized" the workplace.

## The Broader Context: Industrial Relations at Du Pont

These efforts to apply techniques of scientific management to cut costs and enhance managerial control should be considered within the broader context of Du Pont's industrial relations environment. As early as the early 1930s, Du Pont officials launched a none-too-subtle effort "to create an atmosphere of understanding . . . which will permit management to make and carry out those decisions which must be made if we are to operate successfully." During the 1930s and 1940s, this campaign relied on plant and companywide employee magazines, leaflets, films, posters, and lectures.[78] In 1950, the company began a broader, more ambitious effort—its "HOBSO" ("How Our Business System Operates") program, in which workers received classroom training on the American system of free enterprise. By 1953, over 80,000 employees had attended HOBSO sessions.[79] Among the messages employees received through such forums was the need to lower costs, maintain quality, and increase productivity. Du Pont held out the promise of job security, longer service, and "better living" (also the title of its company employees' magazine) in exchange for "more work, better work, and more continuous work" from employees.[80] The alternative was stated implicitly or even explicitly: as one worker recalled being told, "If we didn't modernize we couldn't compete with other companies and it would mean all our jobs."[81]

These actions helped to create a climate for efficiency within the company. Moreover, from the 1920s through the 1950s, one essential fact distinguished Du Pont's overall employee relations environment: unions never mounted a serious challenge to management. Although various national unions, including the CIO, District 50 of the United Mine Workers, the Textile Workers Union of America, and the International Chemical Workers Union, at different times waged vigorous campaigns to organize Du Pont employees, they never represented more than eleven percent of the company's eligible work force. Instead, until 1937 most employees were represented by Works Councils, and thereafter by their successor organizations, independent plant unions (in most cases the break between the two amounted to little more than a name change). The Works Councils were dominated by the company, which actively resisted any efforts by representatives to hold meetings off plant property or to join their colleagues in other plants. With few exceptions, the independent unions were poorly financed, waged few strikes, and gained few concessions from plant managers. Although some independents tried to federate for greater strength, Du Pont's policy of local bargaining blocked their efforts; the company was never forced to negotiate at the corporate level.[82]

For its part, Du Pont management took a tough and unyielding stance towards unions, whether national or independent. Company managers refused to cede any authority over production. They denied unions any voice in setting work rules and output quotas, evaluating jobs, developing labor standards, and determining work schedules; they also refused to link wage hikes to productivity increases.[83] In the early 1950s, senior executives reassessed Du Pont's policy *vis-a-vis* unionism; the result was a shift from a preference for independent unions, to a goal of eliminating existing unions and maintaining, at all costs, the nonunion status of the company's unorganized plants. The Employee Relations Department conducted industrial relations training seminars for managers, sent specialists on "fire-fighting" visits to plants to head off any labor problems, and prepared wage surveys so that departments could time increases to defeat organizing efforts. At the same time, managers sought to reduce interest in unionism by cultivating workers' loyalty to the firm. The company paid high wage scales (at or above local going rates for comparable work) and offered a full package of benefits, including pensions, disability wages, vacations, termination allowances, group life, accident, and health insurance, and a thrift program. Managers used safety contests, recreational programs, plant tours, and other occasions to continually reiterate the theme that mutual interests linked managers and workers. These efforts had dramatic results: the percentage of unionized workers fell from 94 percent in 1946 to 66 percent by 1960, while none of the twenty-five new plants built by Du Pont during the same period was successfully organized.[84]

From management's perspective, most workers responded favorably to the company's efforts to improve their efficiency. The director of Du Pont's Employee Relations Department, Emile du Pont, maintained that the effort to educate workers led them to work more efficiently, lessened their resistance to technological change, and caused productivity to increase.[85] Indeed, levels of output per man-hour rose by 165 percent while labor costs rose only 12 percent from 1939 to 1955, suggesting that many workers *had* become more efficient.[86]

Generalizing about how workers responded to the efforts of industrial engineers to install scientific management at Du Pont is made difficult by the size of the work force and the virtual absence of employee records (most independent unions, for example, did not maintain files). The available evidence, however, indicates that at least some workers responded negatively—and even aggressively—to industrial engineers' attempts to alter their jobs. Even if management was unwilling to negotiate, workers persisted in making wage incentives, work loads, job evaluations, and other job-related concerns the focus of union organizing efforts and grievance sessions. Indeed, as recently as 1988, an internal company memorandum on unionism voiced concern over increased "militancy and opposition to management initiatives around the issues of O[perational] E[ffectiveness], wage increases . . . and productivity improvements."[87]

If the surviving evidence of one unauthorized work stoppage is any indication, workers were willing to take shop floor actions to protest changes in their jobs. In 1946, some 150 operators at the Seaford, Delaware, nylon plant left their stations and went to the cafeteria to protest their increased duties resulting from a recent analysis of their jobs. They were required to tend twice as many machines, but at the same wages as before. The workers complained that they had "too many machines to run"; while they "agreed that they could do the work," they refused to do so unless management increased their wages. The standoff was brief (lasting only a few hours) and production never stopped; foremen of the affected sections ran the machines.[88] But the incident demonstrated that at least some workers were unwilling to accede silently to unilateral efforts by management to alter their work. The available records shed no light on whether workers engaged in day-to-day actions to maintain some element of control over their work. In his study of operators in an automated chemical factory in New Jersey, David Halle found that workers "[became] well versed in concealing information and practices [about their jobs] from management so as to manipulate them."[89] Presumably, at least some Du Pont workers responded in similar fashion to the efforts of industrial engineers to "Taylorize" the workplace.

## Conclusion

Addressing a group of supervisors and employees at the Dye Works in 1919, Du Pont Company president Irénée du Pont denounced as "fallacious" the notion that workers served their interests when they restricted output. Instead, he maintained, workers should adopt "the principle of 'all-pull-together' [to] produce as efficiently as possible." The key, he said, was for

"every employee [to become] a unit in the brain of the company."
Lest anyone gain a misguided notion of what he meant, however,
he quickly elaborated on this comment:

> I do not mean by this that a skilled mechanic ought to try to
> work out some complicated chemical reaction. . . . We want
> thought applied where it will do the most good. Intelligent
> following of detailed instructions worked out by the chemists
> and technicians will yield astounding results in this extraordi-
> nary complex manufacture. That is: if experience shows that a
> certain material should be boiled ten minutes, boil it exactly ten
> minutes — not nine or eleven. If a charge should require 1,000
> pounds of caustic, put in 1,000 pounds and not 950 and put it in
> just when instructions require that it should be put in.[90]

The worker's role in production was limited to carrying out
accurately the instructions of superiors.

Irénée's remarks echoed those of Frederick W. Taylor. Here was
the substitution of scientific knowledge for the judgment of the
workmen. Here, too, was the task set forth for industrial engineers:
reducing workers' jobs to a set of "detailed instructions," which they
would be given by supervisors and told to execute. From first to
last, Du Pont's industrial engineers sought to achieve that objective.

### NOTES

1. Lucien Brouha, *Physiology in Industry: Evaluation of Industrial Stresses by the Physiological Reactions of the Worker* (Oxford, 1960), p. xii. See also DeNord B. Kirk, "Increased Efficiency Through Production Planning," *Advanced Management* 18 (April 1953), p. 25–28; Organisation for European Economic Co-Operation, European Productivity Agency, *Fitting the Job to the Worker: A Survey of American and European Research into Working Conditions in Industry* (Productivity Missions to the United States, Project no. 355, Report of Mission to the United States of September 5, 1956–November 3, 1956), pp. 17, 35; Harry Braverman, *Labor and Monopoly Capitalism: The Degradation of Work in the Twentieth Century* (New York, 1974), pp. 113–22, 140; John Storey, *Managerial Prerogative and the Question of Control* (London, 1983), pp. 147–49.
2. Remarks of Frederick W. Taylor, in testimony before the Special House Committee: a reprint of the public document "Hearings Before Special Committee of the House of Representatives to Investigate the Taylor and Other Systems of Shop Management Under Authority of House Resolution 90," in Frederick W. Taylor, *Scientific Management* (New York, 1947), p. 31.

3. Alfred D. Chandler, Jr., *The Visible Hand: The Managerial Revolution in American Business* (Cambridge, MA, 1977), pp. 438–50 (quote on p. 450). See also Chandler, *Strategy and Structure: Chapters in the History of the American Industrial Enterprise* (Cambridge, MA, 1962), chap. 2; Chandler and Stephen Salsbury, *Pierre S. du Pont and the Making of the Modern Corporation* (New York, 1971); H. Thomas Johnson and Robert S. Kaplan, *Relevance Lost: The Rise and Fall of Management Accounting* (Boston, 1987), chap. 4; JoAnne Yates, *Control through Communication: The Rise of System in American Management* (Baltimore, 1989), chap. 8.

4. See John C. Rumm, "Mutual Interests: Managers and Workers at the Du Pont Company, 1802–1915" (Ph.D. diss., University of Delaware, 1989), chaps. 1–4; Glenn Porter, *The Workers' World at Hagley* (Wilmington, DE, 1981), pp. 7–16; Norman B. Wilkinson, *Lammot du Pont and the American Explosives Industry, 1850–1884* (Charlottesville, 1984), chap. 1.

5. See, for example, comments of Hamilton M. Barksdale and W. B. Lewis in minutes of High Explosives Operating Department (HEOD) Superintendents' Meeting No. 13 (November 1905), and minutes and discussions in other HEOD Superintendents' Meetings, 1904–1909, Longwood Manuscripts, Group 10, Series A (Pierre S. du Pont Papers), File 418, Box 13 (hereafter cited as "LMSS/10/A/418, followed by box number). See also Yates, *Control through Communication*, pp. 235–53; Ernest Dale and Charles Meloy, "Hamilton MacFarland Barksdale and the Du Pont Contributions to Systematic Management," *Business History Review* 36 (1962), pp. 127–52.

6. The following discussion of the efforts made by the HEOD to apply scientific management at Du Pont is derived from Rumm, "Mutual Interests," chap. 6. A somewhat different perspective, emphasizing conflicts between scientific management and safety work, appears in Donald R. Stabile, "The Du Pont Experiments in Scientific Management: Efficiency and Safety, 1911–1919," *Business History Review* 61 (187), pp. 365–86.

7. Hamilton M. Barksdale to Frederick W. Taylor, March 28, 1911, Acc. 500, Series II, Part 2 (Post-1902 Du Pont Company Records), Box 1005 (hereafter cited as "Series II/O2," followed by box number); Fin Sparre to Charles L. Reese, December 5, 1911, Series II/2, Box 205. Several Du Pont Company executives knew Taylor and were familiar, at least in general terms, with his ideas. In 1897, for example, T. Coleman du Pont and Pierre S. du Pont had retained him as a consultant at the Johnson Company, manufacturers of equipment for electric street railways. Chandler and Salsbury, *Pierre S. du Pont*, p. 32; Stabile, "Du Pont Experiments," pp. 367–68.

8. Harry G. Haskell, "Opening Address," HEOD Superintendents' Meeting no. 34 (April 1912), manuscript transcript (MT), pp. 3–4, LMSS/10/A/418, Box 15; Haskell, "Opening Address," HEOD Superintendents' Meeting no. 33 (April 1911), printed text (PT), p. 7. Copies of the printed texts of HEOD Superintendents' Meetings 30–36 (1909–1914) are found in the Hagley Library.

9. Frank C. Evans to Charles H. Herrick, April 1, 1943, Acc. 1078 (Edward M. Harrington Papers), Item 5; Arthur P. Van Gelder and Hugo Schlatter, *History of the Explosives Industry in America* (New York, 1927), p. 547; Stabile, "Du Pont Experiments," p. 371.

10. See, for example, reports and memoranda issued by the Efficiency Division (ED), including "Scientific Management as Applied to High Explosives Works," HEOD Superintendents' Meeting no. 34 (April 1912), PT, p. 181–93; W. M. Moore to W. C. Spruance, Jr., "Report on Box Packing House Operations at Du Pont Works," HEOD Bulletin 311 (May 22, 1912), Series II/2, Item 553; ED, "Efficiency as Applied to High Explosives Works," HEOD Superintendents' Meeting no. 35 (April 1913), PT, pp. 571–96; ED, "Mechanical Dumping of Powder from Box to Hall Machine Belt," HEOD Bulletin 413 (September 12, 1913), Series II/2, Item 554; ED, "Efficiency," HEOD Superintendents' Meeting no. 36 (April 1914), PT, pp. 615–26; [Edward M. Harrington], "Annual Report [of ED]—1914," Jan. 25, 1915, Acc. 228 (Irénée du Pont Papers), Box 104. Harrington's notebooks, containing notes on plant processes and data from time and motion studies of workers, are found in Acc. 1078. See also Stabile, "Du Pont Experiments," pp. 372–76.

11. "Efficiency as Applied to High Explosives Works," PT, pp. 573, 580; "Efficiency," PT, pp. 616–17, 622–24.

12. See, for example, comments of W. M. Moore and H. G. Haskell in discussion section, "Efficiency as Applied to High Explosives Work," PT, pp. 602, 607; comments of W. B. Lewis, F. T. Beers, and W. C. Spruance in discussion section, "Efficiency," PT, pp. 632–34; Stabile, "Du Pont Experiments," pp. 369, 381–82. In 1912, T. Coleman du Pont arranged a meeting between senior Du Pont executives and John Dunlap, editor of *Factory* magazine, to discuss the work of the Society for the Promotion of Scientific Management (the Taylor Society); Harrington and Moore were not invited to attend, nor, apparently, did du Pont inform Dunlap of the Efficiency Division's existence. Du Pont to Dunlap, February 19, 1912 (copy), Series II/2, Box 1005.

13. "Scientific Management as Applied to High Explosives Work," PT, pp. 184–85; "Efficiency as Applied to High Explosives Work," PT, pp. 581–82; "Efficiency," PT, p. 622 (quote). On incentives, see comments of Frederick W. Taylor in discussion section, "Shop Management," American Society of Mechanical Engineers *Transactions* 24 (1903), p. 1470; see also Hugh J. Aitken, *Scientific Management in Action: Taylorism at Watertown Arsenal, 1908–1915* (1960; reprint ed., Princeton, 1985), pp. 34–47; Daniel Nelson, *Managers and Workers: Origins of the New Factory System in the United States, 1880–1920* (Madison, WI, 1975), pp. 51–54.

14. "Efficiency as Applied to High Explosives Works," PT, pp. 574, 584, 589; "Efficiency," PT, p. 619.

15. Comments of A. P. Van Gelder in discussion section, "Scientific Management as Applied to High Explosives Works," MT, p. 134; see also comments of W. B. Lewis and T. W. Bacchus, pp. 128, 141; and comments of C. A. Patterson in discussion section, "Efficiency as Applied to High Explosives Works," PT, p. 596.

16. "Efficiency as Applied to High Explosives Works," PT, pp. 594–95.

17. Comments of Hamilton M. Barksdale and other officials in discussion section, "Efficiency as Applied to High Explosives Works," PT, pp. 605–6 (quote on p. 606); see also Stabile, "Du Pont Experiments," p. 376.

18. Edward M. Harrington, "Explosion in Building #539, 'C' Line Gelatin Mixing House, Repauno, December 8, 1913," n.d., Acc. 1078, Item 4; "Efficiency," PT, p. 621, and comments of C. A. Patterson in discussion section, p. 631; *Philadelphia Public Ledger*, December 9 (quote), December 10, 1913; L. A. DeBlois, "Repauno—Explosion 'C' Line Gelatin 'Old Mix' Mixing House—Sept. 22, 1913," and "Repauno—Explosion 'C' Gelatin Mixing House—Dec. 8, 1913," March 29, 1922, Acc. 1615 (Records of Du Pont Employee Relations Department), Box 4; Stabile, "Du Pont Experiments," pp. 376–77.

19. Harry G. Haskell to HEOD Plant Superintendents, HEOD Bulletin 552 (January 27, 1915), Series II/2, Item 554; Stabile, "Du Pont Experiments," pp. 375–76.

20. Reports of Mr. Oglesby, Efficiency Department, in minutes of weekly Haskell Plant staff meetings, March–October 1918, Series II/2, Box 135; comments of E. N. Johnson (Superintendent, Hopewell Plant), minutes of Hopewell Plant "B" Staff Meeting, April 4, 1918, p. 13, Series II/2, Box 138.

21. See, for example, "Industrial Engineering Division," in Organic Chemicals Department, Chambers Works Plant, Du Pont Company, *Chambers Works History*, 4 vols. (typescript, Carneys Point, New Jersey, 1956–1959), vol. 4, *Auxiliary Services*, chap. 4, pp. 1–2, Acc. 1387 (Miscellaneous Records of Chambers Works Plant), reel 1 (hereafter cited as *Chambers Works History*).

22. Arlington Plant, Du Pont Viscoloid Company, *Pyralin-Articles* 1 (Feb. 16, 1921), p. 1.

23. E. S. Cowdrick, "E. I. Du Pont de Nemours & Company," in "Methods of Wage Payment: Report of a Fact-Finding Study in the Companies Associated with the Special Conference Committee," August 8, 1927, pp. 2–3, copy in Acc. 1699 (Records of Bethlehem Steel Corporation), Box Lot 235 (hereafter cited as "Methods of Wage Payment"); Lammot du Pont to W. C. Spruance, April 13, 1928; Spruance to du Pont, April 18, 1928; W. B. Foster to Spruance, April 17, 1928, Acc. 1662 (Administrative Files of Du Pont Company), Box 46. On Gantt's task and bonus system, see Taylor, "Shop Management," pp. 1376–78; Nelson, *Managers and Workers*, p. 57.

24. "Methods of Wage Payment," pp. 8–11; Industrial Relations Division, Service Department, Du Pont Company, "Village Study, Old Hickory Works, Du Pont Rayon Company, February to April 1926," pp. 4–5, Acc. 1771 (Records of Textile Fibers Department, Du Pont Company), Box 2; Rayon Division, Rayon Department, Du Pont Company, tabulation of employment levels and rates of turnover at rayon plants, 1925–1949, in Rayon Department scrapbook, Series II/2, Item 618; author's interview with Ralph K. Smith, Wilmington, Delaware, September 27, 1984. Smith was a supervisor in the Production Department of the Richmond rayon plant during the 1920s and 1930s.

25. "Methods of Wage Payment," p. 1; W. C. Spruance to Departmental Heads and Executive Committee members, memorandum on Du Pont Welfare Plans, June 30, 1924, Acc. 1662, Box 75; discussion of Merit Pay in minutes of Explosives Department Convention, January 1925, pp. 1–1 to 1–13,

Series II/2, Item 353; H. O. Blumenthal, "Compliance with Fair Labor Standards Act," in minutes of Meeting of Managers and Directors of the Explosives, Technical, and Nitrocellulose & Sporting Powder Divisions, Explosives Department, May 1946, pp. 47, 56, Series II/2, Item 395.

26. Du Pont Company Annual Reports, 1921–1929 (copies in Hagley Library); *Chicago Journal of Commerce*, February 10, 1932; Treasurer's Department, Du Pont Company, "Twenty-One-Year Financial and Operating Record, Years 1923 to 1945, Inclusive," in Du Pont Company, *This is Du Pont* (Wilmington, DE, 1949), p. 31 (copy in Hagley Library). On Du Pont's postwar diversification and research efforts, see Chandler, *Strategy and Structure*, pp. 91–113; David A. Hounshell and John K. Smith, *Science and Corporate Strategy: Du Pont R & D, 1902–1980* (Cambridge, England, 1988).

27. "Twenty-One-Year Financial and Operating Record"; *Chicago Journal of Commerce*, February 10, 1932; Willis F. Harrington to E. G. Robinson, April 28, 1930, Acc. 1813 (Willis F. Harrington Papers), Box 2; Service Department, Du Pont Company, "Argument Against the Five-Day Work Week," circa June 15, 1930; minutes of General Managers' [monthly] Meetings, 1930, Acc. 1813, Box 3; President's Report to Board of Directors, Grasselli Chemicals Company, November 13, 1931, Acc. 1813, Box 8. See also R. Presgrave, *Dynamics of Time Study* (New York, 1945), p. 31.

28. E. G. Ackart, "Some Notes and Anecdotes Concerning the Work and Men of the Engineering Department," August 1946, pp. 47–48, Acc. 1608 (Henry Belin du Pont Papers), Box 51; Granville M. Read, "Fundamentals in Organizing for Cost Reduction," in American Management Association, *Organizing for Cost Reduction*, AMA Production Series no. 122 (1940), pp. 11–12 (quote).

29. Jasper E. Crane to Executive Committee, report on "Economy Measures," August 31, 1937; Executive Committee resolution, September 22, 1937 (quote), Series II/2, Box 1031.

30. Ackart, "Some Notes and Anecdotes," pp. 46, 48–49; Read, "Fundamentals," pp. 11–21; Henry Belin du Pont, "The Engineering Department of the Du Pont Company," draft text of speech, circa 1950, Acc. 1608, Box 2.

31. Walter S. Carpenter, Jr. to Major-General T. J. Hughes, January 20, 1943, Series II/2, Box 840 (quote); see also Read, "Fundamentals," p. 12; Ackart, "Some Notes and Anecdotes," pp. 48–49; Industrial Engineering Division, Engineering Department, Du Pont Company, memorandum, "Field Engineering Department, Du Pont Company, memorandum, "Field Engineering—Scope of Work," circa April 1932, Acc. 1813, Box 12; R. T. Van Ness to E. G. Ackart, memorandum on Industrial Engineering, Development Engineering, and Planning Divisions, February 4, 1946, Series II/2, Box 832; and "The Du Pont Company Wants Management Engineers," advertisement in *Advanced Management* 16 (February 1951), p. 28.

32. *Chambers Works History*, p. 1.

33. Donald F. Carpenter (vice president, Remington Arms Company, a wholly owned Du Pont subsidiary), "Management's Responsibility in Increasing Manufacturing Productivity," in *Organizing for Cost Reduction*, p. 4.

34. Quoted in Kirk, "Increased Efficiency," p. 27.

35. John Q. Heritage, "Work Measurement for Better Maintenance," *Factory Management and Maintenance*, 113 (January 1955), p. 89.

36. James D. Quinn, "A Discussion of Objectives in Maintenance Engineering," in *Maintenance Management: Report of the International Plant & Maintenance Engineering Conference, Held at Alexandra Palace, London, June 17–21, 1963* (London, 1964), part A-2(iii), p. 8.

37. Howard Rossmoore and Robert S. Aries, "Time and Motion Study in the Chemical Process Industries," *Chemical and Engineering News* 25 (October 27, 1947), pp. 3142–44 (quote on p. 3144); see also J. R. Bailey to G. M. Read, memorandum on motion study and chemical workers, August 30, 1938, Acc. 1662, Box 28; Bailey, "Work Simplification in a Chemical Industry," American Institute of Chemical Engineers, *Transactions* 36 (1940), pp. 227–32; L. Baumeister, "Fitting Scientific Management to the Chemical Industry," *Chemical & Metallurgical Engineering* 32 (June 1925), pp. 551–52.

38. E. K. Bolton to Irénée du Pont, 1926, Acc. 228, Box 97; William Haynes, *Men, Money and Molecules* (New York, 1936), pp. 129–30; Theodore S. Kreps, *The Economics of the Sulfuric Acid Industry* (Stanford, 1936), pp. 225–37; Robert M. Crawford, "Economic Comparison of Batch and Continuous Processing," *Chemical & Metallurgical Engineer* 54 (May 1945), pp. 106–7; *Spruance Cellophane News*, "25th Anniversary Issue," November 1, 1955; Robert Blauner, *Alienation and Freedom: The Factory Worker and His Industry* (Chicago, 1964), pp. 127–33; Samuel Hollander, *The Sources of Increased Efficiency: A Study of Du Pont Rayon Plants* (Cambridge, MA, 1964), pp. 58–60; P. J. Wingate, *The Colorful Du Pont Company* (Wilmington, 1982), pp. 148–49, 193–96.

39. "Outline of Objectives in an Industrial Engineering Plant Survey," in Minutes of Explosives Plants Managers' Meeting, May 1933, pp. 45–46 (quote); see also Read, "Fundamentals," pp. 9–10. For examples of changes or improvements resulting from industrial engineering surveys, see Industrial Engineering Division, "Field Engineering—Scope of Work"; President's Report to Board of Directors, Grasselli Chemical Company, November 13, 1931; "Minutes of Contact Sulphuric Acid Meeting, Grasselli & Du Pont Plants, Nov. 19 & 20, 1931," Acc. 1813, Box 8; and E. W. Furst to G. L. Naylor, memorandum, September 1, 1936, Acc. 1813, Box 23.

40. "Methods of Wage Payments," pp. 3, 9; Bailey to Read, August 30, 1938; *Fitting the Job to the Worker*, p. 56; "Light Patterns Can Help You Get Your Ideas Across," *Factory Management and Maintenance* 8 (August 1950), pp. 74–75; Ralph M. Barnes, *Motion and Time Study*, 4th ed. (New York, 1958), pp. 112–15; F. F. Middleswart, "Time Standards for Indirect Operations" (paper presented at Society for Advancement of Management/American Institute of Industrial Engineers "Time and Motion Study Conference," Winston-Salem, North Carolina, January 29, 1954), pp. 2–4, copy in "Du Pont D.A. [Destruction Authorization]" Records, Series 708 (Records of Engineering Department, Du Pont Company), Item 54–5; *Fitting the Job to the Worker*, p. 56. On predetermined time values, see Braverman, *Labor and Monopoly Capital*, pp. 173–76; David B. Porter and Ercole Rosa, Jr., "Work Sim-

plification and Work Measurement," in Management Division, American Society of Mechanical Engineers, *50 Years Progress in Management 1910–1960* (New York, 1960), pp. 136–38.

41. "Methods of Wage Payment," pp. 3–5, 8–10; *Chambers Works History*, pp. 2–6; "The Incentive Wage and Its Possible Application to Explosives Plants," Explosives Plant Managers' Meeting, May 1933, pp. 47–49; R. G. Clough to F. A. Wardenburg, memorandum on Bedaux System, March 8, 1933 (copy), Series II/2, Box 1045; Wingate, *Colorful Du Pont Company*, p. 194.

42. Comments of Loren I. King in discussion section, "Incentive Wage and Its Possible Application," pp. 47–49 (quote on p. 49); *Chambers Works History*, pp. 1–2; Emile F. du Pont to F. S. Johnson, memorandum on "Motion Economy," October 13, 1938, Acc. 1813, Box 27; minutes of General Managers' Meeting, June 20, 1932, Acc. 1813, Box 12; minutes of General Managers' Meetings, February 20, March 20, 1933, Acc. 1813, Box 16; H. F. Sedwick to Jasper E. Crane, May 5, 1936, Series II/2, Box 1046; E. R. Murch to F. C. Evans, report, "Extent of Wage Incentive Coverage Within Du Pont Company," September 1, 1938, Acc. 1813, Box 27 (hereafter cited as "Wage Incentive Coverage").

43. *Chambers Works History*, pp. 3–12; Sedwick to Crane, May 5, 1936; Wendell R. Swint to E. G. Ackart, October 10, 1932, Series II/2, Box 537; Jasper Crane to W. M. Irish, May 7, 1936, Series II/2, Box 1046; Wingate, *Colorful Du Pont Company*, pp. 193–96; Foster to Spruance, April 17, 1928, Acc. 1662, Box 46 (quote); R. C. Clough to F. A. Wardenburg, March 8, 1932; Wardenburg to Crane, March 9, 1932, Series II/2, Box 1045.

44. "Wage Incentive Coverage," p. 3; *Chambers Works History*, p. 2; Charles Lytle, *Wage Incentive Methods: Their Selection, Installation and Operation* (New York, 1942), p. 254. One of the KIM engineers, Loren I. King, in 1933 became Du Pont's first "Wage Incentive Consultant." Ackart, "Some Notes and Anecdotes," p. 49; minutes of Explosives Plant Managers' Meeting, May 1933, pp. 47–49; G. E. Minshull to Plant Managers, Department Heads, and Presidents of Subsidiaries, October 3, 1933, Acc. 1662, Box 9.

45. Foster to Spruance, April 17, 1928; *Chambers Works History*, pp. 1–3; Wardenburg to Crane, March 9, 1932 (quote); author's interview with Ernest R. Habicht, Wilmington, Delaware, May 3, 1985. Habicht, who later became manager of Du Pont's Belle Plant in West Virginia, installed a version of the Bedaux System at Belle in the early 1930s.

46. Crane to Irish (quote); "Wage Incentive Coverage"; Incentive Wage and Its Application," pp. 47–49; Emile du Pont to Johnson, "Motion Economy"; Wingate, *Colorful Du Pont Company*, pp. 194–95.

47. King comments, "Incentive Wage and Its Application," p. 48.

48. "Methods of Wage Payment," p. 4 (quote); *Chambers Works History*, pp. 7–9.

49. *Chambers Works History*, pp. 9–11; "Wage Incentive Coverage"; Habicht interview (quote); Read, "Fundamentals," p. 13; Wingate, *Colorful Du Pont Company*, pp. 194–95.

50. Author's interview with John L. Barnhill, Wilmington, Delaware, January 23, 1984. Barnhill worked at the Dye Works from 1919 until about 1962.

51. Habicht interview.

52. Arlington Plant, Du Pont Viscoloid Company, "Around the Plant," *Pyralin-Articles*1 (May 5, 1920), p. 6.

53. Minshull to Plant Managers, Department Heads, and Presidents of Subsidiaries, October 3, 1933; see also H. F. Sedwick to Works Managers, November 16, 1933, LMSS/10/A, File 1173-5; Service Department, Du Pont Company, report to Executive Committee on "Employees' Representation Plan," January 1, 1935, Acc. 1662, Box 74; Willis F. Harrington, notes on General Managers' Meeting of March 1936, Acc. 1813, Box 22.

54. Lloyd E. Halsted to Lammot du Pont, January 22, 1942, Acc. 1662, Box 28.

55. Employees Mutual Association to "Lamont [*sic*] du Pont," March 21, 1938 (quote); B. D. Beyes to du Pont, March 23, 1938, Acc. 1662, Box 67. See also M. A. Brown to Employees Mutual Association, November 1937 (copy), Acc. 1813, Box 25.

56. Barnhill interview (quote); *Chambers Works History*, p. 8; Wingate, *Colorful Du Pont Company*, p. 195.

57. Frank C. Evans to General Managers, Department Heads, and Presidents of Subsidiaries, memorandum on "Works Council Activities," March 10, 1936, Acc. 1662, Box 74; "Wage Incentive Coverage," pp. 4-7 (quote on p. 4); *Chambers Works History*, pp. 8-9, 12; Wingate, *Colorful Du Pont Company*, pp. 195-96; *Dyeworks News*, January 5, March 2, 1939 (on microfilm in the Hagley Library).

58. William Richter to F. C. Evans, May 4, 1936; L. A. Yerkes to Evans, May 8, 1936, Acc. 1813, Box 22; E. W. Furst to G. L. Naylor, September 1, 1936; Organic Chemicals Department, "Orchem — Operating Efficiency," circa July 1936, Acc. 1813, Box 23; "Wage Incentive Coverage," pp. 4-5; *Chambers Works History*, pp. 7-8; Wingate, *Colorful Du Pont Company*, pp. 194-95.

59. Habicht interview (quote); "Wage Incentive Coverage," pp. 1-3, 6-8; Wingate, *Colorful Du Pont Company*, pp. 197-99; *Chambers Works History*, pp. 12-14.

60. Emile du Pont to F. S. Johnson, "Motion Economy" (quote); Middleswart, "Time Standards," p. 8; *Fitting the Job to the Worker*, p. 56; Service Department, report to Executive Committee on "Company Labor Policy," July 14, 1941, Acc. 1813, Box 35.

61. "Wage Incentive Coverage," pp. 3-4 (quote), 6; *Chambers Works History*, pp. 13-14; Read, "Fundamentals," p. 13; Habicht interview.

62. Kirk, "Increased Efficiency," p. 27. For similar statements, see Middleswart, "Time Standards," pp. 3-12; Heritage, "Work Measurement," pp. 86-93; John S. Sayer, "The Measurement of Maintenance Labor" (paper presented at joint meeting of Society for the Advancement of Management-American Society of Mechanical Engineers, New York City, April 28, 1954), pp. 1-9, D.A. 708, Item 54-58; Quinn, "Discussion of Objectives," pp. 7-8. See also Robert H. Roy, "Commentary on the Future of Work Measurement," in Seymour M. Selig and Morton Ettelstein, eds., *New Horizons in Industrial Engineering* (Baltimore, 1963), pp. 196-97.

63. Heritage, "Work Measurement," pp. 88, 92.

64. Heritage, "Work Measurement," p. 88 (quote); Kirk, "Increased Efficiency," p. 26; Carpenter, "Management's Responsibility," pp. 4-5; U.S. War

Manpower Commission, Training Within Industry Service, report, "Instructor Training Program, Remington Arms Company, Bridgeport, Conn., April–August 1941," exhibit E-3, pp. 22–24, copy in files of George Jacquot, Series A-5, Record Group 211 (Records of the War Manpower Commission), U.S. National Archives, Suitland, Maryland.

65. Kirk, "Increased Efficiency," pp. 25–27 (quote on p. 27); Heritage, "Work Measurement," pp. 86–92; Middleswart, "Time Standards," pp. 2–12; Sayer, "Measurement of Maintenance Labor," pp. 1–9; "Instructor Training Program," exhibit E-3, pp. 2–4, 19–24; Hugh Richmond (Personnel Division, Service Department), "Some Problems Encountered in Substituting Women for Men in Industry" (paper presented at National Industrial Conference Board Meeting, March 19, 1942), pp. 1–3, 5–8, copy in Acc. 1813, Box 38.

66. Heritage, "Work Measurement," p. 92.

67. "Instructor Training Program," exhibit E-3, pp. 22–25 (quote on p. 24).

68. Kirk, "Increased Efficiency," pp. 25–26.

69. "Instructor Training Program," exhibit E-3, pp. 22–25 (quote on p. 22); see also Heritage, "Work Measurement," pp. 90–93; Middleswart, "Time Standards," pp. 9–11.

70. Sayer, "Measurement of Maintenance Labor," p. 1; see also Kirk, "Increased Efficiency," pp. 27–28; Heritage, "Work Measurement," pp. 86–88, 92; Middleswart, "Time Standards," pp. 12–14.

71. Heritage, "Work Measurement," p. 88.

72. "Wage Incentive Coverage," p. 6; Habicht interview; *Fitting the Job to the Worker*, p. 56.

73. Kirk, "Increased Efficiency," pp. 25–28; "Methods of Wage Payment," pp. 5–8; Heritage, "Work Measurement," pp. 86–88; Sayer, "Measurement of Maintenance Labor," pp. 1–12; Middleswart, "Time Standards," pp. 7–14 (quote on p. 14); Wingate, *Colorful Du Pont Company*, pp. 198–99.

74. Bailey, "Work Simplification," p. 232 (quote); Emile du Pont to F. S. Johnson, "Motion Economy"; Read, "Fundamentals," p. 13; Kirk, "Increased Efficiency," p. 26; Rossmore and Aries, "Time and Motion Study," p. 3144; W. R. Bonwit, "Work Simplification—Applications to Plant Maintenance" (paper presented at Sinclair Refining Company Maintenance Symposium, Philadelphia, October 12, 1954), Du Pont D.A. Item 54-79.

75. Kir, "Increased Efficiency," p. 26 (quote); Bonwit, "Work Simplification—Applications," pp. 1–7; Bailey, "Work Simplification," pp. 232–33.

76. Bonwit, "Work Simplification—Applications," pp. 4–11 (quote on p. 4); Bailey, "Work Simplification," pp. 232–33; Read, "Fundamentals," p. 13.

77. Kirk, "Increased Efficiency," p. 25.

78. Emile F. du Pont, "'How Our Business System Operates (HOBSO)': Discussion of Company Objectives and Guiding Principles of the Program with Trained Leaders," February 17, 1950, p. 1 (quote), Emile du Pont Papers (EDP); George Miller, report, "Dissemination of Economic Information Among Employees," October 14, 1938, Acc. 1813, Box 26; C. M. Hackett to L. F. Livingstone, circa September 1946; James Q. du Pont, "List of Present Du Pont Public Relations Department 'Objectives' Versus 'Targets,'" May 2, 1949, both in Acc. 1415 (James Q. du Pont Papers), Box 31;

R. E. Curtin, Jr., report, "Review of Current Public Relations Aims and Idea Content," May 23, 1952, Acc. 1415, Box 17. See also L. L. L. Golden, *Only by Public Consent: American Corporations Search for Favorable Opinions* (New York, 1968), chap. 4. On the effort made to "sell" workers on the American system of free enterprise, see Richard S. Tedlow, *Keeping the Corporate Image: Public Relations and Business, 1900–1950* (Greenwich, CT, 1979), pp. 117–25; Howell J. Harris, *The Right to Manage: Industrial Relations Policies of American Business in the 1940s* (Madison, 1982), chap. 7.

79. Emile F. du Pont, "How Our Business System Operates"; du Pont, remarks to Du Pont Board of Directors, September 17, 1951; du Pont, "Suggested Thoughts for 'HOBSO II' Luncheon Talks," March 14, 1952, EDP; Employee Relations Department, Annual Report to Executive Committee for 1952, February 13, 1953, Acc. 1615, Box 3.

80. Service Department, "Outline of Collective Bargaining Within the Du Pont Company," January 20, 1942, Acc. 1813, Box 38; Emile F. du Pont, "Current Statue of Labor Relations within the Du Pont Company," September 4, 1952; du Pont, "Oral Report before Board of Directors," September 15, 1952, EDP; Employee Relations Department, Annual Reports to Executive Committee, 1952–1960, 1615, Box 3; Julius Rezler, "Labor Organization at Du Pont: A Study in Independent Local Unionism," *Labor History* 4 (1963), pp. 178–95; Ken Tucker, "It Got My Back Up," in Alice Lynd and Staughton Lynd, eds., *Rank and File: Personal Histories by Working-Class Organizers* (Boston, 1973), pp. 224–32; James Phelan and Robert Posen, *The Company State: Ralph Nader's Study Group Report on DuPont in Delaware* (New York, 1973), chap. 3. See also Walter S. Carpenter, Jr. to Willis F. Harrington, November 10, 1941, Series II/2, Box 827; Harrington to Robert B. Wolf, October 13, 1942, Acc. 1813, Box 38; Lammot du Pont to William H. Dow, October 31, 1946, Acc. 1662, Box 69; Emile F. du Pont, speech at Plant Managers' Meeting, Textile Fibers Department, November 3, 1955, EDP; E. F. du Pont, remarks at Ilion Plant Supervisors' meeting, 1956, EDP; "Questions Which Might Border on Employee Relations Raised in Other Panels," July 1959, EDP; Lammot du Pont to John Suman, November 5, 1946 (quote), Acc. 1662, Box 28; Harold Brayman to Walter S. Carpenter, Jr., March 31, 1947, Series II/2, Box 834; *This is Du Pont*, pp. 38–39.

81. Quoted in "No Shuttlecocks at Parlin," *Fortune* 63 (February 1962), p. 190. The curious title refers to a comment by the manager of Du Pont's Parlin Plant, quoted in the article, that the aim behind efforts to furnish information to employees about the need for technological improvements was "to keep things down in the area where people know each other and aren't just badminton birds in somebody's game."

82. Service Department, "Outline of Collective Bargaining"; du Pont, "Current Status of Labor Relations"; du Pont, "Oral Report before Board of Directors"; Employee Relations Department, Annual Reports, 1952–1960; Rezler, "Labor Organization at Du Pont"; Tucker, "It Got My Back Up"; Phelan and Posen, *The Company State*, chap. 3.

83. Service Department, "Outline of Collective Bargaining"; du Pont, "Current Status of Labor Relations"; du Pont, "Oral Report before Board of

Directors"; Employee Relations Department, Annual Reports, 1952–1960; Rezler, "Labor Organization at Du Pont"; Tucker, "It Got My Back Up"; Phelan and Posen, *The Company State*, chap. 3. See also Carpenter to Harrington, November 10, 1941; Harrington to Wolf, October 13, 1942; L. du Pont to Dow, October 31, 1946; E. F. du Pont, speech at Plant Managers' Meeting; E. F. du Pont, remarks at Ilion Plant Supervisors' meeting; and "Questions Which Might Border on Employee Relations."

84. G. Gordon Mitchell, "A Look into the Future of Labor Relations," 1946, EDP; Spencer Brownell to Walter S. Carpenter, Jr., March 18, 1946, Series II/2, Box 841; Carpenter, "Comments before the Personnel and Industrial Relations Conference, Nemours Auditorium, Sept. 19, 1947," August 20, 1947, Series II/O2, Box 842; "Company's Philosophy on No-Union Status," January 4, 1956, EDP; Employee Relations Department Annual Reports, 1953–1960; Rezler, "Labor Organization at Du Pont," pp. 181–82, 187–88; Smith interview; author's interview with George Miller (Special Assistant, Employee Relations Department, Du Pont Company), January 16, 1984.

85. See, for example, du Pont, "Current Status of Labor Relations"; Emile F. du Pont, remarks at Seaford Plant Supervisors' meeting, June 23, 1949, pp. 7–8, EDP; see also "No Shuttlecocks at Parlin," pp. 189–90.

86. See the table accompanying Ira T. Ellis, "Topics for Discussion with Executive and Finance Committees, Tuesday, May 15, 1956," Series II/2, Box 103-A.

87. Quoted in *Wilmington News Journal*, April 24, 1988. For earlier instances, see, for example, Halsted to Lammot du Pont, January 26, 1942; minutes of General Managers' Meeting, June 16, 1941, Acc. 1813, Box 36; F. C. Evans to General Managers, "Premium Pay to Shift Workers for Sunday Work," May 29, 1946, Series II/2, Box 834; lists of pending grievances, in Employee Relations Department Annual Reports, 1952–1956; "CIO's Program for du Pont Plant Announced," Staunton, Virginia, *Leader*, June 11, 1947; "2-Hour Work Stoppage Precedes Du Pont Pact," *Newburgh [NY] News*, June 20, 1955.

88. Pierre S. du Pont, notes of interview with Edgar Smith *re* Seaford Plant, July 7, 1946, pp. 4–5, LMSS/10/A, File 418-14.

89. David Halle, *America's Working Man: Work, Home, and Politics among Blue-Collar Property Owners* (Chicago, 1984), pp. 119–26, 145–47 (quote on p. 146). See also Theo Nichols and Huw Beynon, *Living with Capitalism: Class Relations and the Modern Factory* (London, 1977), which also examines the extent of workers' control in a modern chemical plant.

90. Address of Irénée du Pont before Dye Works Employment Conference, August 13, 1919, reprinted in "Plant Pioneered Labor Relations Steps," *Chambers Works News*, December 1, 1967, p. 8 (copy in Hagley Library).

STEPHEN P. WARING

# 9 Peter Drucker, MBO, and the Corporatist Critique of Scientific Management

In the years following World War II, Peter F. Drucker was the most prominent management writer and consultant in the world. One commentator has claimed that Drucker's writings were "read by more managers than those of any single author, living or dead."[1] Such popularity allowed Drucker to become the foremost postwar champion and critic of Frederick W. Taylor's scientific management. Drucker's critique, unlike those of the union officials of the 1910s, was not based on some specific deficiency or danger. Rather it reflected a sense of the limitations of contemporary business practice in contrast with the potential of an approach based explicitly on internal cooperation and harmony — an approach rooted in European corporatist philosophy and Drucker's early theoretical training.

Drucker often expressed respect for Taylor, who had created "an all but systematic philosophy of worker and work." The influence of Taylor's philosophy, he added, was "the most powerful as well as the most lasting contribution America has made to Western thought since the Federalist Papers."[2] Later Drucker praised Taylor for anticipating the human relations ideas that developed after World War II.[3]

Because such comments represented only one side of Drucker's ideas, he had been hard to understand. At least one scholar has taken the praise of scientific management out of context from the rest of Drucker's writing and has thus overlooked the ways in which Drucker criticized Taylorism and proposed alternatives.[4] Indeed Drucker has seldom been credited for having his own theory of management. Commentators have typically described him as an inconsistent thinker, an enigma, a "guru." As one business journalist put it, Drucker has been "known for many concepts" despite the absence of "a clear and identifiable message, body of research or theory to his name." Such perceptions may be due in part to the "eclectic" way in which he has illustrated his essays and lectures, using examples drawn from history or music or art as well as contemporary business.[5] Because of his apparently unsystematic style, one historian has concluded that Drucker's "real contribution" to management had been not so much in "the cash value of his ideas as in the rigorous activity of mind" by which they were formulated and that managers could learn more from "watching him think than from studying the content of his thought."[6]

Nevertheless, searching beneath stylistic impressions reveals that Drucker developed a managerial theory that sought to go beyond Taylorism. With such writers as Douglas McGregor and Chris Argyris, Drucker charged that Taylor's ideas had helped make American management excessively bureaucratic.[7] Taylor's principles had called for managers to centralize power, separate planning from performing, and specialize tasks. This had helped lead to bureaucratic firms with managers divided from managed. Managers were thus isolated from, and ignorant of, many production matters. And managers manipulated people just like any other factor of production, thus oppressing and underusing their personnel. Consequently Taylorism, so the critics charged, created problems that debilitated American business.

Drucker's therapy for Taylor's bureaucratic disease, like that of McGregor and Argyris, was for managers to integrate planning with doing and synthesize tasks. This quest for an alternative to Taylorism and bureaucracy was a quest for new, corporative principles of management. It called for managers to stop treating people, especially professional employees, as factors of production and begin treating them as members of a community. One scholar has wrongly concluded that "nothing" in American thought has been similar to the German idea that the business corporation was a "social institution" and "the central locus of identity, loyalty, and community." Such a conclusion seems to have been made without knowledge of what American managers have learned from Peter Drucker, an Austrian immigrant, and how they have voiced a desire for "an ethic of mutuality" and a disgust for "bourgeois egotism."[8]

The key to Drucker's corporatism is the technique he labelled "management by objectives and self-control," called "MBO" in the business vernacular. The story of Drucker's method and managers' reaction to it has not been told by a historian.[9] But the story tells much about recent efforts to transcend Taylorism and establish corporatism. And the story also illustrates the failure of Drucker's efforts, largely because his corporatist principles differed little from Taylor's bureaucratic ones. Druckerism, rather than being antibureaucratic and a genuine alternative to scientific management, proposed new Taylorist techniques.

## European Philosophy, American Practice

Drucker's search for remedy for Taylorism began in the 1940s and early 1950s, when he set out to synthesize European political theory with American business practice. The synthesis became management by objectives, a technique designed to make capitalism corporative and corporatism capitalist.[10]

Capitalism and corporatism had been important parts of Drucker's youth in Vienna, Austria. He absorbed ideas from the conservative, Fascist, and especially Catholic versions of corporatist thinking popular in Austria after World War I. Such thinkers as Heinrich Pesch and Othmar Spann had been disturbed by the selfishness, irresponsibility, and class conflict that accompanied industrial capitalism. They believed that these trends alienated workers, fostered socialism, endangered private property, and threatened freedom. To overcome these problems, they envisioned a harmonious polity composed of functional economic groups, or corporations.

These corporations, as corporatists defined them, took precedence over their members. Corporate goals were not merely the sum of the goals of their members. Yet because corporations were by definition organic groups, members would recognize that their needs and group needs were identical and would spontaneously subordinate themselves to the group. In exchange, individuals received income, status, and fulfillment. Seeking freedom from the group amounted to self-destructive and antisocial behavior, for real freedom was *in* the corporation, especially in service to it. Because corporatists envisioned natural harmony between members and groups, moreover, popular sovereignty was at best irrelevant, at worst divisive and counterproductive. Government would come from a natural elite; and since this elite possessed superior wisdom and virtue and performed necessary functions by mediating conflicts and leading members toward common goals, its power was self-justifying.[11]

Given the lack of harmony in interwar Austria, however, these corporatists had from the beginning faced the problem of creating either corporate eggs or corporate chickens. In other words, they had either to convince individuals to adopt common goals so that together they could construct a corporatist system, or they had to construct a corporatist system that synthesized the goals of conflicting individuals. Above all, they needed a natural elite, but could not find one. The authority of traditional leaders of corporatist schemes, clerics and aristocrats, had been discredited in an increasingly industrial, scientific, and democratic society, and business managers were unsuitable given workers' distrust. Eventually some of the idealogues would help establish a fascist dictatorship that used coercion to establish cooperation, a solution that contradicted their presumption of corporate consensus but sustained the hierarchy, privilege, and private property that they had been anxious to defend.[12]

After fleeing the Nazis and beginning an academic career in America in the 1930s, Drucker wrote at length about the good and bad of European culture. In 1939 he expressed admiration for three corporatist thinkers of the Restoration era, conservatives Joseph de Maistre and Vicomte de Bonald and right Hegelian Friedrich Stahl (about whom he had written his first book). He admired their "Christian" conception of "authority," which stressed the "duties" of property ownership, not merely its "privileges," and which called for responsible exercise of power in the interest of "its subjects."[13] Beyond this, according to his "oldest friend" Berthold Freyberg, he was trying to do for the twentieth century what Stahl had attempted for the nineteenth. He wanted to create a social and political structure adapted to the present but preserving the best of the past, and offering through "responsibility" and "commitment" a "synthesis" of power and freedom. Stahl had failed because he could not find the appropriate institution. But Drucker came to believe that he had found the right vehicle in the properly managed business corporation.[14]

That Drucker should turn to a capitalist institution was another legacy of his central European roots. Bourgeois intellectuals in interwar Austria had been torn between desires for a corporatist and a liberal-capitalist order, reflecting a social conflict between an old professional and a new entrepreneurial middle class. Drucker had been affected by the old and the new. He had been born into a prominent family that respected public servants more than businessmen. But as a young man he had worked in business and his education, while scarcely technical, was more practical and professional than most of his class.[15]

Drucker had also respected another Viennese, the economist and historian Joseph Schumpeter, and had learned from him the importance of the entrepreneur. For Schumpeter the entrepreneur was the economic leader whose marketing and administrative skills converted "inventions" into "innovations" and thus created jobs and new wealth. But late in life Schumpeter had come to believe that entrepreneurial success was undermining capitalism and entrepreneurialism. Above all, a new elite of business managers increasingly thought like employees, was interested in perpetuating current projects, and felt little incentive to innovate. These managers were motivated by an ethic of consumption rather than production, and were committed to short-term personal gratification rather than long-term service to family and society. Capitalism, Schumpeter lamented, was in the process of transforming itself into socialism.[16] This prospect apparently appalled Drucker. By 1940 his search for a new social order became a quest for ways of integrating Schumpeter's innovating entrepreneur with Stahl's conservative, responsible ruler. He wanted business managers who could reconcile capitalist with corporative values.

In *The End of Economic Man*, published in 1939, Drucker explained what had happened when central European managers had failed to meet social responsibilities. They had, he said, valued people only for their labor and treated them as factors of production. Treated like things, people had felt isolated and governed by irrational, "demonic forces" beyond their control. Society had ceased to be a "community of individuals bound together by a common purpose" and had become a "chaotic hubbub of purposeless isolated monads." Confused and desperate, some were drawn to the nihilism of Marxism, which in turn undercut traditional values and institutions and paved the way for Fascist dictatorships. Both Fascism and Marxism, as Drucker saw them, were escapist; they could establish order but never fulfill human needs. What people needed was a new "noneconomic society" that could provide freedom, "status," and "function," and it was the task of business managers to help create such a society by shaping the proletarian into the industrial citizen and the company into a community.[17]

In subsequent works, particularly in *The Future of Industrial Man* (1942), *Concept of the Corporation* (1946), and *The New Society* (1949), Drucker emphasized that only satisfying work could fulfill the needs of individuals for autonomy, security, dignity, usefulness, belonging, and peer respect. Work was needed as much to provide "status and function" as income and only the hierarchical corporation could provide satisfying work. People were frustrated when managers valued labor only as a commodity or when workers just sought money from their jobs. In these cases, the firm and the worker valued each other only as a means to an end. But the "apparently irresolvable conflict between the absolute claim of the group" and "the absolute claim of the individual" could be resolved if each accepted responsibility for satisfying the needs of the other. Through responsible acts of "citizenship" by manager and worker alike, the "two autonomous sets of purposes," the ends of society and of the individual, could be brought into "harmony" and thus "fulfilled in one and the same movement."[18]

Drucker found such corporative ideas both in German traditions and in American management publications of the 1930s. The German ideology of industrial leadership held that management was a "calling," which was more than an avenue to status and wealth; it imposed obligations on managers to serve employees and the public good.[19] American management theorists such as Chester Barnard claimed that the manager integrated organization and its members.[20] A manager, Drucker said, took "responsibility for the whole" by getting his subordinates to work toward a common goal. But true to his European heritage, he expressed these responsibilities in a Viennese way and compared the managerial task to that of an orchestral conductor. The conductor selected the piece, the goal. Each musician knew the score and played one instrument. But the conductor harmonized all the parts so that the goal was achieved. "The conductor himself," Drucker explained, "does not play an instrument. He need not even know how to play an instrument. His job is to know the capacity of each instrument and to evoke optimal performance from each." "Instead of 'doing,' he leads."[21]

Drucker liked the orchestral metaphor because it assumed that harmony in the corporation came from consensus rather than from control. Concurrently it assumed that firms could no more do without managers than orchestras without conductors. The "hierarchy of command" in the business enterprise was a natural "hierarchy of skills and functions." Managers were skilled in selecting goals and in integrating specialized tasks. And without hierarchy, organization was not possible. There was no escape from management; the choice was between management and mismanagement. For Drucker management was "grounded in the very economic and technological nature of modern industrialism."[22]

As for managerial goals, Drucker acknowledged that economic goals must come before social ones. If the firm went bankrupt, managers would be unable to create a corporate community. Corporate "survival" depended on making a profit that not only covered costs but provided insurance against future risks. To make such a profit, managers must "create" customers by providing them with useful products and services. Profit, in Drucker's analysis, was the result of, and reward for, economic service, not the cause of it. But profit was "the ultimate test of business performance," indeed "the only possible test."[23]

The primacy of economic performance, however, should not obscure that the business corporation was "as much a social organization, a community and society" as it was "an economic organ." In the "new society," which was an employee society, the firm had a responsibility to realize social values and fulfill individual needs.

Still, as Drucker developed his theories, a central problem emerged, a problem that originated in his admission that the survival of the firm took precedence over the needs of any employee.[24] This priority could prevent the firm from acting responsibly toward its citizens. It means that the interests of individual and firm might not be in harmony, a condition that contradicted his belief that managerial power was indispensable and self-justifying. Two dimensions of legitimacy were involved, one dealing with the assumed usefulness of a managerial elite to society as a whole, the other with the congruence between particular elite decisions and the needs of every organizational member. In other words, employees could condone management as an institution but condemn individual managers or specific decisions. Reconciling these two dimensions of legitimacy would continue to cause Drucker difficulty.

For Drucker legitimate power was "authority" based not on "submission to force," but on "the rule of right over might."[25] The ruled, in other words, must voluntarily grant the ruler's right to command and thereby their own obligation to obey, thus empowering the ruler. Real legitimacy, however, would transcend passive submission to managerial authority. It would inspire the ruled to active commitment to organizational goals, and instill the "self-discipline" that would produce peak performance.[26] They would voluntarily subordinate personal needs to corporate needs. Then the firm could become a harmonious community.

Yet Drucker acknowledged that managerial power, because the firm could never "act primarily in the interests of those over whom the enterprise rules," would always have some illegitimacy. The firm served customers, not employees; managers could not solve this problem through paternalistic forms of "enlightened despotism." When corporate interests conflicted with employee interests, managers had to sacrifice those of the employee. Nor could the problem be resolved through schemes of employee ownership and democratic decision making. Even if the enterprise were a "government of the people and by the people," it could never be a "government for the people." Hence, workers could passively submit to corporate authority, withdraw their efficiency, and refuse to "subordinate" their needs to the corporate "welfare."[27]

Legitimacy caused Drucker so much trouble because he was trying to find ways of authorizing despotic bureaucracy in a society that valued liberal democracy. In a liberal government citizens granted legitimacy by freely choosing a constitution, leaders, and political ends and means. Yet legitimizing corporate government in a liberal way would of course undercut Drucker's management theory of value, so he rejected free citizenship and would only allow employees to choose personal goals within the limits of managerial objectives. Such choices were less acts of consent by citizens than of convenience and necessity by subjects. Constrained in "voice," employees could only "exit" to become entrepreneurs.

As Drucker struggled with the conflict between the need of society for managerial power and the need of the individual for satisfaction, he concluded that conflict could be minimized through methods that would lead employees to adopt "managerial attitudes" and seek fulfillment through commitment to the corporate good. Workers needed to be persuaded that employment as a social contract was both an agreement of "association" and one of "subjection." But they could experience some degree of "self-government" at work. Control over jobs, work methods, and work environments would allow workers to be participants in their "government." Participation would lead them toward the "Christian" conception of freedom, which was ethical, "responsible choice," not "license" or a right to "freedom from something." In addition, he thought that the firm should reward the committed worker.[28]

In the 1940s Drucker believed that labor unions could become a "loyal opposition" and help inculcate a "managerial attitude."[29] After 1949, however, Drucker largely dropped this idea. With the waning of organizing drives, unions no longer concerned him much. And more importantly, he became attentive to a new type of nonunionized worker.

Initially Drucker labelled these new workers the "new industrial middle class," but eventually he called them "knowledge workers."[30] More recently several historical economists have named them "independent" workers. Formally educated, independent workers applied general knowledge and skills to unique situations. These managers, professionals, technicians, and scientists had been in part created by the way Taylorism and bureaucracy had centralized controls and specialized tasks. But Taylorism did not work well to manage them. Their work was difficult to "routinize," and so they had substantial autonomy. Managers expected independent workers to "internalize the formal objectives" of their organization and to accept "a kind of implicit contract," exercising initiative and solving problems while at the same time respecting "corporate authority."[31]

Managers depended on the skills and autonomy of knowledge workers but were also threatened by them. Druckerism responded to that threat in the same way that Taylorism had responded to industrial craftsmen. Indeed, Drucker would argue that "just as the economic conflict between the needs of the manual worker and the role of an expanding economy was the social question of the nineteenth century," so "the position, function, and fulfillment of the knowledge worker is the social question of the twentieth century."[32]

Knowledge workers, as he saw it, were the new skilled workers, and their tasks and self-perceptions were different from those of manual workers. They used knowledge rather than "physical force or manual skill" and produced ideas rather than things. Each saw himself as a professional, if not as an intellectual, and collectively they saw themselves "as 'part of management' without being 'managers,' and as 'workers' without . . . considering themselves 'proletarians.'" They did not command people, but their command of information influenced management.[33]

Because of their independent tasks and bourgeois self-images, these "knowledge professionals" caused peculiar problems for managers. Their work had to be managed because most of them were dedicated to their careers, professional "ethos," or technical specialty rather than to the enterprise. They possessed the knowledge that the firm needed but not the "responsibility" to see that their projects were often irrelevant to "the goals of the whole," especially to the survival of the firm. Yet they could not be easily managed through the traditional forms of bureaucracy. They refused to be treated as inferiors or subordinates, and bullying tactics would likely lead them to sabotage or exit.[34]

For independent workers, Drucker doubted that Taylorism was useful because planning could not be separated from doing. The worker was hired to apply professional knowledge, to think, innovate, adapt to change. He was both planner and performer, and managers could not "take the knowledge out of the work" without destroying its usefulness. Furthermore, since the knowledge worker must design his own work, a control system in which managers regulated work through formal, written rules was self-defeating. Unskilled labor and machines could seldom be adequate substitutes for professionals. Nor could the productivity of independent work be measured in quantitative terms. Other ways would have to be found that could make the necessity of autonomy into a virtue and get the new workers to manage themselves.[35]

Thus, as early as the mid 1950s, long before "intrapreneurship" became a fad, Drucker was calling for corporatist government consistent with entrepreneurship.[36]

To reconcile corporatism and entrepreneurship and achieve legitimacy and rationality, Drucker called for business reorganization. Knowledge work organizations would be less "pyramids" of power like those of the military or the church, but more "concentric, overlapping, coordinated rings" like those of a university or a hospital. In such decentralized structures, the relationship of managers to knowledge workers would be one of mutual dependence. Although managers would still select corporate goals, they would allow professional "juniors and colleagues" to choose work processes and standards. And in conjunction with their integration of corporate effort, managers would teach the knowledge worker to work "under orders" and "subordinate the authority of knowledge to organizational objectives and goals." A new operational "organization ethics" would emerge, leading to a new corporate "common law" and "constitution." The knowledge worker could become a corporate "citizen" with corporate "virtue." He could help the firm, develop himself, and "harmonize" organizational goals and individual needs."[37]

Before Drucker, such management writers as Chester Barnard, Henri Fayol, and especially Mary Parker Follett had emphasized that goals should be clear and legitimate. Follett had argued that managers should obey "the law of the situation" to "depersonalize" directives.[38] To learn more about management "as an integrating mechanism," Drucker in the late 1940s sought work inside a major corporation. He approached Westinghouse but was turned away because he talked like "a Bolshevik."[39] He turned to General Motors and in 1942 the company asked him to study its top management structure. Before finishing his study in 1945, he became acquainted with a managerial tool that seemed to provide at least some of what was needed. Alfred P. Sloan had used something very similar to management by objectives at GM since the 1920s. Donaldson Brown had given the method theoretical expression in a 1927 paper entitled "Decentralized Operations and Responsibilities with Coordinated Control."

Sloan developed his technique to cope with the problem of operating a large, complex agglomeration of business units that sometimes worked at cross purposes. It worked through designing a central marketing strategy, creating several semiautonomous operating divisions, and using a central staff to provide advice, coordinate efforts, and measure performance of the divisions. Managers made policy by negotiating with one another up, down, and across the organizational chart. The system combined, in Sloan's words, "the initiative, responsibility, development of personnel, decisions close to the facts, [and] flexibility" of decentralization with the "efficiencies and economies" of centralization. Drucker found such business "federalism" intriguing, and he discussed it in some detail in his 1946 book on General Motors, *Concept of the Corporation*.

In his autobiography, Drucker recalled that Charles E. Wilson of GM had told him that a generation of "Federalists" had designed the "structure" and "constitutional principles" of big business, and that the subsequent generation of "Jeffersonians" would have to foster "citizenship and community."[40] Drucker would attempt to do so when he helped convert Sloan's technique for managing a multidivision firm into a technique for managing managers and knowledge workers.

## Management by Objectives and Self-Control

Drucker worked out his ideas with Harold Smiddy, a vice president at General Electric who had been impressed by Drucker's book on GM. Smiddy hired Drucker as a consultant, and with Drucker's prompting began using participative management techniques. Superiors, the two men decided, could best get subordinates to work under "self-control" if goals and methods were jointly defined. Smiddy began clarifying objectives with his employees and in 1952 made the process part of company policy. Drucker labelled it "management by objectives and self-control."[41] Its purposes were to direct managerial vision, to promote monetary rationality, to legitimize managerial power and corporate goals, to fulfill individual needs, to guide knowledge work, and to unify ethics and entrepreneurship. By achieving these aims, he intended it to synthesize capitalism and corporatism.

Drucker first prescribed management by objectives in the sections entitled "Managing a Business" and "Managing Managers" in 1954 in *The Practice of Management*. He altered the prescriptions slightly thereafter. He quickly broadened it, for example, from a technique for managing managers to one for managing knowledge workers.

The technique had four parts: centralized determination of corporate goals, decentralized definition of operational targets and task organization, measurements of performance against objectives, and a system of rewards and punishments based on results.

First of all, Drucker wanted managers to set corporate strategy. Corporate goals comprised the "compass bearing" of the corporate ship, guiding it to its destination and preventing it from becoming "the plaything of weather, winds and accidents." Management must have a clear understanding of the "mission and purpose" of the firm. And determining this purpose required more than study of what the firm was doing, for studying present efforts might perpetuate obsolete processes and projects. It required careful market analysis of business opportunities because the customer decided "whether the efforts of a business become economic results or whether they become so much waste and scrap." Managers must learn who their customers were, who they could be, what their unsatisfied wants were, what they regarded as value, and what products would satisfy them. After such questions had been answered, entrepreneurial goals could then be set.[42]

The second step in clarifying goals was to convert these broad aims into specific operational objectives. Managers should proceed, in other words, from learning what their business was and envisioning what it could be to marshalling the means to achieve its goals and devising a plan for utilizing these means. Operational objectives must set forth what was to be achieved in marketing, product innovation, output, resource allocation, personnel performance, corporate social responsibility, and performance measurement. The objectives must then be kept current with changing market conditions. There should be no attempt to "outguess" the business cycle or project the past into the future, for such attempts to escape risk were dangerous in a competitive and innovative economy. Profit making, Drucker emphasized, should not be the only objective. Overemphasis on profits would lead to shortsightedness, postponement of desirable investments, and continuation of obsolescent projects. Commitments to future actions should be used to make decisions about "present means" to achieve "future results." When everyone in the firm knew these objectives, they could better organize their efforts to produce market results.[43] Obviously Drucker realized that clear goals could contribute not only to entrepreneurial effectiveness of managers, but to their political effectiveness as well.

He believed that only top managers should select goals. But central control could lead to goals that subordinates did not understand or accept. Balancing despotism and legitimacy was always precarious, and initially Drucker offered only a few isolated examples of how to juggle both. But by the 1960s he would point to the "consensual decision-making" of Japanese corporations as the one best way to set goals, and would even claim that his books and seminars had taught the Japanese this system.[44] His celebration of Japanese management anticipated the American Japanophilia of the 1980s.[45]

His view of decision making in Japanese corporations overplayed how initiatives came from the bottom up and downplayed how managers used consultations to legitimize decisions from the top down. He claimed that employees throughout the firm began by defining the problem to be solved. They decided what the question was before answers were solicited. Then discussions explored alternatives and their implications. The result usually was that "every decision comes up from below" and was "an expression of a general will." Finally, top management selected "the appropriate people" to make the decision, and once it had been made, their orders would be "obeyed without argument or reservation." Implementing ideas came swiftly because the decision process was seen as a means to action rather than as an end in itself. And because plans resulted from "consensus" rather than "compromises," the peculiar combination of "autocracy" and "democratic participation" insured that decisions never had to be sold to subordinates; "authority from the top down" was always matched by "responsibility from the bottom up." The system, Drucker said, could never be completely imitated by the West since it was rooted in Japanese culture. But the underlying principles, he thought, might "point the way to solutions for some of our most pressing problems."[46]

After top management had established corporate strategy and made general operational objectives clear, subordinate managers and knowledge workers were to negotiate with their superiors and draw up very specific work assignments, performance goals, expected contributions, production targets, timetables, and resource allocations. In negotiating with his superior, each subordinate was to set personal objectives that would substitute for narrow, systematic work rules and job descriptions imposed from above. The negotiation was to go beyond a human relations counselling interview that merely intended to give the worker a "sense of participation." Real participation, defining jobs and goals "actively and responsibly," would cause each to "commit himself" with "a positive act of assent" to "the ultimate business goals" and assume "genuine responsibility." His manager could then hold him to "exacting demands." This would be "upward responsibility," which would be formalized in what Smiddy had called the "manager's letter."[47]

> In this [biannual] letter to his superior, each manager [or knowledge worker] first defines the objectives of his superior's job and of his own job as he sees them. He then sets down the performance standards which he believes are being applied to him. Next, he lists the things he must do to attain these goals — and the things within his own unit he considers the major obstacles. He lists the things his superior and the company do that help him and . . . that hamper him. Finally, he outlines what he proposes to do during the next year to reach his goals. If the superior accepts this statement, the "manager's letter" becomes the charter under which the manager [or knowledge worker] operates.[48]

Such goal setting was in many ways reminiscent of the nineteenth century "inside contracting" system for managing skilled workers in manufacturing firms. Under this system skilled craftsmen had acted as subcontractors who bid on specific projects and organized the work themselves. Managers had found the workers hard to control and had converted the subentrepreneurs into employees.[49] But management by objectives could combine the advantages of subcontracting with those of bureaucracy. The negotiation process would atomize workers and get each to contract to individual goals, possibly encouraging Schmidt-like effort and Stakhanovite competition. Moreover, because the negotiations assumed that managerial power was legitimate, conflict would be transformed from quarrels over control to disagreements over goals. And since managers could better control their new skilled workers without directly controlling their work, they could benefit from contract and control, entrepreneurship and employeeship.

The transparency of negotiations and written contracts would help managers bridge the "communications gap." "Downward" communication, Drucker said, did not work because superiors did not understand the problems and goals of subordinates, and effective communication depended on some "prior agreement on meaning." Only after subordinates had communicated "upward" their "values, beliefs, and aspirations," could superiors reconcile corporate and individual goals. The manager and subordinate would understand one another and could better cooperate. A "common language" would help each person "see" what the other "sees." Superior and subordinate could concentrate on their shared "objectives of performance" and unify their efforts in genuine team work.[50]

The third part of management by objectives was some system for measuring performance of employees relative to self-determined objectives. Drucker emphasized that measurements of "results against goals" must be beneficial to both the individual and the corporation. "Feedback" would give the individual worker information that could be used to exercise "self-control" over the work. And while measurements should not become merely tools of "control from above," they should encourage rationality. With proper feedback, each employee could make independent decisions that would product market results.[51]

Finally, management by objectives would set up rewards and punishments based on clear standards of performance. Appraising performance, Drucker concluded, was one of the most important tasks of the manager, and doing it fairly required "integrity," "the one absolute requirement of a manager." The system should develop "managerial vision," foster "internal, self-motivation," and encourage employees to "drive themselves." Employees should not be judged on potential or personality. Superiors should hold them "strictly accountable" for results and periodically review their contributions. And all rewards and punishments, including salaries, perks, promotions, demotions, and terminations, were to be based on performance relative to the objectives of the company. Performance was not to be judged purely on the "bottom line," however, as that measured only business results, not individual ones.[52]

According to Drucker, the combination of business goals, personal objectives, feedback on performance, and appropriate rewards would "harmonize the goals of the individual with the commonweal." It would substitute "management by self-control for management by domination," making management by objectives as much a "constitutional principle" as a managerial technique. Each worker would become a "manager" and assume responsibility not only for his job and work group, but for the economic and social welfare of the organization. "Control from the inside" would be stricter, more exacting, and more effective than "control from the outside." As a "manager," each worker would take action not because he was ordered to, but because "the objective needs of his task" demanded it. Hence, "by converting objective needs into personal goals," management by objectives could guarantee performance and "genuine freedom, freedom under the law."[53]

Since corporate law was determined by managers, freedom for Drucker was, as one commentator has suggested, a Hegelian "rationale for subordination."[54] Given his presumption that the managerial will should override individual wills, his ideal of corporatist virtue amounted to Max Weber's concept of bureaucratic rationality and Taylor's notion of a "mental revolution." All three assumed that functionaries would suppress goals in conflict with the corporation, accept managerial ends as givens, and methodically select means to attain them. Still Drucker realized, as Weber had, that rationality and harmony depended on the legitimacy of managers and their goals.

In later years Drucker expanded his ideas by insisting that managers select socially responsible goals. He rejected the notion that a "hidden-hand" in the marketplace naturally converted "private vices" into "public virtues." He had never believed that competition automatically solved social problems or absolved managers of moral obligations.[55] Nor had he accepted Milton Friedman's argument that businessmen should stick to "business" and should refrain from appointing themselves guardians of the common good. They were running social organizations that could help society and realize "social values." Like anyone else, they also had "a self-interest in a healthy society," and so they should follow normal ethical imperatives.[56] Moreover, for Drucker, managers were the only true "leadership group" in modern society. If they did not "take responsibility for the common good," then no one else could or would.

Managers, then, had to find ways of achieving economic goals and meeting social responsibilities. But they should transcend Andrew Carnegie's notions of business philanthropy. The idea of doing well in business in order to do good outside business, Drucker said, could justify using immoral methods to accumulate wealth.[57] Managers should strive to do the opposite—do good in order to do well. They should choose profitable strategies that also solved social problems. He admired Japanese managers who "put national interest first" and pursued their private interests in ways that promoted the public interest.[58]

For American examples, Drucker cited Henry Ford, who raised wages to sell more cars, and Julius Rosenwald of Sears, Roebuck, who promoted county agents and 4-H programs.[59] Similarly, he argued that business managers should forego strategies that might help their firms but hurt the commonweal. They should adopt the fundamental principle of the Hippocratic oath, "Above all, not knowingly to do harm," and find out whether a prospective strategy would be dangerous. Chemical companies should have tested the health and environmental impacts of DDT and then kept the product off the market.[60]

Later Drucker endorsed what he called the "Confucian approach" to ethics. In an interdependent "society of organizations," he said, everyone, from the highest manager to the lowest worker, should accept that they had responsibilities to everyone else. They should establish networks of "mutual obligation," help others achieve their goals, and nurture "harmony and trust." This "ethics of interdependence," he acknowledged, had no conception of "rights" with which members could claim "entitlements" and exemption from mutual obligations. For instance, he thought "whistle-blowers," rather than being heroic champions of the public good, were virtueless "informers" who violated their responsibilities. All organizational members should be good citizens, obey "Confucian" imperatives, and accept "the fundamental relationships" of society.[61]

By acts of "statesmanship," by selecting goals that tried to solve social problems and avoid creating new ones, responsible business managers could help to harmonize private and public interests in ways that the market alone could not. Of course all this assumed that corporate leaders could, in Drucker's words, attain the "private virtue" that alone could define genuine social problems, achieve consensus, and mediate private and public interests.[62]

## For and against MBO

In the quarter century after 1954, Drucker's management by objectives stimulated great interest among managers and academics much as Taylor's scientific management had before. Interest was measured in a fifty-five page survey of American, British, and Canadian publications on MBO, which listed over 700 books, articles, monographs, dissertations, and theses.[63] Also like Taylor, Drucker had to defend his ideas from managerial critics. Empirical studies of MBO in practice and political discussions of Drucker's principles showed the essentially bureaucratic form of his corporatism.

Several reasons account for the popularity of MBO. The formation of more multidivision and conglomerate firms isolated top managers, produced more middle managers, and made governing difficult.[64] Structural changes affected the labor market; independent workers increased from 27.8 percent of the work force in 1950 to 32.8 percent in 1970, and that percentage grew even larger during the 1970s.[65] Managers complained that knowledge workers and middle managers were hard to evaluate and discipline; professional people were creative resources and resented being treated as factors of production.[66] And given a demand for alternatives to Taylorism, academics and consultants in addition to Drucker were supplying corporative solutions.[67] Douglas McGregor, for instance, advised managers to abandon the oppressive tactics of a Taylorist "Theory X" and adopt a "Theory Y" that organized work to satisfy workers' needs and meet organizational goals. McGregor recommended management by objectives because it evaluated workers based on performance and encouraged them to assume responsibility for improving their work. He had learned about the technique from managers at General Mills, who had been among the first to adopt Drucker's management by objectives when their company had reorganized into divisions.[68]

Even though the system was popular, empirical studies of its practice did not emerge until the late 1960s. It was adopted more because of logical appeal than because of proven usefulness.[69]

In 1974 two business educators surveyed the Fortune 500 largest industrial firms to determine how many used the system. They found that nearly one-half claimed to use the technique but considerably fewer used it throughout the company and fewer still regarded it as a success. Additional study found that many companies that thought they were using Drucker's brand of management by objectives really were not. Many were simply setting corporate objectives and implementing them using traditional centralized authority. Subordinates were not being granted autonomy, either on the job or in setting performance goals. Goals and work rules were imposed from above. In some cases a laissez-faire method was used; managers told subordinates that results mattered but did not engage in any systematic negotiations. All things considered, the authors concluded that only about ten percent of the Fortune 500 used a management by objectives system like Drucker's, a proportion that compared favorably with the early application of Taylorism. And while these companies generally regarded it as having been successful, it was not clear in what sense it had been successful, whether in terms of consensus, productivity, or control.[70]

Although bureaucratic criticisms of Drucker have been few (which shows how bureaucratic his ideas have been), managers and business academics have often denied that participatory management was rational. Interpreting participatory management as a dangerous form of anarchism, they believed corporative techniques such as MBO coddled workers rather than controlled them.[71] As the sociologist Richard Edwards has argued, managers saw advantages in written directives, narrow job descriptions, and close supervision even if it came at the cost of lower performance and less commitment. They preferred predictable performance to peak performance because it was more easily controlled and less risky; or they believed conformity to company rules was more realistic than commitment to the corporate community.[72]

Drucker recognized the continued popularity of bureaucratic thinking and scientific management and in 1976 he sought to deflect criticism by praising Frederick W. Taylor for first expressing corporative management principles. Revising his previous interpretation of scientific management in his typical cranky and polemical style, Drucker said that Taylor had wanted to reorganize unhealthy and burdensome tasks, to replace the "boss" with "servants" of labor, and to develop workers' potentiality and personality. Taylor had believed "above all" that managers should select, train, and develop the individual for the job he was "best fitted for" and help him become a "first rate man" by scientifically designing his task and providing him with the necessary information and tools.[73] By emphasizing Taylor's corporatist rhetoric and by ignoring how his technical principles had called for simplified jobs and separate planners and performers, Drucker tried to camouflage the iron cage with a corporatist curtain. In the process, he acknowledged that his corporatism was only superficially different from scientific management.

Numerous observers concurred, concluding that MBO did not go beyond Taylorism. These observations were verified by the most thorough case study, which was carried out by Stephen J. Carroll and Henry L. Tosi at Black and Decker in the late 1960s and early 1970s. Their opinion surveys showed that management by objectives did not work quite the way Drucker had expected. Managers at all levels believed that the system improved communication and planning. But they complained about MBO's red tape, the excessive attention given to quantifiable goals, the slighting of self-improvement goals, and the anxiety that resulted when they were held responsible for failures that were beyond their control. Upper-level managers felt their authority was threatened by the negotiations and lower-level managers complained that they had little discretion.[74]

Carroll and Tosi doubted that corporatism was either more harmonious or more productive than bureaucracy. After the introduction of management by objectives, managerial employees "were no more satisfied with pay or their jobs than before," and they did not experience "any more control over their work, any changes in their jobs, or any more job interest . . . than before." Management by objectives best created harmony and improved performance, Carroll and Tosi concluded, when superiors relinquished power to subordinates. But redistributing power itself required a change in "both the philosophy and practice of management." And managers had little incentive to make such changes given that clear goals and feedback improved performance much more than participation in setting goals.[75]

In the late 1960s several psychologists accused Drucker of trying to achieve corporatist harmony through cooptation and control rather than cooperation and consensus. They charged that Drucker's MBO was too bureaucratic to achieve corporatist virtue. Most prominently, Harry Levinson contended that Drucker's system could not satisfy employee needs. The system, Levinson said, put corporate goals first and gave the individual no power to pursue ends that conflicted with job assignments. It insured that the individual would feel like "an object," an "instrument for reaching a goal." To make matters worse, the employee was forced to set personal goals within the confines of corporate strategy so that if he failed to reach them, he would be "hoisted on his own petard." Workers under these conditions felt "like rats in a maze" who only got to choose their own "bait." The underlying reward-punishment psychology only made things worse. Carrots and sticks caused employees to act less out of virtue and more out of selfishness; they were being bribed and bullied, not self-motivated. By treating people as "patsies to be driven, urged, and manipulated," management by objectives often intensified "the hostility, resentment and distrust" between manager and managed that it was supposed to eliminate and encouraged the withdrawal of efficiency that it was designed to overcome. Because of its contradictions, it was "self-defeating," "really just industrial engineering with a new name, applied to higher managerial levels." It could achieve self-motivation, Levinson concluded, only if it began with the needs of the individual, then proceeded to corporate goals and work assignments.[76]

Another psychologist, Abraham Maslow, revealed the utopian qualities of Drucker's corporatism by exposing its assumptions. The system, Maslow argued, assumed a sound market standing so that "eupsychian growth and self-actualization" would be compatible with corporate performance. (In this regard Maslow proved prophetic, the firm in which he had observed MBO in operation dropped the system when it went through hard times in the early 1970s.)[77] It also assumed that people wanted challenging, responsible jobs; that all work would be "self-actualizing," that subordinates could respect, even love, their superiors; that bosses would surrender power; that managerial "wolves" would not prey on corporate "lambs." And more generally it assumed that employees and managers were healthy and homogeneous, not "psychopaths, schizophrenics, paranoids, brain injured, feeble-minded, perverts," or "addicts," among other things.[78]

Finally Maslow contended that management by objectives assumed that corporations could become "synergic" institutions in which persons pursuing selfish ends "automatically" helped others and persons acting altruistically "automatically" helped themselves. In synergy, all choices were good, all acts rebounded to personal and public advantage, and "virtue" paid. Not surprisingly, the only examples he could find of this were from a nonindustrial culture, the Blackfeet Indians.[79] Although Maslow believed these prerequisites for management by objectives could be met, others might be doubtful.

Drucker conceded that Maslow's observations were cutting and made a "real impression."[80] He also admitted that his system had become a "fad" in the 1960s and had been "oversold and over-promoted." But he thought that when applied properly, it had worked. In 1974 in *Management*, his 839-page magnum opus, he restated his old arguments. His version of management by objectives, he acknowledged in addressing Maslow, was "a stern taskmaster" and was not "permissive." The "responsibility and self-discipline" that it demanded required "strong and healthy" people. But he denied that there were realistic alternatives. Taylorism, with its carrot-and-stick approach, no longer worked in "developed countries." Knowledge workers must be "self-directed"; they needed negotiation and some autonomy.

Nor did Drucker think that basing management by objectives on individual rather than corporate goals could ever be as rational as Levinson claimed. Corporate survival had to take precedence over individual goals. To think otherwise, to want "organization without alienation," was the illusion of "romantics," for in a real sense, "organization is alienation." Finally, Drucker argued, the survival of the firm required "clear, unambiguous, designated command authority vested in one person." Production collapsed when managers were removed, as "proven" when industries were nationalized.[81] Management, he later emphasized, "will not 'wither away.'"[82] Such a defense of management helped make Drucker a best-selling author. In 1974 the sales of *Management* temporarily surpassed those of another technical book, *The Joy of Sex*.[83]

Nevertheless, in recent years Drucker has downplayed the formal technique of "MBO" as a means of making business bureaucracy more corporative. This was less a change in philosophy than in public relations. While distancing himself from MBO, he continued to argue for task synthesis and integrated planning and doing. He has also asserted that in the last forty years managers have listened to him and learned to treat "professionals" as "colleagues."[84]

In the 1980s, he tried to teach bureaucrats how entrepreneurship could make them into more rational capitalists. One commentator claimed that Drucker's lesson on the creation of customers has been central to marketing theory from the 1950s on.[85] But by the 1980s, after a decade of penetration of American markets by foreign firms, many were denying that American managers had attained Drucker's ideal of the entrepreneur who combined private profits and social service. Rather, managers had become ivory-tower number-crunchers and bureaucratic parasites who preyed on producers and the public and feasted on short-term profits.[86]

Drucker, of course, had always held that profit was the ultimate test of business performance, a lesson that was still followed. But if the critics were right, managers had ignored his simultaneous insistence that corporate survival, indeed the survival of capitalism itself, required long-term planning and intelligent risk taking, constant technical innovation with accompanying elimination of obsolete products and processes, effective protection of market standing, and strategies that served workers and the public.[87]

Drucker himself denied that any national decline in entrepreneurship had occurred during the 1970s.[88] Indeed he contended that entrepreneurial pressures and computer technology were hastening the evolution of a "new" form of business organization that was reuniting planning and doing. The new environment was creating "information-based organizations" with self-directing employees such as hospitals, universities, and symphony orchestras. Each would employ, Drucker predicted, more knowledge workers and two-thirds fewer middle managers than Taylorist "command-and-control organizations."[89]

Such messages helped Drucker's reputation grow ever larger in the 1980s. Admirers hailed him as the "father of the new management," who first combined entrepreneurial and corporative management principles.[90] Tom Peters, the decade's leading entrepreneurial prophet, expressed his "amazement" and "perhaps dismay" that Drucker had written "everything" on managing for innovation in 1954 in *The Practice of Management*.[91]

Born-again Druckerites, however, ignored history and the way that Drucker's corporatism duplicated Taylor's bureaucratism. Particularly Druckerism replicated the centralized power of Taylorism. Even as Drucker described the "low hierarchy" of the "new" organization, he emphasized that "central management" was needed; even orchestras needed conductors and hospitals administrators. Top managers still had to impose control through something like management by objectives.[92]

Drucker's insistence on the importance of top management revealed that he never called for a full fusion of planning and doing. His persistent advocacy of decentralized operations and centralized coordination still depended on professional managers. And if such managers were isolated from production, the objectives they helped to set could be as confined to quantitative standards and short-term profits as they had been in the old bureaucracies.[93] These same managers could remain primarily concerned with controlling subordinates and minimizing risk, not with allowing freedom to innovate. Transcending bureaucracy would seem problematic since Drucker has admitted that at best only three to five percent of American firms have been well managed.[94]

To conclude, management by objectives did not go beyond the principles of scientific management. Managers who applied it were typically unwilling to reverse Taylorism, surrender power, and synthesize planning and performing. To do so would have deprived them of their reason to exist. Nor did Drucker's criticism of Taylorism ever call for managers to abdicate from power. Such a revolutionary call would have cut him off from his managerial audience. Indeed, he was never revolutionary; he simply called for managers to be responsible and rational, especially in governing professional workers. Drucker's theory always made managerial will superior to all other wills, and this made him very popular among managers.

Accepting the prevailing Taylorist conception of the manager also helps explain why Drucker's avowedly corporatist prescriptions actually led to bureaucratic management practice.[95] The sociologist Rosabeth Moss Kanter, echoing Maslow, has called Drucker a "management utopian" who had an excessive faith in managers' ability to apply his ideas. His vision of "the world-as-it-ought-to-be" obscured sight of "the world-as-it-is." Faith prevented his understanding the "human limitations," managers' lust for power and money, and the "organizational limitations," those bureaucratic imperatives for centralization and specialization, that so often prevented significant restructuring.[96]

Accordingly, Drucker's management by objectives mainly perpetuated a Taylorist separation of planning and performing. His advice that managers establish harmony in a hierarchy was little different from Taylor's advice that they get control over a hierarchy. Corporatist advice was only one part of a shift from the "authoritarian" management of the first half of the twentieth century to the "hegemonic" kind of the last half.[97] But Taylor and Drucker had essentially the same theory of good business government. Both believed that the best government was that ruled by scientific managers. Drucker and other corporatists transcended Taylor's techniques but not his management principles. Thus Taylorism, reborn and transformed, was alive and well after the Second World War.

NOTES

1. William Clarkson, "Drucker: Closing the Theory/Practice Gap," *New Management* 2 (Winter 1985), p. 23.

2. Peter F. Drucker, *The Practice of Management* (New York, 1954), p. 280.

3. Peter F. Drucker, "The Coming Rediscovery of Scientific Management," *Conference Board Record* (June 1976), pp. 25–37.

4. Hindy Lauer Schacter, *Frederick Taylor and the Public Administration Community: A Reevaluation* (Albany, NY, 1989), pp. 17, 121. Schachter cited only Drucker's "Coming Rediscovery" article. For my interpretation of this article, see discussion in "For and Against MBO" herein.

5. Amanda Bennett, "Management Guru: Peter Drucker Wins Devotion of Top Firms with Eclectic Counsel," *Wall Street Journal*, July 28, 1987, p. 1ff.

6. Alan M. Kantrow, "Why Read Peter Drucker," *Harvard Business Review* 58 (January–February 1980), pp. 74–82, quoted on p. 76.

7. See Stephen P. Waring, *Taylorism Transformed: Scientific Management Theory Since 1945* (Chapel Hill, 1991); Douglas McGregor, *The Human Side of Enterprise* (New York, 1960); Chris Argyris, *Personality and Organization: The Conflict Between the System and the Individual* (New York, 1957).

8. R. Jeffrey Lustig, *Corporate Liberalism: The Origins of Modern American Political Theory, 1890–1920* (Berkeley, 1982), pp. 255–56.

9. Brief, incomplete, and favorable accounts that leave out its connections with corporatism or conceptions of social responsibility include George S. Odiorne, "MBO: A Backward Glance," *Business Horizons* 21 (October 1978), pp. 14–24; Dale D. McConkey, "MBO: Twenty Years Later," *Business Horizons* 16 (August 1973), pp. 25–36; R. G. Greenwood, "Management by Objectives: As Developed by Peter Drucker, Assisted by Harold Smiddy," *Academy of Management Review* 6 (April 1981), pp. 225–30.

10. Two studies have mentioned Drucker's corporatism, one by a political scientist, M. Morton Auerbach, *The Conservative Illusion* (New York, 1959), pp. 211–12, and another by a journalist, John J. Tarrant, *Drucker: The Man Who Invented the Corporate Society* (Boston, 1976), pp. 53–59. Neither traced corporatism to Europe or showed how management by objectives was a technique designed to synthesize corporatism and capitalism.

11. On corporatism in general, see Philippe Schmitter, "Still the Century of Corporatism?" *Review of Politics* 36 (1974), pp. 86–131; Ralph Bowen, *German Theories of the Corporate State with Special Reference to the Period 1870–1919* (New York, 1947), pp. 1–5, 11–118, 210–19; Matthew H. Elbow, *French Corporative Theory, 1789–1948: A Chapter in the History of Ideas* (New York, 1966), pp. 11–22, 29–96, 197–204; Eugene Golob, *The Isms* (New York, 1954), pp. 540–44, 548–60. For the Austrian thinkers, see Fritz K. Ringer, *The Decline of the German Mandarins: The German Academic Community, 1890–1933* (Cambridge, 1969), p. 232; Alfred Diamant, *Austrian Catholics and the First Republic: Democracy, Capitalism, and the Social Order, 1918–1934* (Princeton, 1960), pp. 11–14, 22, 24, 29–30, 36, 54–57, 61, 72, 160–64, 168, 194, 203–7.

12. Diamant, *Austrian Catholics and the First Republic,* especially pp. 238, 286–87.

13. Peter F. Drucker, *The End of Economic Man: The Origins of Totalitarianism* (New York, 1939, 1969), pp. 106–7, chap. 4. See also Peter F. Drucker, *Friedrich Julius Stahl: Konservative Staatslehre & Geschichtliche Entwicklung* (Tuebingen, 1933); John Edward Toews, *Hegelianism* (Cambridge, 1980), pp. 232, 246–48.

14. Berthold Freyberg, "The Genesis of Drucker's Thought," in Tony H. Bonaparte and John E. Flaherty, eds., *Peter Drucker: Contributions to Business Enterprise* (New York, 1970), pp. 17–22.

15. Marshall McLuhan and Barrington Nevitt, "The Man Who Came to Listen," in *Peter Drucker,* p. 36; Diamant, *Austrian Catholics and the First Republic,* p. 90; Ringer, *German Mandarins,* pp. 75–76; "Peter Ferdinand Drucker," *Current Biography: 1964* (New York, 1964), p. 112; James O'Toole, "Peter Drucker: Father of New Management," *New Management* (Winter 1954), pp. 18, 24, 32.

16. Peter F. Drucker, *The Age of Discontinuity: Guidelines to Our Changing Society* (New York, 1968), pp. 145–51; Peter F. Drucker, "Schumpeter and Keynes," *Forbes* 131 (May 23, 1983), pp. 126–28; Joseph A. Schumpeter, *Capitalism, Socialism, and Democracy* (New York, 1942, 1950), part II, especially pp. 132, 141–42, 156.

17. Peter F. Drucker, *Adventures of a Bystander* (New York, 1978), p. 35; Drucker, *The End of Economic Man: The Origins of Totalitarianism* (New York, 1942, 1969), pp. 55, 77, 242, 268. Kantrow has also stressed how "the lessons of fascism" shaped Drucker's thought; see "Why Read Peter Drucker," p. 81.

18. Peter F. Drucker, *The Future of Industrial Man: A Conservative Approach* (New York, 1942, 1955), pp. 78–85; Peter F. Drucker, *Concept of the Corporation* (New York, 1946, 1964), pp. 114–38; Drucker, *New Society*, pp. 47–49, 151, 153, 229, chaps. 15 and 25. See also J. B. McKee, "Status and Power in the Industrial Community: A Comment on Drucker's Thesis," *American Journal of Sociology* 58 (January 1953).

19. See H. Hartmann, *Authority and Organization in German Management* (Princeton, NJ, 1959), especially pp. 8–10.

20. See Chester I. Bernard, *The Functions of the Executive* (Cambridge, 1938), especially pp. 215–34.

21. Drucker, *Practice*, pp. 119, 126–27; Peter F. Drucker, *Management: Tasks, Responsibilities, Practices* (New York, 1974), pp. 398–99; Drucker, *Discontinuity*, p. 235. This symphonic analogy, one scholar has argued, was a "sort of mental habit" amongst German university professors in the early twentieth century; see Ringer, *German Mandarins*, pp. 108, 114–19, 122–23, 128–29, 234–35, 446–47.

22. Drucker, *Industrial Man*, p. 15; Drucker, *New Society*, pp. 5–7, 20–26, 343, 350; Drucker, *Practice*, p. 4.

23. Drucker, *New Society*, pp. 47, 50, 52, 61, 204, 314; Drucker, *Practice*, pp. 35–37, 46, 47, 60, 91, 76; Shigetaka Mohri, "Neo-Fordism," in *Peter Drucker*, pp. 196–99.

24. Drucker, *New Society*, p. 99.

25. Drucker, *Industrial Man*, pp. 35, 36.

26. Drucker, *Industrial Man*, pp. 35, 36.

27. Drucker, *New Society*, pp. 99, 100, 103; Drucker, *Corporation*, pp. 35–36, 42.

28. Drucker, *Industrial Man*, pp. 62, 109–11, 115; Drucker, *New Society*, pp. 49, 157, 160.

29. Drucker, *New Society*, pp. 106–113, 146, 150, 282–88. Although losing concern with unions, Drucker was an early promoter of job enrichment for manual workers. See Waring, *Taylorism Transformed*, chap. 6; Drucker, *Practice*, pp. 258, 262, 270, 280, 283–84, 296, 303–4, 310.

30. Drucker, *New Society*, pp. 42–43.

31. David M. Gordon, Richard Edwards, and Michael Reich, *Segmented Work, Divided Workers: The Historical Transformation of Labor in the United States* (London, 1982), pp. 202, 211, 222, 224. See also Richard Edwards, *Contested Terrain: The Transformation of the Workplace in the Twentieth Century* (New York, 1979), pp. 88–89, 174–77, 192–93.

32. Peter F. Drucker, *The Effective Executive* (New York, 1966), p. 173.

33. Drucker, *Effective Executive*, pp. 3, 61; Drucker, *Discontinuity*, pp. 276–77; Peter F. Drucker, *People and Performance: The Best of Peter Drucker on Management* (New York, 1977), pp. 24, 74–78.

34. Drucker, *Management*, pp. 450–51, 454; Peter F. Drucker, *Managing in Turbulent Times* (New York, 1980), p. 131.

35. Drucker, *Effective Executive*, p. 34; Drucker, *Management*, pp. 32–33, 183; Drucker, *Landmarks*, pp. 60–73.

36. See J. S. DeMott, "Here Come the Intrapreneurs," *Time* 125 (February 4, 1985), pp. 36–37. Drucker also doubted that the theories and techniques of

Elton Mayo and the "human relations school" helped in managing knowlede workers; see Drucker, *Practice*, pp. 274–80.

37. Drucker, *Managing in Turbulent Times*, pp. 132–33; Drucker, *Landmarks*, pp. 78–82, 106; Drucker, *Effective Executive*, pp. 173–74.

38. Mary P. Follett, *Dynamic Administration: The Collected Papers of Mary Follett*, ed. Henry C. Metcalf and Lyndall Urwick, (New York, 1941), pp. 50–70.

39. Richman, "Wide-ranging Mind," p. 10.

40. Tarrant, *Drucker*, p. 77; Drucker, *Corporation*, especially pp. 49–50, 64, 67, 78, 121; Drucker, *Adventures*, p. 272. For information on GM and Sloan, see also Alfred D. Chandler, Jr., *Strategy and Structure: Chapters in the History of the American Industrial Enterprise* (Cambridge, MA, 1962), chap. 3; Alfred Sloan, *My Years with General Motors* (New York, 1964), chap. 23.

41. Ronald G. Greenwood, "Management by Objectives: As Developed by Peter Drucker, Assisted by Harold Smiddy," *Academy of Management Review* 6 (April 1981), pp. 225–30.

42. Drucker, *Practice*, pp. 60–61; Drucker, *Management*, pp. 81, 91, 94, chap. 7; Peter F. Drucker, *Managing for Results: Economic Tasks and Risk-taking Decisions* (New York, 1964), pp. 5, 94, 127, chap. 11.

43. Drucker, *Managing for Results*, pp. 222–26; Drucker, *Management*, pp. 99–100, chap. 8; Drucker, *Discontinuity*, pp. 42–57; Drucker, *Landmarks*, p. 52; Drucker, *Practice*, pp. 62–81, 88; Peter F. Drucker, "Long-Range Planning," in Peter F. Drucker, *Technology, Management and Society* (New York, 1970), pp. 132–33, 136.

44. Peter F. Drucker, "Management as a Liberal Art," in Peter F. Drucker, *The Frontiers of Management: Where Tomorrow's Decisions are Being Shaped Today* (New York, 1986), chap. 27.

45. Waring, *Taylorism Transformed*, chap. 8:

46. Drucker, *Management*, pp. 257, 466–70; Peter F. Drucker, "What We Can Learn from Japanese Management," in Peter F. Drucker, *Men, Ideas and Politics: Essays by Peter F. Drucker* (New York, 1971), pp. 203–10; Peter F. Drucker, "A View of Japan Through Japanese Art," in Peter F. Drucker, *Toward the Next Economics and Other Essays* (New York, 1981), p. 188.

47. Drucker, *Management*, p. 309; Peter F. Drucker, "What Results Should You Expect? A User's Guide to MBO," in Drucker, *Towards the Next Economics*, pp. 87–89; Drucker, *Practice*, pp. 126–30; Drucker, *People and Performance*, pp. 63–70.

48. Drucker, *Practice*, p. 129.

49. See John Buttrick, "The Inside Contract System," *Journal of Economic History* 12 (1952), pp. 205–21; Daniel Clawson, *Bureaucracy and the Labor Process* (New York, 1980), chap. 3; Harry Braverman, *Labor and Monopoly Capital: The Degradation of Work in the Twentieth Century* (New York, 1974), chap. 2.

50. Drucker, *New Society*, p. 195; Drucker, *Management*, pp. 490–93; Drucker, *Practice*, p. 136.

51. Drucker, *Management*, pp. 218, 494–504; Drucker, *Practice*, pp. 131–32.

52. Drucker, *Practice*, pp. 133, 147, 150, 267, 303, 304, 310; Drucker, *Managing in Turbulent Times*, pp. 67–71; Drucker, *Management*, pp. 460–61.

53. Drucker, *Management*, pp. 284, 441–42; Drucker, *People and Performance*, p. 78; Drucker, *Practice*, pp. 131, 135–56.
54. See Brant W. Abrahamson, "Corporate Capitalism: An Analysis of Peter Drucker's Conception of Industrial Society" (University of Iowa, M.A. thesis, 1961), pp. 35–36, 87–88, 90–91.
55. Drucker, *Practice*, pp. 382–83, 391; Drucker, *Corporation*, pp. 27–29, 206, 214.
56. Drucker, *Practice*, pp. 9–10, 382–83; Drucker, *Management*, pp. 319–25, 348, 350, 366; Drucker, *People and Performance*, pp. 28, 299. See also Milton Friedman, *Capitalism and Freedom* (Chicago, 1962), pp. 133–34; Theodore Leavitt, "The Dangers of Social Responsibility," *Harvard Business Review* 36 (September–October 1958), pp. 41–50.
57. Drucker, *People and Performance*, p. 293; Drucker, *Management*, pp. 325, 348–49; Peter F. Drucker, "Converting Social Problems into Business Opportunities: The New Meaning of Corporate Social Responsibility," *California Management Review* 26 (Winter 1982), pp. 53–58; Drucker, *Discontinuity*, chap. 10.
58. Peter F. Drucker, "Behind Japan's Success," *Harvard Business Review* 59 (January–February 1981), pp. 83–90.
59. Drucker, *Practice*, pp. 383–6, 389–91; Drucker, "Converting Social Problems," pp. 53–63; Drucker, *People and Performance*, pp. 307–10.
60. Drucker, *People and Performance*, pp. 301–5; Drucker, *Management*, pp. 325–29, 368–69.
61. Peter F. Drucker, "What is 'Business Ethics'?" *The Public Interest* 63 (Spirng 1981), pp. 18–36, especially pp. 32–35.
62. Drucker, *Corporation*, pp. 27–28; Drucker, *Practice*, p. 391.
63. Odiorne, "MBO," p. 14; Richard Mansell, "A Management by Objectives Bibliography," mimeograph (Waterloo, Ontario: University of Waterloo, 1977).
64. See Alfred D. Chandler, *The Visible Hand: The Managerial Revolution in American Business* (Cambridge, MA, 1977), pp. 476–83; Neil Fligstein, "The Spread of Multidivisional Form Among large Firms, 1919–79," *American Sociological Review* 50 (June 1985), pp. 377–91.
65. Gordon, Reich, and Edwards, *Segmented Work*, p. 211; see also Eric O. Wright and Bill Martin, "The Transformation of the American Class Structure, 1960–1980," *American Journal of Sociology* 93 (July 1987), pp. 1–29.
66. McConkey, "MBO," p. 26.
67. See Waring, *Taylorism Transformed*, chaps. 6–9.
68. Douglas McGregor, "An Uneasy Look at Performance Appraisal," *Harvard Business Review* 35 (1957), pp. 89–94; Douglas McGregor, *Leadership and Motivation: Essays of Douglas McGregor*, ed. Warren G. Bennis, Edgar H. Schein, and Caroline McGregor, (Cambridge, MA, 1966), chaps. 3, 4, 5, 10; McGregor, *Human Side of Enterprise*. See also Odiorne, "MBO," p. 20; McConkey, "MBO," pp. 26–27.
69. McConkey, "MBO," p. 27.
70. Fred Schuster and Alva Kindall, "Management by Objectives: Where We Stand," *Human Resource Management* 13 (Spring 1974), pp. 8–11.

71. See Waring, *Taylorism Transformed*, especially chaps. 3, 4, 9. Among hundreds of bureaucratic critiques of corporatism, see Thomas H. Fitzgerald, "Why Motivation Theory Doesn't Work," *Harvard Business Review* (July–August 1971), pp. 37–44; Mason Haire, Edwin Ghiselli, and Lyman W. Porter, "An International Study of Management Attitudes and Democratic Leadership," *Proceedings CIOS XIII, International Management Conference* (New York, 1963), pp. 101–14.

72. See Edwards, *Contested Terrain*, pp. 146–47.

73. Drucker, "Coming Rediscovery of Scientific Management," pp. 23–27.

74. Henry Tosi and Stephen Carroll, "Managerial Reactions to Management by Objectives," *Academy of Management Journal* (December 1968), pp. 514–26; Henry Tosi and Stephen Carroll, *Management by Objectives* (New York, 1973), pp. 14, 15, 26–31, 44, 50–51, 74–75.

75. Tosi and Carroll, *Management by Objectives*, pp. 3–5, 7–10, 36, 39–41, 43, 64, 66, 76. See also J. J. Villarreal, "Management by Objectives Revisisted," *S.A.M. Advanced Management Journal* 39 (April 1974), pp. 28–30; L. Dyer and W. Weyrauch, "MBO and Motivation: An Empirical Study," *Academy of Management Proceedings* (1975), pp. 134–36; M. L. McConkie, "Clarifying and Reviewing the Empirical Work on MBO," *Group and Organization Studies* 4 (December 1979), pp. 461–75.

76. Harry Levinson, "Management by Whose Objectives?" *Harvard Business Review* (July–August 1970), pp. 125–34. The sociologist Alan Fox has made a similar evaluation, pointing out its similarity to Soviet-style techniques and noting that middle managers sometimes referred to MBO as a "Do-It-Yourself Hangman's Kit"; see *Beyond Contract: Work, Power and Trust Relations* (London, 1974), p. 358. See also George Strauss, "Management by Objectives: A Critical View," *Training and Development Journal* 26 (April 1972), pp. 10–15; Douglas S. Sherwin, "Strategy for Winning Employee Commitment," in Harvard Business Review, *On Management* (New York, 1975), pp. 54–69; C. F. Molander, "Management by Objectives in Perspective," *Journal of Management* 9 (February 1972), pp. 74–81.

77. "Where Being Nice to Workers Didn't Work," *Business Week* (January 20, 1973), pp. 98–100. Managers abandoned participative techniques so they could impose tougher performance standards. See also E. L. Malone, "The Non-Linear Systems Experiment in Participative Management," *Journal of Business* 48 (January 1975), pp. 52–64.

78. Abraham H. Maslow, *Eupsychian Management* (Homewood, IL, 1965), pp. 7, 41, 139–140, 150–53.

79. Maslow, *Eupsychian Management*, pp. 88–91, 103.

80. William F. Dowling, "Conversation: An Interview with Peter F. Drucker," *Organizational Dynamics* (Spring 1974), p. 36.

81. Dowling, "Interview," pp. 36, 46; Drucker, *Management*, pp. 192, 231–45, 268, 526.

82. Peter F. Drucker, *The Unseen Revolution: How Pension Fund Socialism Came to America* (New York, 1976), p. 114.

83. Marylin Bender, "Consulting Guru for Managers," *New York Times*, April 14, 1974.

84. Peter Drucker Management Seminar Teleconference, George Washington University Continuing Engineering Education Program, February 8, 1990.

85. Arnold Corbin, "The Impact of Drucker on Marketing" in *Peter Drucker*, pp. 147–65.

86. See Robert Hayes and William Abernathy, "Managing Our Way to Economic Decline," *Harvard Business Review* 58 (July–August 1980), pp. 67–77; Robert B. Reich, *The Next American Frontier* (New York, 1983), especially parts 2 and 3; Ira C. Magaziner and Robert B. Reich, *Minding America's Business: The Decline and Rise of the American Economy* (New York, 1982), pp. 4–5, 65–66, 109–46, 191–94.

87. See Drucker, *Practice*, pp. 62–63, and also Peter F. Drucker, "Business Objectives and Survival Needs" in Drucker, *Technology, Management and Society*, pp. 149–65; Peter F. Drucker, "The Performance Gap in Management Science: Reasons and Remedies," *Harvard Business Review* 51 (1973), pp. 41–48; Peter F. Drucker, "Management Science and the Manager," *Management Science* 1 (1955), pp. 115–26.

88. See Peter F. Drucker, *Innovation and Entrepreneurship: Practice and Principles* (New York, 1985), especially the Introduction and pp. 139–40, 254, 258.

89. Peter F. Drucker, "The Coming of the New Organization," *Harvard Business Review* (January–February 1988), pp. 45–53.

90. O'Toole, "Father of the New Management," pp. 4–32, especially pp. 4–5.

91. Thomas J. Peters, "Drucker: The Other Half of the Message," *New Management* 2 (Winter 1985), pp. 14–17.

92. Drucker, "Coming of the New Organization," pp. 45–53.

93. See Business Week, *The Reindustrialization of America* (New York, 1982), p. 57. See also Waring, *Taylorism Transformed*, chap. 3; H. Thomas Johnson and Robert S. Kaplan, *Relevance Lost: The Rise and Fall of Management Accounting* (Boston, 1987).

94. See J. F. Gibbons, "An Interview with Drucker on the Role of a Consultant" in *Peter Drucker*, p. 319.

95. For comments on the gap between Drucker's theory and management practice, see O'Toole, "Father of New Management," pp. 4–32.

96. Rosabeth M. Kanter, "Drucker: The Unsolved Puzzle," *New Management* 2 (Winter 1985), pp. 10–13.

97. Michael Burawoy, *Manufacturing Consent: Changes in the Labor Process under Monopoly Capitalism* (Chicago, 1979), pp. 180–83.

# EPILOGUE

Focusing on influential individuals, business organizations that ranged in size from a few hundred to several thousand employees, and comparatively brief periods in the decades after 1915, the essays in this volume cannot supply definitive judgments about the fate of scientific management after Taylor's death or about the evolution of managerial technique in the twentieth century. Yet because the activities of Richard Feiss, the Gilbreths, Edwin Gay, Mary Van Kleeck, Charles Piez, Charles Bedaux, Peter Drucker and Joseph & Feiss, Link-Belt, and Du Pont managers were notable parts of the post-1915 history of scientific management in the United States, these essays help to illuminate the larger picture.

They show, for example, that Taylor's death did not halt the evolution of scientific management and may, in fact, have accelerated the pace of innovation. Just as Taylor did not invent scientific management, his death did not leave it in a final or definitive form. The movement that Taylor inspired retained its vitality through the 1920s and probably later. The reconciliation of the Taylor society veterans and the Gilbreths led to the emergence of a more sophisticated conception of time study and more powerful analytical tools, precisely the kinds of innovations Taylor had in mind when he initially subsidized Sanford Thompson's time study research. The potent synthesis of industrial engineering and personnel work, anticipated at Joseph & Feiss, and common at such firms as Link-Belt by the 1940s, was another notable instance of this process. Additional research would presumably supply other examples. In terms of managerial technique, then, Taylor's successors had transcended his work by the 1920s. Taylor remained an important and provocative historical figure, but his works were no longer a relevant or reliable guide to industrial practice. As Edward Eyre Hunt wrote in 1924, the progress of scientific management since his death had been "sure and swift."[1]

Certainly the broader implications of scientific management became clearer after Taylor's death. In 1915, Taylor's work was largely discussed and debated in terms of industrial production. A decade later, no one would have suggested that scientific management was "just" industrial engineering or even that its most important impact was on the operation of the factory. World War I was the most immediate stimulus to a larger perspective, but the conversion of substantial groups of academics and intellectuals to the cause of scientific management and the continued growth of large organizations with extensive administrative bureaucracies committed to management as a self-conscious activity were also significant contributing factors. The possibilities of improving the performance of nonbusiness institutions also help explain the popularity of the principles of scientific management. Comparatively few Americans went as far as Mary Van Kleek, but there was widespread recognition of the possibilities of economic and social planning.

Ironically, in view of this apparent influence, the impact of scientific management on the shop floor, and on the worker and working conditions, is difficult to summarize. In the 1940s, as in the 1910s, the manager's conception of the challenge of production management and the consequent need for change and improvement varied widely. Richard Feiss, Charles Piez, and the Du Pont and Bedaux engineers were all devoted to scientific management, but that fact provides only the most general guide to their activities and to the experiences of employees they managed. If someone had convened a meeting of Link-Belt, Du Pont and Bedaux client employees in 1940, the workers could have discussed at length their employers' commitments to cost cutting and anti-unionism, but it is not clear what other concerns they would have had in common. Judging from these accounts, a history of scientific management "from the bottom up" would be no more conclusive about the impact of managerial initiatives in the middle decades of the century than studies examining scientific management and labor during Taylor's lifetime. The addition of evidence from the service sector would likely introduce even more variations.

Thus, while scientific managers were unquestionably interested in work, they were preoccupied with details. The executives who appear in these essays were only rarely concerned with the distribution of skills or with distinctions between planning and implementation of policy. They took the existing system of production as a given and tried to perfect the fine points. The experiences of the Du Pont and Bedaux companies suggest that there were many details to attend to, and that such attention paid substantial dividends. When scientific management was used to the workers' disadvantage, as it was at some of the Du Pont plants and in many of the Bedaux installations, it was usually applied in a traditional way to reduce wage rates and to increase, not decrease, the worker's responsibilities.

Nevertheless, Taylor reemerged in the 1940s as an apostle of narrow, specialized tasks and the removal of decision making from the shop floor. This Taylor was the figure that Drucker rebelled against and the straw man of other social scientists' accounts. That their antidotes, like MBO, did not represent a meaningful break with existing practices is hardly surprising. What was surprising was their disregard for the part of Taylor's message that was as relevant in 1955 as it was in 1915. As the real Taylor had emphasized, scientific management was "not any of the devices which the average man calls to mind when scientific management is spoken of. . . ." It was a commitment to knowledge, reason, and continuous attention to detail that was equally antithetical to old-fashioned empiricism and to new-fashioned panaceas.

These essays suggest, then, that the ideas that Taylor and his allies promoted in the early years of the century have continuing value for understanding the operation of the business firm and for many efforts to organize and direct other activities in the half century after Taylor's death. They provide no evidence of centralized direction, uniform goals, or predictable results. Scientific management encompassed diverse and often contradictory activities. It was not an automatic or inevitable consequence of economic development; Taylor, his followers, and his critics did matter. But they were less important for their specific contributions than for their role in creating an intellectual milieu that encouraged contemporaries to think about organizations and the principles of organized activity, and to act accordingly. If Taylor had returned in the 1940s, he might well have concluded that his call for a mental revolution had been answered.

NOTES

1. Edward Eyre Hunt, ed., *Scientific Management Since Taylor: A Collection of Authoritative Papers* (New York, 1924), p. xii.

# CONTRIBUTORS

Guy Alchon is Associate Professor of History at the University of Delaware. He holds a doctorate from the University of Iowa, and is the author of *The Invisible Hand of Planning: Capitalism, Social Science, and the State in the 1920's*. He is writing a book about Mary Van Kleeck.

Kathy Burgess is a doctoral candidate in history at the University of Pennsylvania and is writing a dissertation entitled "Confronting the Labor Problem: Industrial Relations at the Link-Belt Company, 1890–1950."

David J. Goldberg is Associate Professor of History at Cleveland State University. He is the author of *A Tale of Three Cities: Labor Protest and Organization in Paterson, Passaic, and Lawrence, 1916–1921* and is currently working on a book about social and political conflict in the United States after World War I.

Steven Kreis is Adjunct Instructor in British and European History at Florida Atlantic College and Broward College. He received a Ph.D. in history from the University of Missouri and is working on a book entitled "Efficiency for Sale: Scientific Management in Britain, 1890–1945."

241

Daniel Nelson is Professor of History at the University of Akron and the author of several books and articles on scientific management, including *Managers and Workers: Origins of the New Factory System, 1880–1920* and *Frederick W. Taylor and the Rise of Scientific Management.*

Brian Price received his Ph.D. in history and American studies from Purdue University. He teaches interdisciplinary, multicultural, year-long programs in humanities, social sciences, and political economy at The Evergreen State College in Olympia, Washington.

John C. Rumm is an assistant editor at the Joseph Henry Papers, Smithsonian Institution. He is revising for publication his University of Delaware doctoral dissertation, "Mutual Interests: Managers and Workers at the Du Pont Company, 1802–1915."

Stephen P. Waring has degrees from Doane College and the University of Iowa. He is Assistant Professor of History at the University of Alabama in Huntsville and is the author of *Taylorism Transformed: Scientific Management since 1945.*

# INDEX